BASEMENT

DISPLACEMENT & DIFFERENCE Contemporary Arab Visual Culture in the Diaspora

Displacement & Difference

CONTEMPORARY ARAB VISUAL CULTURE IN THE DIASPORA

Edited by

FRAN LLOYD

DISPLACEMENT & DIFFERENCE Contemporary Arab Visual Culture in the Diaspora

Edited by Fran Lloyd

ISBN 1 872843 22 0

Cover: Collage from Batool al-Fekaiki, *Children of the Future,* 1999 (detail); Zineb Sedira, '*Hide' and 'Seek*', 1999, computer generated photographic image; and (back cover) Mai Ghoussoub, *Diva*, installation, 1999

Published by Saffron Books, an imprint of Eastern Art Publishing

Managing Editor Sajid Rizvi

Eastern Art Publishing
P O Box 13666
London SW14 8WF
United Kingdom

Telephone   +44-[0]20 8392 1122
Facsimile   +44-[0]20 8392 1422
E-mail   saffron@eapgroup.com
Web   www.eapgroup.com
                 www.eapgroup.co.uk
                 www.artbyte.co.uk

Designed by Prizmatone Design Consultancy
Printed and bound in the United Kingdom

British Library Cataloguing in Publication Data
A catalogue record of this book is available from the British Library

Published with the
financial assistance of

THE
ARTS
COUNCIL
OF ENGLAND

Contents

Batool al-Fekaiki, *Children of the Future,* 1999
installation of painted stone and gravel, from *Dialogue of the Present: Site and Performance,*
Pitshanger Manor and Gallery, London, July - August 1999

Sabiha Khemir, *The Happy Island*, 1994 (detail), illustration from *The Island of Animals*

Acknowledgments

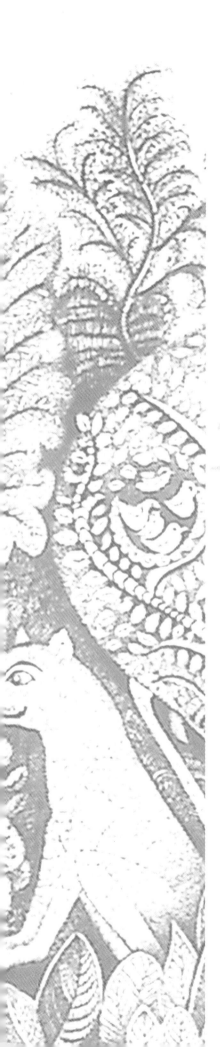

This publication would not have been possible without the support of several individuals, organisations and institutions. In particular, I would like to thank Siumee Helen Keelan, the curator of *Dialogue of the Present: the Work of 18 Arab Women Artists*, who had the inspired idea of the exhibition and who has worked throughout to bring several related projects to fruition. This book is a direct result of that exhibition and her invaluable help in organising the related symposium, *Displacement and Difference: Arab Identity in the Contemporary World*, held at the Brunei Conference Centre, University of London, on Saturday, 24 April 1999. Jointly organised by the School of Art and Design History, Kingston University and the Centre of Near and Middle Eastern Studies, School of Oriental and African Studies, University of London, the symposium was supported by the British Academy, the London Arts Board, Visiting Arts, the Centre of Near and Middle Eastern Studies, SOAS, and Kingston University. I would like to thank all concerned for their support, and the Arts Council of England for financial assistance with this publication.

My thanks also go to all of the speakers who contributed to the success of the symposium, including Gilane Tawadros, Director of the Institute of International Visual Arts (inIVA), London. The following essays were developed from the symposium and I would like to thank all of the writers for their contributions and for being such a delight to work with across various geographies. In addition, I would like to thank all of the artists involved for answering my many questions and for granting permission to reproduce their works.

Further thanks to Melanie Roberts for her invaluable recording skills; Althea Greenham and the other staff of the Women's Art Library, Fulham Palace, London for their support; AAVAA, based at the University of East London, for use of their library, and Kingston University for some research leave to enable me to undertake this publication. Many thanks to Sajid Rizvi, the commissioning editor, for his unfailing support in the production of this publication, and to colleagues, friends and students who helped me to rethink visual culture. Not least, I would like to acknowledge the unreserved support of my husband Patrick Warren and my children Luke, Camille, Duncan, Nathan and Saskia.

The authors and the publishers are indebted to all the artists for permission to reproduce their works and to Flammarion, Paris, for permission to reproduce the Andrèe Chedid poem from *Poëmes pour un texte (1970-1991)*, 1991. **F L**

Mary Tuma, *Body Count* (detail), 1995
wire, stockings, tulle, pins, thread 20 x 32.5 x 12cm

Images, Diasporas and Difference

Displacement and Difference: Contemporary Arab Visual Culture in the Diaspora focuses on the multiplicity and diversity of Arab identities imaged by contemporary Arab artists in the diaspora. Centring on images produced by Arab artists, it brings together several interconnected areas of enquiry which have been the subject of recent writing across and within a number of disciplines. Most importantly, these include the complex and often contradictory processes which constitute 'belonging' (and therefore 'unbelonging') through gender, geographies, race, ethnicity, religion, and sexuality; the changing nature of diaspora/diasporas, and the different ways in which shifting and intersecting points of identification are re-presented and embodied in visual art practices in the contemporary world.[1]

Contrary to the stereotypical images that circulate, particularly in the western world, Arab identities are not monolithic, uniformly constituted or reducible to singular categories, whether by religion, language, geography or gender.[2] Like all identities, they are produced by the different ways in which embodied subjects are situated and situate themselves along multiple lines, according to gender, race, religion, ethnicity, generation, sexuality and so forth. These multiple and shifting points of identification, negotiated through sameness and difference, are always formed through and against an other or other points in time and space: through multiple and often contradictory histories, politics and social interactions.

Thus, by focusing on the imaging of Arab identities in the diaspora, this publication is not concerned with defining or fixing Arab identities or, indeed, with Arab identity *per se*. Instead, it is concerned with the continuous process of negotiation, challenge and resistance through which Arab identities are imaged, and continuously re-imaged, in contemporary visual culture, across and within multiple diasporas. This emphasis on imaging foregrounds visual culture as an active site of the renegotiation of identities and meanings, both for the artist and the spectator. For, far from being dead objects or images, with pre-determined and fixed meanings, visual culture is part of the production of knowledge which is constantly open to new meanings, negotiated through points of identification and difference.[3]

However, although meanings are multiple and not pre-determined, asymmetries of positioning exist, and the questions of which identities are imaged, how they are imaged, by whom, against or through what, and for what purposes have become crucial ones. In this respect, the scarcity of material on contemporary Arab visual culture, whether in Arab countries or the diaspora, is marked.[4] Despite the presence of such major international artists as Mona Hatoum, a Palestinian born in exile in Lebanon (who now lives in Britain), little attention has been paid to the Arab diaspora within contemporary art practice.[5] This is especially striking when compared, for example, to the fast expanding, and much needed, body of literature on contemporary black women's art, on Arab women's writing, and the number of recent publications focusing on Jewish identities.[6] Fully aware of the dangers of monolithic categories, such as Arab or women, and the delimitation of territories by nation, race, ethnicity or religion, it is this omission that the authors seek to address within the discipline of western art history.[7]

Paradoxically, therefore, in presenting a variety of perspectives on the imaging of contemporary Arab identities, the following collection of essays aims to confound and resist attempts to separate contemporary Arab subjects into marginalised or proscribed cultural spaces. It emphasises the often overlooked fact, that contemporary visual culture is produced across and within multiple geographical sites, including the diasporas of Britain, the United States and Palestine, and that these artists are important as active subjects in the contemporary art world. (Figure 1.1)

The possibility of imaging this project has emerged as a result of radical changes, connected with the multifarious conditions of postmodernity and postcolonialism, which have, in effect, slowly eroded, both from within and without, the previously held privileged and self-assured position by the western world, geographically, politically and culturally.[8] In an age of increasing mobility, whether through travel, migration, voluntary or involuntary exile or the developments of new global communication technologies, it is no longer possible (if ever it was) to conceive of cultural identity as predominately associated with a fixed site of a nation, a particular geography or a unified culture. Instead, the emphasis has shifted, for a variety of reasons, to an awareness of multiplicity both within and across these sites in a number of different ways. These changes have had a profound effect on how we view ourselves and others.

Ever since Edward Said's seminal book on Orientalism, published in 1978, there has been much written on the imaging of the Orient, particularly the Oriental and/or Arab woman as other.[9] While Anglo-American feminist writing on visual culture has provided a powerful critique of the universalised, male gaze associated with empire, mastery, and the gendering of the Orient,[10] other scholars, working within various disciplines, have critiqued both western totalising and eurocentric discourses, and the linking of nation, state and gender in colonial and postcolonial geographies, by both revolutionary and/or conservative groupings.[11] For, as Inderpal Grewal has noted, "What needs to be examined is how gendering is a disciplinary practice in all societies, without relying on notions of First World 'freedoms' and 'Third World' repressions."[12]

Thus, in much recent writing, the focus has shifted from the rather singular and oppositional categories of the West and the East, and the coloniser and the colonised, to an awareness of more complex, multiple and contradictory positionings, according to geographies, gender, race, class, language and sexuality, where subjects occupy more than one positioning — they may be empowered by class, for example, but not by

1.1 Leila Kawash, *Diaspora* (detail), 1992, mixed media collage on canvas, 90 x 75cm

Photo: Mark Gulezian

1.2 Malika Agueznay, *Regard,* 1990, zinc etching, 49 x 34cm

race or gender. Frequently informed by cultural studies, anthropology, and the relatively new discipline termed postcolonial studies, feminist writers such as Reina Lewis, for example, and Meyda Yeğenoğlu, have shown the shifting relationships between race, gender and culture in their respective studies of women Orientalists, and women and veiling.[13] Others, such as Ella Shohat, Irit Rogoff and Lisa Bloom, arguing for a multicultural feminism, have used such interdisciplinary methods to analyse the different ways in which ethnic and racial categorisation are linked to issues of national identity, and the making and reception of visual culture in various geographies.[14] (Figure 1.2)

In terms of cultural identity, one of the most evident shifts is in the renewed interest in the diaspora, the movement of a nation or a group of people from one homeland to another. In Britain, the writings of Stuart Hall and subsequently Paul Gilroy,[15] have been of immense importance in dismantling the concept of a singular, unified national identity and of establishing the concept of the diaspora as a site of transformation and difference where cultural identities are continually remade both through and against past and present conditions. Together with the work of Homi Bhabha on hybridity and in-betweenness,[16] such approaches, as Gilroy states, "skirt the sterile opposition between tradition and modernity by asserting the irreducible priority of the present"[17] and have enabled a fundamental rethinking of inherited categories and classifications.

Building upon this work, Nicholas Mirzoeff's recent writing on African and Jewish diasporas argues that the diaspora can no longer be seen in the singular and predominately along a trajectory of the homeland and the place of displacement.[18] For many in the 20th century, the diaspora has become more frequently a new home from which a return may not be envisaged or indeed possible and "the hybridity generated by diaspora is not just with the 'host' nation but among diasporas themselves."[19] This awareness of the historical and continuing interactions between different diasporas, the increasing frequency with which individuals may inhabit various successive diasporas in the course of a single lifetime as multiple immigrants, and the further complexities of what Irit Rogoff calls the "diaspora's diaspora,"[20] points to the numerous and often

1.3 Maysaloun Faraj, *Sisters of Black and Gold*, 1988, glazed stoneware with onglaze and gold metal, height 57cm, width 28cm. Collection Raya Jallad

contradictory intersecting points of cultural identification that we are just beginning to envisage. (Figure 1.3)

Discussing her experience of living and working in the diaspora of America, Chandra Talpade Mohanty, notes, for example, that "there is no clear or obvious *fit* between geography, race, and politics for someone like me. I am always called on to define and redefine these relationships — 'race,' 'Asian-ness,' and 'brownness' are not *embedded* in me, but histories of colonialism, racism, sexism, and nationalism, as well as of privilege (class and status), are involved in my relation to white people and people of color in the USA."[21] Aware that "such definitions and understandings do provide a genealogy," Mohanty stresses, however, that it is a "genealogy that is always relational and fluid as well as urgent and necessary."[22] Furthermore, within the framing of multicultural feminism, which crosses national and regional borders, "Questions of 'home,' 'belonging,' 'nation,' and 'community' thus become profoundly complicated."[23]

Concepts of nation, or what Benedict Anderson refers to as "imagined communities,"[24] are radically changing in numerous ways. While the boundaries of nation-states are redefined in a post-Soviet Bloc and realigned Europe, the interconnected effects of American power, recent events in Afghanistan and the Middle East after the 11 September 2001 attacks in the United States, the Gulf War, and resultant new alliances formed across the globe, both locally and nationally, have produced ever more complex and multiple sites of identification. At the same time, the not unrelated rise of religious fundamentalism, both in colonial and postcolonial spaces, has led to the increasing racialisation of religion. More specifically, and "especially," as Nira Yuval-Davis notes in relation-ship to Islam and Britain, this "reached a new peak after the Rushdie affair" and more recent events where "groups previously known by national or regional origin … are now all seen as part of a single Muslim community. This categorization of minority communities in primarily religious terms assumes them to be internally unified, homogeneous unities with no class or gender differences or conflicts."[25] Equally, as Hatem shows, in the context of America and the Gulf War, the anti-Iraqi political statements quickly became aligned with a "broad anti-Arab one" where "'Arabs' continued to be homogeneously represented as a cultural and political 'other'."[26]

These essays disrupt this homogeneity by concentrating on the specificities of differing geographies, generations and positionings. Arab identity cannot be ascribed to a particular territory or nation. As Sabiha Khemir's essay shows, there is no one originary homeland nor one singular religion. Arab is not synonymous with Muslim — there are Christian Arabs, Jewish Arabs and so forth. Conversely, Muslim is not synonymous with Arab, as the large communities of Southeast Asian and Iranian Muslims show. Similarly, links of language are again compli-cated by differing dialects and the effects of colonisation where whole generations in Morocco or Algeria, for example, may have not written or spoken in Arabic.[27]

1.4 Azza al-Qasimi, *Geometrics 1,* 1997, etching and collage, 75 x 54cm

As noted previously, issues of geography and nation are equally as important to the current rethinking of visual representa-tion and its meanings. Numerous writers have shown that the history of art has, until recently, been written from a eurocentric view and constructed primarily in terms of nation and the classificatory systems of the West.[28] Art from colonial and non-western geographies has been presented in the museums as ethnography or, when it has entered art galleries, it is usually as a traditional culture removed from the modernity of the West.

This is problematic for all geographies, but it is particularly problematic for colonised and postcolonial geographies of which the Arab world represents a substantial part. Frequently educated within a western art system, at home or abroad, such subjects are often refused access to the exhibition spaces of western modernity and a place in its history, while simultaneously existing outside of the 'traditional'. Doubly displaced through modernity and tradition, they represent an almost overlooked history of hybridity that has yet to be written.[29] (Figure 1.4)

However, it is not a case of simply writing these artists back into history, although this is an important and necessary project. It also requires a radical rethinking of the way that history has been written and from whose perspective. For, as Aline Brandauer incisively notes, what is at stake here "are the identity conditions of modernity itself, and how these begin to shift as we look at its development outside of the metropolitan centers of Europe and North America, or alternatively, from points of view of those whose agency has been ignored or suppressed."[30]

Moreover, writing on the western modernist myths "of pure creativity and expressivity," Trinh T Minh-ha, the Asian American writer, filmmaker and composer, eloquently argues that these western constructs of the artist depoliticise "the tools of creation ('Forget ideology: let the work come out from the vision you have: otherwise it is impure,' or, 'Forget aesthetics: only bourgeois indulge in the luxury of aesthetic experience')."[31] Thus, "what is passed over or reduced to the technical realm is the question: How is it made?" For Minh-ha, like many of the artists discussed here, the act of "(Re)Creating" is more complex; it involves questioning "... it is an excursion. More often than not, it requires that one leave the realms of the known, and take oneself there where one does not expect, is not expected to be."[32]

1.5 Mai Ghoussoub and Souheil Sleiman, *Displaces,* 1998, plaster installation in three rooms

1.6 Saadeh George, *Today I Shed My Skin: Dismembered and Remembered,* 1998, detail of installation, life size

As indicated earlier, this collection of essays is concerned with such shifts of naturalised assumptions about visual culture. Written from different perspectives and locations, the authors of the essays provide multiple perspectives on the imaging of contemporary Arab identities and the issues involved. They do not attempt to provide an all encompassing history of the present Arab world, nor do they claim to speak for a particular geography or community. Instead, the essays are intended as a first step towards the theorising of the imaging of contemporary Arab identities in multiple diasporas. It is an area that has been almost entirely absent from the discipline of art history, particularly in Britain, and the agency of its subjects ignored. Until more attention is given to these different bodies of work, it will be impossible to fully consider multiple diasporas. (Figure 1.5)

The opening part of the book's title, *Displacement and Difference*, is intended to signal the variety of interconnected issues encompassed in this study. Displacement is both geographical, through forced or voluntary exile, and cultural displacement, in the sense of a suppression of other histories, whether in colonial and/or postcolonial or diaspora geographies. (Figure 1.6)

Much has been written recently on the crossing of cultural and territorial boundaries, the effects of displacement and of exile: the loss, ambivalence, in-betweenness, the plurality of vision, the sadness and the new perspectives it can provide.[33] Several writers have seen such 'deterritorialisation' as a particularly productive site for women artists and writers; not just because it can generate new perceptions, but as Janet Wolff argues, it can also "facilitate personal transformation, which may take the form of 'rewriting the self,' discarding the life long habits and practices of a constraining social education and discovering new forms of self-expression."[34] Minh-ha sees such questioning as also offering the possibility of "participating in the changing of received values — the transformation (without mastery) of other selves through one's self. To displace so as not to evade through shortcuts by suppressing or merely excluding."[35]

As Edward Said notes, nationalism has an "essential association with exile" which it seeks to fend off by asserting belonging while, "just beyond the frontier between 'us' and the 'outsiders' is the perilous territory of not-belonging" of exile.[36]

However, as Tina Sherwell's essay on the imaging of Palestine shows, one does not have to leave one's homeland to be displaced.[37] The forced re-drawing of political maps leads to a re-negotiation of space and to the reality of a diaspora within as well as outside of the previous territory. Equally, as Sedira's recent work suggests, displacement and exile has been the fate of numerous Arab females in their homeland, in this case Algeria, and in their various birthplaces in the diaspora. (Figure 1.7)

Crucially, displacement is also used to refer to the displacement of eurocentricity and its accompanying grand narratives, which have prevailed for so long. For, it is only through this displacement, of questioning what has become naturalised, that new ways of looking at ourselves and others may emerge. Using Derrida's two-step strategy of breaking binary oppositions, Yeǧenoǧlu succinctly describes this process whereby: "The aim of shaking the structure itself is possible only when the other and otherness is located in the heart of the subject. In other words, displacement is the move by which the desire for a sovereign, possessive, and unitary position is itself interrupted."[38] Furthermore, it also points to what Shohat refers to as "the multilayered displacement" where, as she shows, categorisations frequently used to monitor ethnicity and race, exclude and assume certain geographies, while "reductive categories like 'Jew,' or 'Arab' or 'Latino/a' similarly hide the racial variety of a chromatic spectrum that includes white, black, mestizo/a, and brown" and "does not allow for the polysemy in the politics of colour."[39] (Figure 1.8)

1.7 Zineb Sedira, 'Hide' and 'Seek', 1999, computer generated photographic image, 21 x 30cm

In a similar way, difference refers to the multitude of differences which operate historically, politically and culturally to separate along the lines of gender, race, nation, religion or sexuality, and to difference within and across such groupings.[40] Seeking to avoid the homogenisation and fixing of identity around any one of these groupings, difference is the recognition of the multiplicity that is the process of identity and becoming, whether as the multiplicity of female subjects, Arab subjects or Muslim subjects. However, this is not to say that such identificatory points are not important, particularly given the realities of those subordinated or disenfranchised by gender, race or sexuality. Further-more, as much recent writing has shown, cultural and sexual difference are not a separate category of women's studies or of cultural studies or a sub-set of a more important subject, of, for example, modernism, colonialism, postcolonial and so forth, but are a central and crucial part of the very formation of the category itself and constitutive of the subject.[41] Thus, as Minh-ha succinctly states, "The struggle is always multiple and transversal — specific but not confined to one side of any border war."[42] (Figure 1.9)

Significantly, the majority of the artists discussed here are women. While this partly reflects the large number of Arab women artists working in Arab countries and the diaspora, it also represents the concerns of the writers, and the specificities of women's experience in differing colonial and postcolonial spaces. While gender has been important in the imaging of national identities, particularly during colonial struggles, the central role that women have directly occupied in visual culture has received little attention until recently. Refusing a singular category of woman or Arab, the writers who are all women, come from different locations and cultural backgrounds. The majority are Arab, but some are not. Each has articulated a different perspective on the imaging of contemporary Arab identities in order not to conceal differences, but to become aware of the process through which difference operates across the multiple sites of visual culture, and to question the different ways in which exclusion and inclusion operate. The essays are therefore an

1.8 Jananne Al-Ani, *Untitled (Veils Project)*, 1997, black and white photograph, first of a pair, each 180 x 120cm

opportunity to rethink Arab identity in all these different and displacing ways both for the artist and the spectator. (Figure 1.10)

The opening essay by Els van der Plas provides a valuable reminder of what is at stake if we really want an international and multicultural art world. In an attempt to push forward the debate about multiculturalism and art, she argues that, if change is going to occur, the normalised and dominant cultural and aesthetic values of the West will need to be reconsidered and radically altered. These changes will need to occur both within and across the educational and art institutions which support, control and mediate access to the international art world.

Salwa Mikdadi Nashashibi's essay further develops these issues by focusing on multiculturalism in America and the place assigned to Arab art. Drawing upon her rich experience as an Arab American curator and writer, Nashashibi outlines the problems of ethnic classificatory systems and the particular difficulties facing Arab American artists who, located between a white mainstream and ethnic minorities, are frequently marginalised by both groupings. Emphasising the multiplicity of Arab American art, generational differences, and its multi-sited sources, Nashashibi discusses the work of three contemporary women artists, and argues for the crucial need to rethink a eurocentric education system, and the museum and gallery policies which currently exclude such multiplicity.

Moving between different registers which include the autobiographical, Sabiha Khemir explores the multiplicity of Arab identity through the unity and diversity of the language, the wide ranging effects of the diaspora, and its relationship to personal and collective memory. Crossing different geographies and histories, Khemir argues for the need to maintain a contact with Arab history and Islamic art, and the importance of seeing these histories extend beyond the nineteenth century affects of colonisation into the 20th century. Committed to the necessity of a dialogue, she demonstrates the possibilities of coexistence of difference through reference to the historical past of Andalusia, and to contemporary developments in musical forms. (Figure 1.11)

Aware of the invisibility of Arab women in both Western Orientalism and

Fundamentalism, Mai Ghoussoub, the Lebanese artist, writer and editor argues for the rethinking of current attitudes towards the orient and the 'other'. Taking the Arab woman's body as a major site for the operation of the gaze, Ghoussoub looks at a wide range of visual culture from 19th-century Orientalist imagery in painting, the popular photographic images of colonial postcards to contemporary Arab book covers and advertisements. Pointing to a number of conflicting and contradictory gazes, both in the East and the West, Ghoussoub questions what is suppressed or silenced and argues for the need to rethink habitualised classificatory systems and hierarchies. (Figures 1.12 and 1.13)

Continuing the theme of geographies and diasporas, Tina Sherwell explores the little researched area of contemporary Palestinian art. Drawing upon the recent history of the Palestinian people within the occupied territories, she outlines the effects that their cultural, economic and political displacement has had on Palestinian art and the imaging of Palestine as a motherland. Aware of imaging as a crucial part of national discourse and the privileging of certain groups, Sherwell shows how this works to suppress or repress difference across a multitude of sites and highlights other neglected histories in contemporary visual culture. (Figure 1.14)

The next contribution further develops the question of imaging identities and the politics of location by firmly placing artistic production in a cross-cultural frame. Here, Houria Niati, the Algerian-born installation and performance artist, provides an insight into her experiences of growing up in colonial and postcolonial Algeria and the crossing of geographical and cultural boundaries. Offering new insights into the limitations of monolithic national definitions, she emphasises the specificities of her work in changing situations, and the

1.9 Laila al-Shawa, *Children of War,* 1992-1995, 100 x 230cm, part of The Walls of Gaza installation of 10 silkscreens

1.10 Wafaa El Houdaybi, *Meknés,* 1998, work in progress, paint and henna on stretched leather

1.11 Sabiha Khemir, *Shipwreck 1,* Illustration for book cover, *The Island of Animals,* 1994, 12.5 x 32cm, Quartet Books, London 1994

1.12 Mai Ghoussoub, *Diva*, 1999, installation, 200 x 50 x 30cm

She stood straight and tilted her head slightly towards her public. I have to bend the aluminium rod harder towards her neck. I stop. I look at her, I have the feeling that she is staring at me. I pull harder and bang heavily on the material but I still can't reduce her to her own figurative self.

Here she is again, triumphant in her myth. A winner. A goddess that we can hear, imagine, long for, scream with, cry for. A goddess that can be worshipped but never touched.

"I will make you touchable again" I say to her while I am unraveling the black woollen threads that will stand severely combed around her face, an austere perfect chignon.

I stretch the wool but I can't get to her. She is absolutely unreachable. She is definitely looking at me now. She can see me, I would swear to it. And I, with the millions who worshipped her, cannot see but her aura.

"AH! AH!" she sings, "YOU KEEP ME WAITING MY OPPRESSOR YOUR DEVASTATING EYES - IF ONLY" - and millions of Arab women and men sigh listening, late at night, to her complaints and becoming increasingly and desperately addicted to her voice.

No I cannot carve her mouth. It would not be right. It would be blas-

1.13 Mai Ghoussoub, *Diva*, 1999, installation, 200 x 50 x 30cm

1.14 Firyal al-Adhamy, *Looking Forward*, 1997, acrylic and watercolour on paper, 55 x 40cm

importance of performativity in the process of making and understanding her work as embodied subjectivity. (Figure 1.15)

By contrast and from a different perspective, my contribution focuses on the work of contemporary Arab women artists exhibited in Britain in *Dialogue of the Present*, 1999-2000.[43] Using recent writing on subjectivities and performativity, I extend the idea of cultural belonging to consider the role of memories and materialities for the artist and the audience. Through an analysis of specific works created in the Arab diaspora of London, I argue for a re-evaluation of memory as an act of performativity and embodiment in the present (rather than a nostalgic re-creation of the past) and the importance of memory for bringing into view the forgotten and repressed histories evident in the work of contemporary Arab women artists. In addition, I suggest that it is through memory that identities are renegotiated and that new meanings can be created by the artist and the spectator.

Thus, moving beyond issues of the gaze and the 'other,' the authors all offer new ways of considering the complex interplay between the cultural politics of location, memory, and embodiment through an investigation of difference and displacement in contemporary Arab visual culture. Furthermore, they address the numerous ways in which difference and displacement can be rethought in a fast changing and volatile world where we are witnessing the displacement and movement of peoples on a scale unknown since World War II, based on perceived cultural and religious difference, with the overwhelming events in Kosovo. This, together with the Palestinian situation, the crisis in Algeria and the continued sanctions in Iraq, and the recent upheavals on the world stage, makes questions of difference, how it is constituted and what it signifies, crucial ones. Acutely aware that 'belonging' is always in relation to 'not belonging,' the understanding of the processes of exclusion/inclusion take on an urgency in a contemporary world where postcolonial experience is radically altering the way we all perceive ourselves, our sense of home, belonging and our identity.

Visual culture has always been part of the struggle of identities, whether national, group, or individual. It is not value free and immune from vested interests and hence, as these essays underline, the particular need to be continually alert to the often underlying ideas of authenticity versus corruption, of pure versus mixed, of homogeneity or unity versus the heterogeneous and multiple. For, although we may be aware of the fictive elements of representation and of the imaging of identities, it does not mean, as many writers have stressed,[44] that these do not have real effects at all levels by reiteration, performativity and widespread dissemination. Conscious, as Mirzoeff quite rightly notes, of not valorising the diaspora,[45] such diaspora identities can embody the disruptive/transformative effects of the diaspora and allow us to re-think assumptions and positionings. As Khemir notes, there is always the risk that the sense of crossing boundaries, characteristic of the new globalism,

1.15 Houria Niati, *Ziriab...Another Story*, 1998, installation detail, *Dialogue of the Present: The Work of Eighteen Arab Women Artists*, installation, Hot Bath Gallery, Bath, 16 January 1999

may finally be a reinstatement of a western power position, but equally the refusal of a unified or unidirectional imaging is necessary for a new fluidity and unfixity at all levels and an increasing self-criticality about the terms and methods used.

Using various approaches and methods, these essays are intended to open up a range of history yet to be written while simultaneously stressing that multiple identities do not necessarily mean fragmented ones. The imaging of contemporary Arab identities in the diaspora are a desire to situate oneself, to question and to re-think identities through an awareness of the politics of location, and equally as importantly, an awareness of the work as a site of discovering, of agency and of questioning in a shifting world where the making and contesting of imaging matters. (Figure 1.16)

Notes

[1] For recent theorisations of 'belonging' in social anthropology, art history and postcolonial studies see Reed, Christopher (ed). *Not at Home: The Suppression of Domesticity in Modern Art and Architecture*, London: Thames and Hudson, 1996; Naficy, Hamid (ed). *Home, Exile, Homeland: Film, Media and the Politics of Place*, London and New York: Routledge, 1998; Mohanty, Chandra Talpade. 'Crafting Feminist Genealogies: On the Geography and Politics of Home, Nation and Community' in Shohat, Ella (ed). *Talking Visions: Multicultural Feminism in a Transnational Age*, Cambridge, Mass: MIT Press, 1999, pp485-500.

[2] Following the 'Rushdie affair,' the Gulf War and the most recent events after the 11 September attacks in the United States and the bombing of Afghanistan, stereotypical images of Arabs and/or Muslims (Arab or not) have become increasingly dominant. See, for example, Hatem, Mervat F. 'The Invisible American Art: Arab American Hybridity and Feminist Discourses in the 1990s' in Shohat, Ella (ed). *Talking Visions: Multicultural Feminism in a Transnational Age*, ibid, pp369-390, and Modood, Tariq 'British Asian Muslims and the Rushdie Affair' in Donald, James and Rattansi, Ali (eds), *'Race, Culture & Difference*. London, California, New Delhi: Sage Publications in association with The Open University, 1992, reprinted 1999.

[3] For issues of performativity in relation to visual culture see, for example, Bloom, Lisa (ed). *With Other Eyes: Looking at Race and Gender in Visual Culture*, Minneapolis: University of Minnesota Press, 1999 and Jones, Amelia and Stephenson, Andrew. *Performing the Body: Performing the Text*. London and New York: Routledge, 1999.

[4] For recent research on different aspects of contemporary Arab visual culture see the following publications in English: Ali, Wijdan. *Contemporary Art from the Islamic World*, London: Scorpion Publications Ltd, Amman: The Royal Society of Fine Arts, 1989. Lloyd, Fran (ed). *Contemporary Arab Women's Art: Dialogues of the Present*. London: Women's Art Library and I B Tauris, 1999; Lloyd, Fran. 'Contemporary Algerian Art: Embodiment and Performing the 'Self': Houria Niati and Zineb Sedira,' *Journal of Algerian Studies*, London, March 2000; Nashashibi, Salwa Mikdadi. *Forces of Change, Artists of the Arab World*. Lafayette, California: ICWA, 1994; Tucker, Judith E (ed). *The Presentation of Culture, Arab Women, Old

1.16 Zineb Sedira, *'Hide' and 'Seek'*, 1999, computer generated photographic image, 21 x 30cm

Boundaries, New Frontiers. Bloomington: Indiana University Press, 1993; Zuhur, Sherifa. *Performance, Art, Image and Gender in the Modern Middle East.* Cairo and Florida: American University of Cairo Press and University of Florida Press, 1995; Zuhur, Sherifa (ed). *Images of Enchantment: Visual and Performing Arts of the Middle East,* Cairo: American University of Cairo Press, 1998.

[5] For a detailed discussion of Hatoum's work, including the effects of exile and displacement, see Archer, Michael *et al, Mona Hatoum,* London: Phaidon Press, 1997. See also, for example, the catalogue essay by Candice Breitz on the American-based Arab Egyptian artist Ghada Amer in *Echolot: Oder 9 Fragen an die Periperie (9 Questions from the Margins),* Museum Fridericianum, Kassel, Germany, 1998 and the essay on the Arab-Israeli artist Sigal Primor by Irit Rogoff, 'Daughters of Sunshine — Diasporic Impulses and Gendered Identities' in Bloom, Lisa (ed), *With Other Eyes, ibid,* pp157-183.

[6] On Jewish identity, for example, recent visual culture publications include Bohm-Duchen, Monica and Grodzinski, Vera (eds), *Rubies & Rebels: Jewish Female Identities in Contemporary British Art,* London: Lund Humphries, 1996; Mirzoeff, Nicholas (ed). *Diaspora and Visual Culture: Representing Africans and Jews.* New York and London: Routledge, 1999; Nead, Lynne and Steyn, Juliet, *The Jew: Assumptions of Identity,* London: Continuum, 2000. By contrast, little has been written on the imaging of Arab identity whether separately or as part of the multiple diaspora which includes African and black visual culture.

[7] This omission is the result of several factors. In part, there is a relatively recent Arab cultural tradition that privileges the word over the visual image, the cultural and political policies in several Arab geographies that reinforce this hierarchy and privilege the traditional, and undoubtedly a question of economics, particularly for women artists. However, it is also the result of recent political and historical events that have positioned the Arab world as a danger to the European-American world, together with an institutionalised eurocentricity in the art world which has tended to ignore work produced in Arab geographies and diaspora. Notable exceptions to this in Britain were the exhibitions *From Two Worlds,* Whitechapel Art Gallery, London, 1986, which included the Algerian-born artist Houria Niati, the momentous *The Other Story: Afro-Asian Artists in Post-War Britain,* at the Hayward Gallery, 1989 which included Mona Hatoum, and *Four x 4,* organised by Eddie Chambers in 1991.

[8] These included, among other influential texts, the outlining of postmodernity in Lyotard, Jean-François, *The Postmodern Condition: A Report on Knowledge,* Minneapolis: University of Minnesota Press, 1979; the deconstruction of naturalised western mythologies by Barthes, Roland, *Mythologies,* translated Annette Lavers, London: Granada; the critique of western history and concepts of the self by Michel Foucault in *An Archaeology of Knowledge,* New York: Pantheon Books, 1972; and the challenges presented by writers in the 1980s on the effects of postcolonialism, including Bhabha, Homi K, 'The Other Question — the Stereotype and Colonial Discourse,' *Screen,* 24, No 6, November-December 1983; Spivak, Gayatri C, *In Other Worlds: Essays in Cultural Politics,* London: Methuen, 1987; Minh-ha, Trinh T, *Woman Native Other,* Bloomington: Indiana University Press, 1989. See also Young, Robert, *White Mythologies: Writing History and the West,* New York and London: Routledge, 1990.

[9] Said, Edward. *Orientalism: Western Conceptions of the Orient.* London: Routledge and Kegan Paul Ltd, 1978. See also MacKenzie, John M, *Orientalism: History, Theory and the Arts.* Manchester and New York: Manchester University Press, 1995; Graham-Brown, Sarah, *Images of Women; The Portrayal of Women in Photography of the Middle East, 1860-1950,* London: Quartet Books, 1988.

[10] See Nochlin, Linda. 'The Imaginary Orient' in *The Politics of Vision: Essays on Nineteenth-Century Art and Society,* New York: Harper and Row, 1989 (first published in *Art and America,* May 1983). For subsequent feminist writing on Orientalism see note 13 below.

[11] See, for example, Kandiyoti, Deniz. 'Identity and its Discontents: Women and the Nation' *Millennium: Journal of International Studies,* Vol 20, No 3, 1991, pp429-43; Kandiyoti, Deniz (ed). *Women, Islam and the State.* Philadelphia: Temple University Press, 1991; Yuval-Davies, Nira and Anthias, Floya (eds).

Woman-Nation-State, London: Macmillan, 1989; Grewal, Inderpal and Kaplan, Caren (eds), *Scattered Hegemonies: Postmodernity and Transnational Feminist Practices*, Minneapolis: University of Minnesota Press, 1994; Grewal, Inderpal, *Home and Harem: Nation, Gender, Empire and the Cultures of Travel*, Durham, NC: Duke University Press, 1996; Mohanty, Chandra Talpade, 'Under Western Eyes: Feminist Scholarship and Colonial discourses' reprinted in Patrick Williams and Laura Chrisman (eds), *Colonial Discourse and Post-Colonial Theory, A Reader*, Cambridge: Harvester/Wheatsheaf, 1993, pp196-220 and P Chatterjee, 'The Nation and Its Fragments: Colonial and Post Colonial Histories,' *Third Text*, Summer 1998, *Reviewing Orientalism*.

[12] Grewal, Inderpal. 'On the New Global Feminism and the Family of Nations: Dilemmas of Transnational Feminist Practice' in Shohat, Ella (ed). *Talking Visions*, 1999, p523.

[13] Both writers provide an incisive and clear discussion of this in relation to Orientalism. See Lewis, Reina. *Gendering Orientalism, Race, Femininity and Representation*. London and New York: Routledge, 1996 and Yeğenoğlu, Meyda. *Colonial Fantasies: Towards a Feminist Reading of Orientalism*. Cambridge: Cambridge University Press, 1998. See also Lewis, Reina 'Cross-cultural reiterations: Demetra Vaka Brown and the performance of racialized female beauty' in Jones, Amelia and Stephenson, Andrew. *Performing the Body: Performing the Text*, 1999, pp 56-75; and Bernstein, M. *Visions of the East: Orientalism in Film*, New Brunswick, New Jersey: Rutgers University Press, 1997.

[14] Shohat, Ella (ed). *Talking Visions*, 1999; Bloom, Lisa (ed). *With Other Eyes, 1999;* Irit Rogoff, 'Daughters of Sunshine — Diasporic Impulses and Gendered Identities' in Bloom, Lisa, as above. See also Ella Shohat and Robert Stam, *Unthinking Eurocentrism: Multiculturalism and the Media*, London and New York: Routledge, 1994.

[15] See Hall, Stuart. 'Cultural Identity and Diaspora' in Williams, P and Chrisman, L (eds). *Colonial Discourse and Post-Colonial Theory, A Reader*. Cambridge: Harvester/Wheatsheaf, 1993; Hall, Stuart. 'New Ethnicities' in 'Race,' Culture and Difference, Donald, J and Rattansi, A (eds), 1992; Gilroy, Paul. *The Black Atlantic: Modernity and Double Consciousness*. London and New York: Verso, 1993.

[16] Bhabha, Homi T. *The Location of Culture*. London and New York, Routledge, 1994.

[17] Gilroy, Paul. *The Black Atlantic*, 1993, p202.

[18] Mirzoeff, Nicholas (ed). *Diaspora and Visual Culture: Representing Africans and Jews*, 1999. See also Brah, Avtar, *Cartographies of Diaspora*, New York and London: Routledge, 1996.

[19] Mirzoeff, Nicholas (ed). *Diaspora and Visual Culture, 1999*, pp3-4.

[20] Rogoff, Irit. 'Daughters of Sunshine — Diasporic Impulses and Gendered Identities' in Bloom, Lisa (ed), *With Other Eyes*, 1999, p163.

[21] Mohanty, Chandra Talpade. 'Crafting Feminist Genealogies' in Shohat, Ella (ed). *Talking Visions*, 1999, p500.

[22] Ibid. p499.

[23] Ibid. p485.

[24] Anderson, Benedict, *Imagined Communities: Reflections on the Origin and Spread of Nationalism*. 2nd edition, London, Verso, 1992.

[25] Yuval-Davis, Nira 'Fundamentalism, multiculturalism and women in Britain' in Donald, James and Rattansi, Ali (eds). *'Race,' Culture & Difference*, 1992, p284.

[26] Hatem, Mervat F, 'The Invisible American Art: Arab American Hybridity and Feminist Discourses in the 1990s' in Shohat, Ella (ed). *Talking Visions*, 1999, p372.

[27] The Algerian-born sociologist and anthropologist Marie-Aimée Hélie-Lucas discusses this in 'Women, Nationalism and Religion in the Algerian Liberation Struggle' in Badran, Margot and Cooke, Miriam (eds). *Opening the Gates: A Century of Arab Feminist Writing*, Indiana: Indiana University Press, 1990, pp105-114.

[28] See, for example, Clifford, James. *The Predicament of Culture: Twentieth Century Ethnography, Literature and Art*. Cambridge Mass: Harvard University Press, 1988, and Bloom, Lisa (ed), *With Other Eyes*, 1999, introduction.

[29] For further discussion see, for example, *The Other Story*, Whitechapel Art Gallery, 1989; Araeen, Rasheed. 'New Internationalism' in *Global Visions, Towards a New Internationalism in the Visual Arts*, edited by Jean Fisher. London: Kala/inIVA, 1994, pp3-11.

[30] Brandauer, Aline. 'Practicing Modernism' in Mirzoeff, Nicholas (ed). *Diaspora and Visual Culture*, 1999, p254.

[31] Minh-ha, Trinh T. 'Cotton and Iron' in Ferguson, Russell *et al. Out There, Marginlization and Contemporary Cultures*, 1990, p334-335.

[32] *Ibid*, p335.

[33] See for example, Rushdie, Salman. *Imaginary Homelands: Essays and Criticism 1981-1991*. Granta Books, 1992; Said, Edward W. 'Reflections on Exile,' 1984 in Ferguson, Russell *et al. Out There, Marginlization and Contemporary Cultures*, pp357-366; Said, Edward W. 'The Voice of a Palestinian Exile,' *Third Text*, Vol 3, No 4, 1988: p39-50; and Bhabha, Homi T. *The Location of Culture*. London and New York: Routledge, 1994.

[34] Wolff, Janet. *Resident Alien, Feminist Cultural Criticism*. Cambridge, UK: Polity Press, 1995, p9. See also Kaplin, Caren. 'Deterritorializations: The Rewriting of Home and Exile in Western Feminist Discourse,' *Cultural Critique*, No 6, Spring 1987; Kristeva, Julia, *Strangers unto Ourselves*. Trans by Leon S Roudiez, New York: Columbia University Press, 1991; Kaplin, Caren. *Questions of Travel: Postmodern Discourses of Displacement*, Durham, NC: Duke University Press, 1996; Rey, Chow. *Writing Diaspora*, Bloomington: Indiana University Press, 1993.

[35] Minh-ha, Trinh T. 'Cotton and Iron' in Ferguson, Russell *et al. Out There*, 1990, p332-333.

[36] Said, Edward W. 'Reflections on Exile,' 1984 in Ferguson, Russell *et al. Out There*, 1990, p359.

[37] Displacement within has been extensively discussed by several writers, including the Martinican revolutionary Fanon, Frantz, *Black Skin, White Masks*, translated Charles Lam Markmann, New York: Grove Press, 1952, and the French feminist Kristeva, Julia. *Strangers unto Ourselves*, 1991.

[38] Yeğenoğlu, Meyda. *Colonial Fantasies*, 1998, p8.

[39] Shohat, Ella (ed). *Talking Visions*, 1999, p7.

[40] For a useful discussion of difference within gender see Teresa de Lauretis (ed), *Feminist Studies/ Critical Studies*, London: Macmillan, 1986.

[41] See, for example, Mohanty, Chandra Talpade, 'Under Western Eyes' reprinted in Patrick Williams and Laura Chrisman (eds), *Colonial Discourse and Post-Colonial Theory, A Reader*, 1993, pp212-4

[42] Minh-ha, Trinh T. 'Cotton and Iron' in Ferguson, Russell *et al. Out There*, 1990, p330.

[43] See Lloyd, Fran (ed). *Contemporary Arab Women's Art*, 1999.

[44] See, for example, Yeğenoğlu, Meyda, *Colonial Fantasies*, 1998; Betterton, Rosemary, *An Intimate Distance: Women, Artists and the Body*, London and New York: Routledge, 1996 and Butler, Judith, *Bodies That Matter: On the Discussive Limits of Sex*, London and New York: Routledge, 1993.

[45] Mirzoeff, Nicholas (ed). *Diaspora and Visual Culture*, p9.

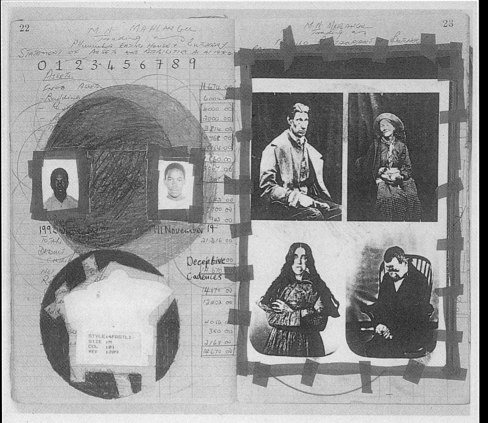

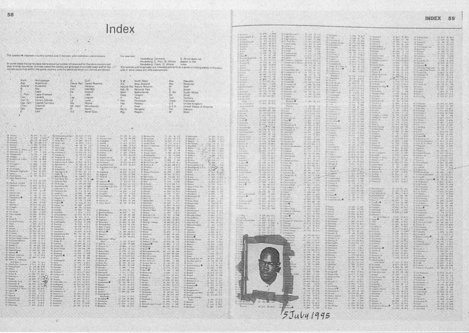

2.1 Moshekwa Mokwena Langa, *No Title*, 1995, collage, 93 x 73cm
Born in 1975 in South Africa, Langa's work was shown in the second Johannesburg Biennale,
12 October 1997 – 18 January 1998

ELS VAN DER PLAS

Internationalism and Art: Re-evaluating the Concepts of Beauty and Individuality in the International Context

Discussions within the framework of internationalism and art, including subjects like 'I and the Other,' 'Globalisation and art,' 'Art in a multicultural society' and 'Under Different Skies' all threaten to fall into repetition and cliché. The international debate seems to keep getting bogged down in issues such as quality and in guilt feelings of the one as opposed to the anger of the other. Postcolonial embarrassment is not dissipating as a result of continued assertions that the work of more black artists should appear in museums or that Arab modern art should be included in the curricula of western universities. It is important therefore to further develop this intercultural debate in order to bring it to a new level. To this end, I propose that we need to identify new values which will breathe fresh life into what has become a tired art debate.

Such a re-thinking could break the status quo of the postcolonial and postmodern situation in the art world and thereby allow us to approach a truer internationalism.[1] These new values could then take the place of the old parameters such as 'originality' and 'quality' — terms that are applied carelessly in reference to both new and historical developments in art.

Originality

Originality is a central concept in western art discourse. It has arisen from the modernist idea of being ahead of one's time — the individual as an original creator — and is frequently aligned with the artist's place being in an ivory tower rather than within society. Originality as a concept has a largely western connotation. It usually stands diametrically opposed to the idea of imitation which, in many non-western cultures, is a highly valued quality indicative of such traditions as the master-apprentice relationship. In these contexts, Mimesis does not automatically mean that the artist's individuality is not expressed in the work.

Quality

Quality is also a much used value judgement in modern art. This concept gets bandied about recklessly in western art criticism. It seems no one knows anymore what it is that defines quality, partly because of the increased proportion of art from other cultures on the world market. Thomas McEvilley, the American critic, has attempted to give the term 'quality' a frame of reference in his essay 'Revaluing the Value Judgement,' published in his book *Art and Otherness* (1992). Rather than seeing quality as a universal value, he argues that it is dependent upon origin, gender, belief and environment.[2] McEvilley's serious attempt to question this concept, to re-think and re-evaluate it, has not yet led to a more substantial theory. However, following this and other developments in theory and practice, art production has become much more diverse in recent years.

The general desire to rethink existing categories seems to have created opportunities for innovative art projects and for works from a variety of cultures to become more visible. (Figures 2.1 and 2.2)

Within such contexts, the concept of quality could again become a valuable one through a process of re-evaluation and reassessment, although it may first be necessary to remove all value from the term. Would it not be useful here to remember the remark of a Tibetan monk, that the best art is created by the most pious monks?[3]

Certainly, the value of quality has recently been put to the test in terms of the distinctions usually drawn between 'low art' and 'high art'. For example, when the painter Chéri Samba (born in 1956 in Zaire) hung his painted signs in the museums of modern art, they prompted a discussion about whether his art was of the same quality as that of, for example, Anselm Kiefer, and whether the work of a folk artist would not be better placed in a folklore museum. In the meantime, Samba has broken through to the so-called legitimate art circuit, an indication that the meaning of value in relationship to contemporary art is certainly subject to change.

However, to avoid falling into the same restrictive institutional traps and repetitive criticisms which such debates usually engender, I suggest we formally declare these two western core concepts of 'quality' and 'originality' bankrupt, certainly as far as they relate to the debate about internationalism and art. Nonetheless, I realise that we must provide alternative terms which can foster an intercultural forum and, in order to work towards this, I suggest that we use the opportunity to re-evaluate two other concepts, namely 'beauty' and 'individuality'. Before I develop these concepts further, I should provide some context for my concerns.

2.2 Malika Agueznay, *Peace (Salem),* 1997, zinc etching, 29.5 x 22.5cm

Most importantly, developments during the colonial and postcolonial eras have created an asymmetry of cultures. Some cultures have played the part of rulers; others were the victims. Some had/have economic wealth, others were/are poor. Some were perceived as rich in culture, others as poor in this respect. Now, as we enter a new century, there appears to be a need — from all sides — to do away with this asymmetry. With new developments in communication and the growing ease with which more people can move around the globe, cultural exchanges and confrontations are becoming more intense — both in the positive and negative sense. There is nothing that can stop this trend. However, these circumstances also stimulate the search for concepts that can provide such meetings with a shared cultural and intellectual foundation.

I and the Other/art as the Other

All countries and all artists have their own cultural history which plays an important role in evaluating one's own culture and that of others. Such evaluations in reference to other cultures — and, thereby in reference to one's own culture — can be characterised by a variety of traits, for instance tolerance, openness (or lack thereof) ethnocentrism, generosity and so forth. These have considerable influence on a country's cultural development and, in turn, on the arts.

If we are to enter into an intercultural debate it is important that all parties are interested in the Other and are open to new ideas and influences. Clinging rigidly to one's own roots, to the exclusion of anything different, will not pave the way to dialogue or communication. Tolerance must stem from an attitude of self-awareness. Very simply, understanding one's own culture, its situatedness, and its multiplicity will allow for greater understanding of another culture.

So, seemingly there is the One and there is the Other. To this idea the German philosopher, Herbert Marcuse (1989-1979) added a third aspect in his book, *The Aesthetic Dimension, Toward a Critique of Marxist Aesthetics*, (1978) when he wrote: "... art is 'unreal' not because it is less, but because it is more as well as qualitatively 'other' than the established reality."[4] What is so interesting about this statement is that Marcuse refers to art as different or as the 'other'. This premise gives us a point of departure from which to escape the art debate as it now stands.

If art is the Other then precisely for this reason it can show us truths — and by 'us' I mean everyone. For, at the very moment that there exists a collective Other, it allows us to find our commonalities by analysing the Other. And, this gives us the chance to create a truly contemporary intercultural art world.

Re-evaluating existing concepts

Beauty: Within the framework of recent art debates, the concept of beauty has been out of favour for many years. It seems to have become taboo to speak of beauty in reference to works of art. In European culture the 'beautiful' is associated with Romantic painting, the Pre-Raphaelites, the writing of Charles Baudelaire and Jane Austen, and the early 19th-century tombs of Canova. But, are the robust works of Joseph Beuys or the confrontational art of Damien Hirst ever discussed in terms of beauty?

In March 1999 in Bombay, the Prince Claus Fund organised a discussion between Indian journalists, philosophers and artists.[5] This was in preparation for a larger event consisting of conferences and presentations, which the Fund plans to organise in 2000 entitled, *Beauty in Context*. The premise of the initial discussion was that beauty is a relative concept which depends on culture, environment, gender, customs, habits and personal preferences. South American artists, writers and critics, also discussed the same topic in Mexico City later in the same year. Obviously, there were enormous differences between the approaches of the two groups — one located in India and one in Mexico. Nevertheless, everyone agreed about one thing; beauty had to be saved from an ignominious end. Once restored to its former discussible status, it could indeed become an important parameter in the discussion of internationalism and art.

The Indian theatre critic Rustom Bharucha, who opened the discussion in Bombay with a paper on 'Beauty in Pain,' observed that:

> If one had to invoke beauty today in literary theory, for example, this would seem like a thoroughly regressive gesture, a return to New Criticism, which has been thoroughly deconstructed over the years. This does not mean that the beautiful does not occasionally appear as an effect, an affect, a compliment in postmodern theory, but it is almost entirely denuded of any specific content. If beauty has to be taken seriously, therefore, it will almost inevitably be problematised.[6]

While not ignoring the problematic of the term, Bharucha allows the possibility of the concept of beauty to be openly discussed once again as part of an international, intercultural debate.

The Spanish-born American philosopher, George Santayana (1863-1952) had a less problematic view of beauty. He described the experience of art as "pleasure" and saw beauty as a quality which can only exist in one's perception as the objectification of pleasure. Indeed, Santayana goes so far as to state that: "Nothing but the good of life enters into the texture of the beautiful."[7] Although this is highly contestable, it does point to the central role that beauty once played in a western discussion of aesthetics. Equally, Melville Herskovits' 1959 writings on a number of western philosophers is still highly relevant today when he observes that: "their studies of aesthetics lacked a cross-cultural dimension" and "that there is a need to widen the base of aesthetic theory, to break through its culture-bound limits. If the aesthetic response is a universal in human experience, it must be studied as such, everywhere it is found."[8]

Working from the idea that an aesthetic reaction is recognisable to everyone, beauty can be used to bridge cultural boundaries. After all, is there anyone who has not known the feeling of experiencing beauty? Although its forms may change, beauty can serve as the foundation on which to develop an international, critical debate on art. I am not just imagining a universal concept of beauty, or of universal art, on the contrary, in fact. It is precisely everyone's ability to recognise the aesthetic experience that offers space for a varied and lively debate about what this might be. For example, the beauty of the lugubrious photographs of blood and semen by the Colombian artist, Fernando Arias (born in 1963) is clear to me, as is that of his installation created from hundreds of blood slides, all checked for HIV, which combine to form a man's body. It's bloody, but it's beautiful. *Images Against Aids* (1994). (Figure 2.3)

2.3 Fernando Arias, *Images against Aids*, poster for Aids, 1994

Individuality: The second concept which could provide a basis for a newly revitalized intercultural discussion of art is that of individuality, a concept no less problematic than that of beauty.

The much-used yardsticks of originality and inventiveness essentially place an emphasis on the degree of innovation, evident most clearly in the 20th-century western desire for an avant-garde. But, as Arthur Koestler noted, new things do not exist; there are only new combinations of existing things. One could argue that this is apparent in the work of Andy Warhol who brought art and

2.4 Shirin Neshat, *Allegiance with Wakefulness,*
1994, black and white photograph with indian
ink, 109.2 x 99cm

commerce together, or in the paradoxical idea of Marcel Duchamp to raise the ultimately mundane to the artistic arena by placing ready-mades in a museum. At the beginning of the 20th century, avant-garde art in Europe was characterised by the desire to bring art and life together while, at the same time, distancing itself from bourgeois society and the existing art establishment. It was a difficult attitude to maintain and could never achieve its goal. But it did cause a revolution in art and questioned the accepted concepts of originality.

The avant-garde has also been characterised by 'breaking for the sake of breaking' and artists from the Futurists onwards have been aware of the fundamental impossibility of the avant-garde surviving its own premise of constant innovation.[9] The desire for constant renewal is, and has become a cliché in 20th-century western art to the point that if something is typified as avant-garde, it loses its avant-garde function. It is for this reason that I am searching for a standard with which to judge art other than the degree to which it is original.

By contrast, individuality could provide a more secure basis for an international dialogue where, based upon a more equal footing, respect for the individual is inherent in the concept. In 1998, I gave a lecture in Stockholm in which I tried to provide such a definition of art within an international context:

An artist expresses an idea or an emotion by means of representation. He or she may be expressing a meaning or a feeling and may be transmitting it to a local, national or international community. An artist has the talent and skill to put this message or emotion in a form that places it on a higher plane than the purely personal, so that it appeals to a wider audience.[10]

Following on from this, I would argue that a work of art becomes interesting, not when it is original or innovative, but when it is more than personal emotion or objective analysis. Individuality embraces more than the purely personal, as described above. It has to do with character, environment, cultural background, talents and desires. It goes further than originality and offers more than just the translation and analysis of everyday, mundane affairs. It is the work's singularity, the characteristics of form, and the reasons for the choice of subject that make the work individual. For example, if we take a work by the Iranian artist Shirin Neshat, this may become clearer

In Figure 2.4, *Allegiance with Wakefulness* (1994) Neshat presents a photograph of two bare feet with the foreboding image of a rifle barrel posed between them. The soles of the feet are decorated with poetic calligraphy. Here, we see a variety of characteristics in her art; the artist is a woman (and she chooses to represent the feet of a woman); she comes from Iran, where she felt threatened as a woman and as an activist (the gun can be interpreted as a threat or as a means of defence); and, now, she lives in New York (and the image contains a mixture of eastern and western symbolism). In combination with each other, I would sum up these characteristics as the individuality of this particular work.

Importantly my concern to provide a positive stimulus to the international art debate is based on the sad fact that little has changed in the international art world in spite of long running intercultural discussions. In the Netherlands, for example, non-western art is still not taught in the universities. In western collections of modern art the presence of non-western art is minimal and, in the western museum circuit, there are few if any non-western curators to be found. Conversely, the libraries in Asia, Africa and Latin America have little information on contemporary modern art, whether from home or abroad. The presence of high quality art periodicals in non-western countries is scarce and exchanges between museums of modern art at a global level still leave much to be desired.

Arthur Koestler, whom I mentioned earlier, drew a distinction between three forms of creativity; namely humour, discovery and art. I have discussed art at length here and discovery in terms of originality, the avant-garde, and individuality. To conclude, I would suggest that the international art debate would probably also benefit from a good dose of humour. Koestler, in fact, compares the catharsis of laughter with the pleasure we feel at experiencing art. For, as the native American said to the totem pole in a museum of modern art, "I know you from a plum tree."[11]

Notes

[1] For a fuller discussion of "true internationalism" see Els van der Plas. 'Internationalism and the Arts: Theory and Practice' in *The Prince Claus Fund Journal*, No1, The Hague: Prince Claus Fund, 1998, pp55-58.

[2] McEvilley, Thomas. *Art & Otherness, Crisis in Cultural Identity,* Kingston, New York: Documentext/McPherson & Company, 1992.

[3] Martin, Jean-Hubert (ed) *et al. Magiciens de La Terre*, exhibition catalogue, Georges Pompidou Centre, Paris, 1989.

[4] Marcuse, Herbert. *The Aesthetic Dimension, toward a Critique of Marxist Aesthetics*, London: Macmillan Press Ltd, 1979 or *Die Permanenz der Kunst: Wider eine bestimmte Marxistische Aesthetik*, Munich: Hanser, 1977.

[5] 5 March 1999. See 'Working Conferences' in *Prince Claus Fund Journal*, No 2, The Hague: Prince Claus Fund, 1999, p6.

[6] Bharucha, Rustom. 'Beauty in Context' in *Prince Claus Fund Journal*, No 2, The Hague: Prince Claus Fund, 1999, p9.

[7] George Santayana 'The Sense of Beauty' (1898) cited in Beardsley, Monroe C. *Aesthetics from Classical Greece to the Present, a Short History*, Alabama: University of Alabama Press, 1966.

[8] Melville Herskovits 'Art and Value' (1959) cited in Beardsley, Monroe C. *Aesthetics from Classical Greece to the Present, a Short History*, Alabama: University of Alabama Press, 1966.

[9] Drijkoningen, Fernand. *Historische Avantgarde*, Amsterdam: Huis aan de Drie Grachten, 1982. Anthology by F Drijkoningen and J Fontijn *et al.*

[10] van der Plas, Els. 'Internationalism and the Arts: Theory and Practice' in *The Prince Claus Fund Journal*, No1, The Hague: Prince Claus Fund, 1998, p56.

[11] Koestler, Arthur. *The Act of Creation*, New York: Macmillan, 1964.

SALWA MIKDADI NASHASHIBI

American-Arab Artists and Multiculturalism in America

During the imperialist conquests of the Orient, art that symbolised the soul of nations was carried off from Africa, Asia and the Americas to museums in the West. A century later, contemporary artists from these same regions are vying for representation in western art institutions. Arab artists are no exception; to many a solo exhibition at these institutions carries considerable value for professional advancement. As several artists have stated, recognition by the western art world secures appreciation for their art in their respective countries. Today, the challenge facing the western art world is to move beyond the perception that ethnic art serves as a testimony to the imperialist legacy and, in the context of America, to acknowledge contemporary art by non-European Americans as a form of personal expression by people who are free to use international methods and techniques.

This challenge is more pertinent now for several reasons. Cultures are more politicised as a result of the economics of the new world order, and they face a world divided not just along ideological lines but also by cultural, ethnic and religious differences. There are also a growing number of minority artists living in the western hemisphere who must be recognised. At the same time, the commercialisation of cultures and the advancements in communication technologies are changing people's perception of cultural differences. The fact that information on art from anywhere in the world is only an instant away (literally under our fingertips) results in a wide range of local, regional and international idioms and models being available to choose from, and to come to terms with. All these factors have also generated new issues for the American-Arab artists to contend with. This essay attempts to explore some of these issues and to shed light on the relevance of 'identity' to American-Arab artists. It will also show how art institutions respond to first and second generation Arab artists living within or outside the boundaries of multiculturalism in the state of California, which was the first state to adopt multiculturalism in the United States.

The past notion that the US is a melting pot of cultures that ends up 'white' has recently been transformed into what Lucy Lippard, in her book *Mixed Blessings*, describes as a flavourful soup in which the ingredients retain their own forms and flavours.[1] Lippard's definition is one way of describing multiculturalism. However, the definition varies, depending on who is asked and in what context the question is posed. Furthermore, the ingredients of this soup are constantly changing. In the year 2000 the percentage of whites was to be 57 per cent compared to 80 per cent in 1970.[2] By the year 2020 minority children will become the majority in California, Texas, New York and Florida.

In the late 1960s, the idea of a 'melting pot' started to give way to diversity and equality among differences under the new policy of 'multiculturalism.' Multiculturalism is about respecting differences among all groups: religious, gender, socio-economic, sexual orientation, age, and the physically challenged. Advocates of multiculturalism have succeeded in promoting educational and social reform policies that aim at the inclusion rather than the exclusion of minorities. Opponents of multiculturalism envisage it as a new form of tribalism that strengthens ethnic loyalties and results in further separation along ethnic and racial lines.

In the early 1980s, California took the lead in multiculturalism when San Francisco State University offered the first course in Ethnic Studies, followed by Stanford University's decision to revise the liberal art courses to include literature from non-European countries. Multicultural programmes were introduced in schools and affirmative action and quotas followed. The latter ensured equality of opportunities for minorities in the state's government job sector and in higher education. However, in the mid-1990s California voted to cancel affirmative action for minority students at state universities. In 1998 a high school principal in California cancelled the observance of black history month and *Cinco de Mayo* because of Black-Latino tensions on campus. More recently a decision to reduce the budget of the Ethnic Studies Department led to a hunger strike by students at the University of California in Berkeley. These incidents underscore the tension surrounding the issue of ethnic diversity on university campuses and serve to inflame the debate on the merits of multiculturalism.

The Arab community in the United States: legal status

Should the Arab community adopt multiculturalism? Will the celebration of Arab heritage in schools and communities result in further isolation of the Arabs? Should the Arabs demand minority status? How do all these questions affect Arab artists?

Currently there are about three million Americans of Arab ancestries. The first wave of immigrants, approximately 250,000, came from Syria and Lebanon before the Second World War, and many of them had only a high school or elementary school education. After the Second World War, Arabs came to the United States mainly for higher education or as professionals. Only Yemenis came as factory workers or farmers, and in contrast with earlier immigrants, the majority were Muslims. Detroit has the largest Arab community in the US with roots in Lebanon, Syria, Iraq, Palestine, Yemen and Egypt. According to the US Census Bureau's definition, Arab Americans are people who trace their ancestry to any one of the countries of the Arab League. In general American Arabs are better educated than the average American. The percentage of those who did not attend college is lower than average, and the percentage of those with postgraduate degrees is twice the average.[3]

Arabs are officially defined as 'white' and are not considered a minority except for the residents of San Francisco, where a 1999 City Council decision gave them minority status. Minority status remains a controversial issue for American Arabs because many feel they can retain both their Arab and American identities without acquiring minority status. Others believe minority status stigmatises them and lowers their social status, and they consider that the recent Arab support of the San Francisco initiative was prompted by the promise of job opportunities in city services and projects.

The marginalisation of American-Arab art

American Arabs face negative stereotypes especially in the media. Dehumanisation and alienation of Americans of Arab descent escalates with every conflict in Arab regions that involves American intervention. During the Gulf war, for example, Iraqis were described as "people without a culture," a sad commentary on a country that was for several centuries the cultural centre of the world.[4] American knowledge of Arab culture and the arts is distorted and minimal at best. As far as the art academia is concerned, the last Arab contribution to art was in Muslim Spain. Even that is attributed to the Moors of Africa! In effect the contemporary Arab has little to offer in the arts aside from the mass-produced imitations of Pharaonic art and other tourist souvenirs. In addition, Arab governments have marginalised contemporary Arab art further by focusing exclusively on the art of ancient cultures of the region and by funding extensive travelling exhibitions from their ancient collections only.

Arab artists in America

The first Arab immigrants arrived at the time when assimilation into one melting pot with a dominant white, Anglo-Saxon Protestant flavour was the dominant ideology. To the first Arabs fleeing starvation, religious persecution, horrors of war and a despotic Ottoman rule, assimilation was a small price to pay for a new start in a promising world. In contrast, recent Arab immigrants are immediately faced with questions of 'identity' in the American context of ethnicity and gender relations. Artists, writers and musicians have to conjure up a definition for their art. Is it Arab, Muslim, Egyptian or an appropriation of western modernism? If they are legally white, does that also mean that their art should be given 'white' or mainstream status? This usually creates a dilemma for American art curators because if art by American Arabs is validated within mainstream western aesthetics, the individual artist or the group he/she represents will most likely have to be recognised. There is at least one documented case of a young Lebanese female artist who, after concluding an agreement to exhibit her work at a gallery in Los Angeles, was told to find another outlet for her work by the gallery owner when he found out that she is an Arab.[5] Although such cases are rare, they provide an accurate picture of the isolation that many first generation American Arabs experience in the US. Those starting afresh in America with limited funds find opportunities and resources with which to learn and experiment, but they miss the recognition and praise they received in the Arab world. In the case of women artists, American art curators find it difficult to believe that they get more recognition and better chances to exhibit in the Arab world than their American counterparts.[6]

Arab artists can be grouped into three categories: the first group of artists identifies with their cultural heritage; they may or may not speak the language, but they keep their ties with the Arab world and are involved in regional politics, and are active in their communities. Their art is inspired by their American or Arab experiences, or a synthesis of both. The second group prefers complete assimilation and has expressed its desire to remain non-hyphenated by gender or ethnicity. These artists may or may not speak Arabic, and they maintain their American identity with the option of adopting selected styles, techniques or themes with an Arab reference. They are usually disconnected from the Arab world, and their knowledge of the art and culture of the region is taken out of context. The third group are multiple immigrants with a hybrid identity who bring with them a truly multicultural experience. This group includes Iraqis or Algerians who immigrated to Europe before coming to the United States. They either identify with the second group, or they maintain their own, unique style and have yet to express the influence of the American experience.

According to recent data, American-Arab artists of the first and second group seem to be successful; approximately 85 per cent of the artists registered in the International Council For Women in the Arts' database (ICWA)[7] have exhibited in group or solo exhibitions in the US. Several women artists belong to art co-operatives, women's art associations or African-American art associations (North African Artists).

The artists I interviewed in the mid-1980s were reluctant to present themselves as Arab artists within a group show for Arabs; they questioned the relevance of an Arab artists' exhibition and felt that their artistic identity had nothing to do with their place of birth. There were several reasons given for their reluctance to join a group exhibition of Arab art.[8] Among the reasons recorded were:

"I want my art to be judged on merits of quality and not ethnicity."

"I have worked hard to be recognised as an international artist and by hyphenating my art it will be read in a totally different context."

3.1 Liliane Karnouk, *Black and Green,* 1992
mixed media on canvas, 75 x 69cm
(see colour plate 1)

"I am not familiar with the other artists' work and therefore cannot commit myself."

"I do not wish to politicise my art."

One artist, who was born in the US and later married an Arab and lived in the Arab world for several years, considered herself American and saw no reason to join an Arab group exhibition.

Almost twenty years later and after organising several Arab art exhibitions, I rarely encounter resistance to the idea of a group Arab exhibition, with the exception of the second group, which is increasingly becoming a minority. Many of the artists who initially refused to join an Arab group exhibition have changed their mind; a common reason given for the change is that they wish to show Americans the Arab achievements in contemporary art. The following selection of artists shows how American/Canadian Arab artists construct a third identity that evolves from their individual experiences that may, or may not, centre on 'Arab' themes.

Liliane Karnouk is a Canadian-Egyptian artist whose work is an example of how the environment can shape a style anchored in one or more traditions. At first glance, her new art work seems deceptively unlike her earlier work which was produced in Egypt before moving to Canada two years ago (figure 3.1). At that time, natural dyes and materials preoccupied Karnouk who was searching for common denominators in nature — a nature which was increasingly being threatened by pollution. Images of tissue culture, from the tree barks of the Canadian forests, blended with Egyptian papyrus, and handmade paper and fibres.

By contrast, Karnouk's recent works are panels or screens of geometric designs. She also produces similar designs in fine lace-like patterns cut in glass (figures 3.2 and 3.3). She describes her art as follows:

3.2 Liliane Karnouk, *Untitled,*
1998
acrylic on canvas, 1 of 3
panels, each 66 X 24cm
(see colour plate 2)

...influenced by the range of colours in my garden in British Columbia and a diverse array of patterns rooted in Native Canadian art and Arab-Islamic art. The major Arab influence is in the fusion of the

3.3 Liliane Karnouk, *Untitled,* 1998
glass, 180 X 360cm
model for public sculpture
(see colour plate 3)

ornamental form where the useful object is also aesthetic. In the new work, the order of geometric measures replaces the shapes and textures of the optic representation of the biological nature of the tree bark; both new and old works emphasise an underlying structure.[9]

The meeting between the East and West also converge in the art of Doris Bittar who spent her early childhood in Lebanon before her family immigrated to New York. Her memories of life in Beirut are depicted through patterns from oriental rugs, French floral fabric, her mother's embroidery and the warm landscape. In art school she was reintroduced to the 'exotic' Orient through Matisse's portrayals of Arabs and his use of pattern. While living in New York, she became familiar with the Jewish culture and looked closely at biblical narratives. The crossing of these three cultures — the Arab, French and Jewish — has been the basis for a series of works where the artist interweaves a personal, historical and political narrative.

Edward Said has argued that Orientalism does not translate into a dialogue between East and West. Rather, it is a fantasy-based discourse that has served western ambitions in the Orient and resulted in colonisation of the East.[10] Bittar's painting, *Watching Jacob*, 1992 (figure 3.4), intervenes in this discourse by recontextualising a painting by the French artist Eugène Delacroix.[11] Bittar's figures are appropriated from Delacroix's *Jacob Wrestling with the Angel* (1857-61) while the text, superimposed on the painting, is taken from an Al Asmar poem. The roses are those she remembers from her grandfather's garden in Beirut.

Delacroix's original work, painted for the church of St Sulpice in Paris, is a large pastoral scene with Jacob and the angel as the main focus. On the extreme right hand side, Jacob's man servant, dressed as an Arab, is 'abandoning' him as the superimposed text explains. By contrast, Jacob is dressed in western clothes and has a fairer complexion. Delacroix's depiction indicates that western history has chosen to describe the Arab-Islamic world as alien and aberrant rather than acknowledging it as stemming from the Judaeo-Christian tradition of Abraham, through his son Ishmael. The depiction of the Arab is an ominous and bigoted portrayal.

In *Watching Jacob*, Bittar re-presents Delacroix's figures. The Arab figure is removed from his passive side role and placed in the central panel thus casting the Arab in an active role as both an observer and a questioner of history. However, although resituated, the Arab figure is still excluded from the emotional centre of the piece and acts as a reminder of the story of Ishmael, Abraham's son, who is forever linked to his brethren and forever excluded. Following on from this, Bittar's scene could be a metaphor for Palestinian exile and identity. Furthermore, the Arabic text, reads, "He who denies his face shall be renounced by all birds of paradise."[12] The words could be a warning against a denial of history; it could be the Jew's denial for his/her link to the Arab, or the Arab's denial of his/her identity.

Bittar's work, like that of several other artists, is grounded in the past and present histories of the Arabs. It is complex work for the average American audience to appreciate

3.4 Doris Bittar, *Watching Jacob,* 1992
oil on three canvases 150 x 455cm
(see colour plate 4)

its content and therefore requires substantial didactic material. By incorporating Arab themes the artist risks misinterpretation or limited appreciation of the thematic content of the art work, a problem common in conceptual art and other multimedia art forms. In the light of the absence of balanced and accurate information about the Arab world in school texts or the media, a broader understanding of the art is unlikely. The problem is compounded by the views held by most art professionals about Arab culture. Many American critics and curators see Arab society as static and have little appreciation of its diversity and the changes taking place in the arts and culture of its numerous regions.

Mary Tuma is a second-generation American Arab of Palestinian origin. Tuma studied textile and costume design. Her long struggle with weight problems inspired much of her work which is concerned with the female body imaged in the American clothing industry. Tuma questions the sizing system in the women's fashion industry, a numerical standardisation that she feels locks women into stereotypical forms which are imposed by a male dominated industry. She sees women as having to contend with a constant redefinition of their body image, which, in the process, denies them the freedom to define their own physical and emotional needs. In *Body Count* of 1995 (figure 3.5) Tuma's bodies, made with wire frames covered in stretched stocking fabric, evoke a variety of emotions that in reality are masked by the imposed fashions that women have to adjust their emotions to.

By contrast, Ghada Jamal emigrated to the United States during the civil war in Lebanon. She is an abstract landscape painter. Her outstanding use of colour evokes moods ranging from the tranquillity of Lebanese mountain villages to the horrors of the Gulf War. A member of an informal Arabic music group in Los Angeles, California, her most recent work is inspired by classical Arabic music played on the *nay, oud* and *qanun*. *The Traveller, No 34* (figure 3.6) is one piece in a series of twelve that interprets her response to musical passages in Arab-Andalusian music. The music materialises through the rhythm of the pure colour, the line and the spatial relationships in a pictorial space that is reminiscent of her earlier landscape paintings. (Figures 3.7 and 3.8)

3.5 Mary Tuma, Body Count, 1995
wire, stockings, tulle, pins, thread 20 x 32.5 x 12cm,
collection of the artist

3.6 Ghada Jamal, Music Series: The Traveller, No 34,
1998, mixed media on wood, 30 x 30cm
(see colour plate 5)

Arab art and American art institutions

A common misconception among American curators (most of whom are 'white,' as many of the art gatekeepers are) is that all art that comes from the 'Middle East,' with the exception of Israeli art, is predictable, looks alike, is too traditional, or is too western to be different. Unfortunately, 'difference' has become the buzz word; it translates into cultural diversity and therefore fits the definition of multiculturalism. In

3.7 Ghada Jamal, *Music Series: The Traveller,* No 25, 1998
mixed media on wood, 30 x 30cm
(see colour plate 6)

3.8 Ghada Jamal, *Music Series: The Traveller,* No 29, 1998
mixed media on wood, 30 x 30cm
(see colour plate 7)

order to avoid another form of 'cultural imperialism,'[13] we must be aware and appreciate the commonalities among cultures and not only the differences.

Only through education can we surmount these attitudes: multiculturalism alone cannot resolve all the issues facing a diverse population. So far multicultural programmes have not targeted education in the art schools, the art professionals or the directors of art institutions. In this context, Graeme Chalmers' argument for a multicultural education that stresses the importance of identifying similarities among cultures, and addressing disciplines such as aesthetics, art criticism, art history, and studio production in this way, is a useful one.[14] Issues of ethnocentrism, bias and discrimination are also important as well as the affirmation and enhancement of pride in each individual's artistic heritage. Art education too must also investigate what art means to other cultures, and how it is conveyed. Another factor that must be taken into consideration is the role of artists in other cultures, their artistic concerns and how they have resolved issues common to all artists.

One organisation that was founded with the singular objective of educating art professionals and the public on the contemporary contributions of Arab artists is The International Council for Women in the Arts, a non-profit, educational organisation dedicated to presenting to the American public and art professionals the achievements of Arab women artists. The initial focus on women grew out of the misconceptions about Arab women's participation and contribution, not just in the arts, but also in all other professional fields. The title of the first exhibition, *Forces of Change: Women Artists of the Arab World* (1994), was intended to draw attention to the social and political changes that can be achieved through art by Arab women. At the same time the success of the exhibition was prefigured in the title, which intended to change the American public's image of the Arab woman.

More recently, the Council has focused on thematic approaches to planning exhibitions, which has drawn much interest and resulted in a wealth of questions and material that necessitates further investigation. This approach provides the public with a shared sense of humanity and emphasises the diverse responses and experiences available in many cultures. Also, the Council's new division, The Cultural and Visual Arts Resource, serves both men and women artists. Until art institutions incorporate the history of Arab art into their curriculum and museums begin to hire curators familiar with the language and contemporary cultures of the Arab world, both the Council and the Resource Centre will continue to offer information on the contemporary contribution of Arabs in the form of exhibitions, publications, lectures and symposiums.

State and community support

Museums in the United States receive major funding from an élite group of 'whites,' who may not be willing to fund multicultural programmes at the expense of Euro-American artists. Some minority artists argue, for example, that modern art institutions in California are receiving state funds for multicultural programmes but marginalising art by people of colour. Instead, they want to see 'cultural democracy' within mainstream art institutions. Certainly, museum education departments have adopted a more diverse stance than most modern art galleries, particularly in the interpretation of indigenous art for museum visitors and as part of the programmes for children. However, overall Arab-Islamic art programmes receive scant attention from museums. Few American Arabs contribute to museums or serve on their boards or volunteer as docents.

Nevertheless, Arab communities in Los Angeles, Detroit, Chicago and, more recently, in New York have benefited from city or state funding for multicultural programmes. They have participated annually in several cultural festivals where contemporary art is occasionally presented in an informal festival atmosphere. Similarly, a few Arab cultural organisations include visual arts by American Arabs but rarely do these events take place on a regular basis and the visual arts usually constitute only a small part of a cultural event that focuses mainly on music, dance or conferences. By contrast, the Alif Gallery in Washington DC, which was the only space dedicated to contemporary Arab art, finally closed down after struggling for 10 years.

In this context, it is important to remember that most American-Arab artists draw inspiration from art trends in the Arab world and those who are responsible for art education in the Arab world must consider incorporating Arab-Islamic art history into the curriculum. Few universities integrate such programmes into the Art Departments and consequently most art students are well versed in European art history and have little or no knowledge of great Sumerian art, Al Wassiti's style, or the works by pioneers of contemporary Arab art, including Mahmoud Mukhtar, Jawad Salim, Effat Nagui and Saloua Raouda Choucair.[15]

In effect, I am arguing that Arab artists must receive the support of government and private agencies to study their heritage and thereby retain a cultural continuity that gives integrity to modern Arab art. By maintaining their links to the past, and being aware of the contemporary social and cultural elements of the society they live in, Arab artists reaffirm Arab cultural values, raise public conscious-ness and help those at home and in the diaspora negotiate the complexities of cultural identities and histories.

Although multiculturalism is not a perfect answer, it does support groups that are seldom represented in the mainstream by drawing attention to their achieve-ments, and this approach may be of value in the short term. In the longer term, mainstream art institutions must rely on their own resources to investigate and introduce art work by artists from diverse cultures. Overall, the 1990s have seen a healthy increase in the number of country-based survey exhibitions at major

American art museums, including travelling exhibitions representing art from Mexico, Africa, Thailand, Latin America, the Arab world, and recently China. These exhibitions not only bring art from other countries to the United States, but they also highlight works by first, second or third generation immigrants from these countries.

In conclusion, I want to stress that it is only through art education at all levels that we can create a truly pluralistic approach to the arts. An education that addresses our commonalties rather than the differences while, at the same time, underscoring humanity in art within all cultures is much needed. Edward Said refers to this present need for a more humane global community when he writes: "The fact is that we are mixed with one another in ways that most national systems of education have not dreamed of. To match knowledge in the Arts and Science with the integrative realities is the intellectual and cultural challenge of the moment."[16]

Notes

[1] Lippard, Lucy. *Mixed Blessings: New Art in Multicultural America,* New York: Pantheon Books, 1990.

[2] Mar, Eric. *1990 Census Poses Challenges for California's Future, California Perspectives Now,* San Francisco, 1993.

[3] Orfalea, Gregory. *Before the Flames: A Quest for the History of Arab Americans,* Austin: University of Texas Press, 1988.

[4] For detailed discussion of the affects of the Gulf War on Arab American women see Hatem, Mervat F, 'The Invisible American Half: Arab American Hybridity and Feminist Discourses in the 1990s' in Ella Shohat, *Talking Visions: Multicultural Feminism in a Transnational Age,* Cambridge, Mass: The MIT Press, 1998, pp369-390.

[5] Nashashibi, Salwa Mikdadi. Unpublished author's notes based on interviews with Arab artists living in Los Angeles. Los Angeles, 1991.

[6] Nashashibi, Salwa Mikdadi (ed). *Forces of Change: Women Artists of the Arab World,* Washington: International Council for Women in the Arts and National Museum for Women in the Arts, 1994.

[7] ICWA: The International Council for Women in the Arts and its division the Cultural and Visual Arts Resource is a non-profit organisation based in Lafayette, California. Founded in 1988 the Council maintains a unique computerised database on Arab artists, in Arab geographies and in the diaspora, and organises contemporary art exhibitions.

[8] Nashashibi, Salwa Mikdadi. Unpublished Interviews with Arab artists, 1991-3.

[9] Nashashibi, Salwa Mikdadi. Correspondence with the artist, British Columbia, 1999.

[10] Said, Edward. *Orientalism,* New York: Random House, 1978.

[11] Much has been written on Delacroix and Orientalism, particularly the painting, *The Women of Algiers,* produced in 1834 following his visit to the port of Algiers in 1832. See Todd Porterfield, 'Western Views of Oriental Women in Modern Painting and Photography' in Nashashibi, *Forces of Change: Women Artists of the Arab World,* 1994, and Hassan, Salah M, 'The Installations of Houria Niati,' *NKA, Journal of Contemporary African Art,* Fall/Winter, 1995.

[12] Bittar, Doris. *Looking at Delacroix....* San Diego: Exhibition Catalogue, 1993.

[13] Collins, G and Sandell, T. 'The Politics of Multicultural Art Education', *Art Education:* Vol 45 No VI, 1992.

[14] Chalmers, Graeme F. *Celebrating Pluralism: Art, Education, and Cultural Diversity.* Los Angeles: Paul Getty Trust, 1996.

[15] Mahmoud Mukhtar (1891-1934), the Egyptian artist, is considered the father of modern Arab sculpture; Jawad Salim (1921-1961) an Iraqi artist was the key figure in the development of modern Iraqi art and taught at the Institute of Fine Arts in Baghdad; Effat Nagui (1912-1998) is a celebrated Egyptian woman artist; the Lebanese woman artist, Saloua Raouda Choucair (born 1916) lives in Beirut.

[16] Said, Edward W. *Culture and Imperialism,* New York: Alfred A Knopf, 1993, p331.

SABIHA KHEMIR

Mobile Identity and the Focal Distance of Memory

According to tradition, the Arabs have one common ancestor: Ishmael, son of Abraham. But a geographical expanse with a complex history characterises identity in the Arab world. Being Arab means different things to different people. The diversity in the Arab world is ethnic and religious. Arab societies actually encompass: Copts in Egypt, Christians in other parts of the Middle East and Jews.

In the Tunisian psyche, the fusion between Arab and Muslim is total. I will therefore speak of the Arab Muslim culture where I was born and brought up. The name of the region, al-Maghrib (North Africa), literally means the Western part of the land of Islam. I am Arab, but as a Tunisian, there is the Roman, the Phoenician, the Berber, the Andalusian, the Turkish and so forth, in my making; various historical ingredients that are not necessarily apparent on the surface. But still, the same land, Arab, Mediterranean with its lingua franca, as I have known it, played a role in the shaping of my identity. The generation that was born after Tunisia's independence from French colonisation (which took place in 1956) lived a kind of 'cultural symbiosis.'

The important, unifying factor between Arab countries is Arabic as a language. The first Arab country I visited was Egypt. I remember the overwhelming feeling when I landed in Cairo: there was a sense of scale and immensity not present in Tunis. There was, before my eyes, this world which I knew well or thought I did through black and white Egyptian films which have been a very extensive industry in all Arab countries. That world was before my eyes in full colour. I felt completely at home. The first evening, I remember telling a long-winded story — as I sometimes do — to a group of Egyptians who were listening to me very intently with great concentration. I extended my narrative, holding their full attention, driving carefully to my punch line at which point, I was expecting an explosion of laughter. Instead, one of them told me '*wallahi law targamti kulli da lil Arabi kunna nitfahim!*' ('Were you to translate all this into Arabic, we would communicate!'). I had told the story in my Tunisian dialect!

The reason I am relating this incident is to bring the factor of diversity into this unifying element that is the Arabic language. The richness of Arabic dialects is quite extraordinary. The Tunisian dialect is different from the Moroccan, the Moroccan different from the Algerian, the Algerian different from the Iraqi, the Iraqi different

Facing Page
Sabiha Khemir, *Phoenix I,*
1998 (detail)

from the Syrian, the Syrian different from the Lebanese, the Lebanese different from the Yemeni, the Yemeni different from the Palestinian, the Palestinian different from the Bahraini ... and I have not mentioned all of them!

Yet the unifying force embodied in classical Arabic is very potent. I transfer this multiplicity in unity which is so characteristic of 'Arab identity' to my sense of existence in the world.

I grew up hearing the saying *'yulad at-tifl ka as-safhat al bayda, fa abawah yuhawwidanih aw yumajjisanih aw yuslimanih.'* (A child is born like a white page, his parents make a Jew, a Christian, a Mazdain or a Muslim out of him). Cultural identity is acquired from the context where one was born and brought up. Sometimes, I wonder, if we do get access to another planet, how would our identity be defined there. I presume until a baby is born in the new planet, his or her parents would be Americans or Russians on 'Planet X'!

In the book *The Little Prince* by Antoine de Saint-Exupery, the little prince, wandering in Planet Earth, comes across a flower and asks her: "Where are the men?" "Men..." she echoes, "one never knows where to find them. The wind blows them away. They have no roots, and that makes their life very difficult."

Unlike plants human beings have the possibility to move anywhere precisely because their roots are not material. Yes, they have been moving more and more. But the little flower was wrong: it has nothing to do with the wind. Her vision was simply conditioned by the environment familiar to her.

The Arab was originally a nomad. Prophet Mohammed migrated from Mecca to Medina which would have been, at the time, akin to leaving for another country. *Al-Isra wa-l-mi'raj* (The Prophet's ascension to Heaven) was also a form of migration. It is very significant, indeed, that the Arab Muslim calendar starts from the date of *al-Hijra*, the Prophet Mohammed's migration to Medina. While the birth of Christ marks the start of the Christian calendar, the Muslim calendar starts with the migration of the prophet, not with his birth. Islam accepts Christianity. The Arab world celebrated the millennium with the West. In some 580 years, the Arab Muslim world will celebrate the *hijra* millennium alone. Anyway, migration is a fundamental aspect in Arab identity.

I take as example one remarkable Arab who lived in exile. The sociologist and philosophical historian Abd ar-Rahman bin Muhammad Ibn Khaldun was a shoulder large enough for both Eastern and Western scholars to stand on. He was born in Ifriqiyya, that is present day Tunisia, in 1332 AD, he lived in Spain, Algeria and Egypt and visited several other places. He died in Egypt in 1406 AD. When asked where he came from he replied: 'from my mother's womb.' Not being sedentary, he did not see it fit to link himself to a fixed place.

The Arab diaspora played a decisive role in the displacement of Arab people. In the case of some, it is what is (practically at least) a self-imposed exile. People leave for different reasons. Different circumstances — political or personal or both — force them to get out, they are often linked to the hindering of freedom.

When you are out of your culture, you are no longer part of the picture. Distance allows you to see better and changes the perspective. But distance allows one to see better up to a certain extent then it turns into the opposite: a life in exile with memory as a companion. From my personal experience, I would say that memories constitute a very important component in the life of a culturally displaced person. With the geographical impossibilities of memories (memories do not create realities but just reflect them) nostalgia can take over.

Rituals that have been inculcated in us from childhood are a powerful tool in the hands of memory and our sense of identity. For example, the 27th of March 1999

4.1 Sabiha Khemir, *Phoenix I*, 1998, drawing, 86 x 41.9cm, private collection

was a Saturday, it was the 'id al-Kebir, the great Muslim feast of the sacrifice of the sheep by Abraham, for his son Ishmael. It was a glorious sunny day in London. I phoned home (in Tunisia) to wish everyone a 'happy Eid.' And alone, I left home (my house in London) and took the tube to the Barbican Centre, where the so-called 'Festival of the Heart' was held.[1] After listening to old story telling from Ireland, I moved to the free stage of the foyer where a great number of people gathered. Irish singers vocalised their joy and pain — they were singing their history and their memory — everyone tapped away to the rhythm; a child, about seven years old, danced his feet off in a frenzy, his arms by his sides, still and stiff in contrast to his energetic feet. Somewhere in my memory's eye, I saw a seven-year-old girl. A colourful scene: the sheep's blood, crimson red, gushing out as the sheep was opened before our very eyes. The sheep, we children had taken for a walk that very morning after having embellished it with colourful ribbons. Back to the Barbican Centre and the Irish singers, the rolling of their RRRs, Arab in its quality, did not clash with the scene in my mind's eye: I could see my nieces and nephews (now), being spared the scene of the killing in the garden and enjoying grilled meat indoors.

To say I was horrified by the killing of the sheep the year I was seven, or any other sheep any other year, would be a hypocritical lie. A black and white photograph which I have in a drawer in London and which has been waiting to be catalogued in an album for years, displays my joy and elation on this ritual day. It shows me as a seven-year-old, holding the sheep's spleen, with a gleeful smile on my face. Tender, grilled lamb in Tunisia was and still is delicious.

One has to watch the lens of memory attentively. The lens of memory has many distortions. My far-reaching memory remembers that Abraham, Ibrahim al-Khalil (Friend of God), was the ancestor of both Muslims and Jews.

Nostalgia is very powerful. It can take you forward or backward. And consciousness has to watch very carefully the distortions of memory's lens. Listening to Arabic sends a thrill through my being. The songs of Um Kulthum wrench the sighs out and the smell of sandalwood and jasmine bring a desire for elation.[2] (See Mai Ghoussoub, *Diva*, 1998). But elation can lead to intoxication. I stand with my being imbibed with a sensual culture. I stand in the cold. My eyes are open. The flamenco of my being aspires to a rigorous passion, it rejects the laziness of the mind.

Out of this displacement can come constant contradictions, powerful forces pulling you asunder. Because, as the proverb goes: 'What is good for the heart is not necessarily good for the spleen.' One perhaps ends up living not in one culture or the other but between cultures. To live in between, one's existence has a direct link to that historical breach. The displaced also stands on a platform for debate where bridges are being built and his or her diaspora will have a significant part, however minuscule, in the building of those bridges. Perhaps, the lives of some of us are about connecting.

According to the 10th century Arab philosopher, Abu Hayyan al-Tawhidi, 'al-ghorba hiyya ghorbat al awtan' ('exile is when one feels in exile at home').

The problems of Arab identity impose themselves on an individual abroad not only because of his or her displacement. The identity of the Arab world is in turmoil at home too. Colonisation, the British in the Middle East and the French in North Africa, has created a breach in the history of Arab identity. By the end of the 19th century, the Arab world, made lethargic by the Ottoman Empire, then exhausted and nonchalant was confronted with western technology and there was too much to take in one go. The result is indigestion on a large scale. The coloniser was not interested in the culture of the colonised. The colonised has been busy trying to catch up. Emptied of its resources to free itself of the coloniser, the colonised is faced with the necessity to free itself of itself, of the sequels of colonisation which have become part of that self. Algeria is an unfortunate example.

The present reality of the Arab world is a difficult one. As an Arab individual, I need and have the responsibility to carry the hope and energy of transformation, of recreating — and I do not mean here reproducing — but recreating my past.

Bob Marley once said to his photographer who was a Jamaican living in London: 'you were born on the earth of Jamaica and now you're in the concrete soil, you have to be very strong.' A displaced person is often standing in the gap and the gap can be a vacuum. So one's sense of identity has to reach back to the seed to assure the continuum of a growth faithful to the nature of

4.2 Sabiha Khemir, *The Nightingale and the Rose* (detail), 1986 illustration inspired by *The Conference of Birds*

one's being. When there is a conflict between the cultural identity and the individual identity which has often been the case for Arab women, the journey takes a route of metamorphosis and transcendence. Reconciliation not rejection of cultural identity seems essential for individual growth and what I would name 'a far reaching memory' is essential. I see memories as being of two types: one immediate, personal, close and another remote and far reaching.

I would link a 'far reaching memory' to a cultural heritage. I believe that there is a need to provide access to Islamic art material, for it to be simply available, for that cultural heritage to be accessible outside the Arab world but especially within the Arab world. The aesthetics and beauty of a particular culture are essential in the way they reflect a different vision of the world. That is the way it gives to humanity at large. It is not a necessity to copy the past, but to animate our present reality with the timeless values of our civilisation. I am not saying producing ceramic tiles with Islamic designs is the answer, nor am I advocating nostalgia for a glorious past. Just the simple availability of that richness, that it becomes part of the present identity, not just the ugliness of war and conflict, the ugliness of politics. To have access to that beauty and for the Arab child to be open to that beauty like a source for the seed. For an artist, not necessarily to paint miniatures but to have fed from the beauty of that source. If we were to reproduce the whole material of the Arab, Islamic artistic expression again, we would not necessarily achieve the link with the past which is vital for our identity. If we are able to take in that artistic expression and interact with it, perhaps we can connect with its source. I feel that its source is immense. It is rich in harmony in contrast to our recent history where that harmony has been broken. (Figures 4.2 and 4.3)

I believe that a knowledge of our past in its contribution to the progress of man will be instrumental in our contribution to the progress of man today. My far-reaching memory is a commitment to my history and its link to a responsibility towards the memory of humanity.

The study of Islamic art in the West is very valuable. Such study is not available in many Arab countries. It is no coincidence, however, that the study of Islamic art history which starts with the Islamic conquest in the seventh century halts at the 19th century. A breach in the artistic expression of the Arab world is a direct reflection of the breach in its history brought about by colonialism. This is one of the reasons why contemporary Arab artistic work is very important, it establishes the vibrancy of life's continuum. Creativity is an expression of the individual's freedom, an essential part of their humanity. Free artistic expression is a reinstatement of

4.3 Sabiha Khemir, *The Happy Island*, 1994 illustration from *The Island of Animals*, 20.8 x 28.8cm, Quartet Books, London, 1994, private collection

identity. Contemporary expression tries to contribute to the formation of a modern consciousness. (Figures 4.4 and 4.5)

Women, by the nature of their reality aspire to positive transformation, to surmount a reality of confinement. Their expression is doubly important. However, there is a danger that the themes expressed by Arab artists living in the West (particularly women) in their creative work, can be exploited. Sometimes, their expression is not taken in itself but is used as a tool to reinforce a negative view of the Arab world. Out of the artist's liberating act, a rope is woven around the artist's neck. For example, in its praise for my novel *Waiting in the Future for the Past to Come*, *The Independent* newspaper described it as "...a strikingly emotional tale of a clever young woman growing up in a traditional Tunisian village and aching to escape to western freedoms."[3]

4.4 Sabiha Khemir, *The King of the Djinn*, 1994 illustration *for The Island of Animals* Quartet Books, London, 1994, 20.8 x 28.8cm, private collection

Meanwhile, *The Irish Times* commented, "...to create a world, an ambience that is so intensely Arab, Tunisian, Muslim through the medium of a language so alien to that culture, is a truly remarkable feat." [4]

It seems to me that a positive meeting between the West and the Arab world requires unlearning as much as it necessitates learning. There is a great deal to unlearn.

Every language has a spirit that is particular to it. I wrote in English with the spirit of the Arabic language. The characteristics which determine my cultural being as an Arab are evident in my writing not just in terms of themes but also in the use of the English language. If, in my creative endeavour, I can give to the world that which is very Arab, I would have hopefully 'enriched' the human experience — in whatever small way. In the writings of writers from the Arab

4.5 Sabiha Khemir, *The Djinns Celebrate*, 1999, one of series of illustrations for a forthcoming collection of stories, 42 x 26cm

world, that world takes shape, the Arab experience becomes accessible. Artistic expression is direct, it is the work of beings who speak Arabic. (Figure 4.6)

The Arab woman, naked in the eyes of the Orientalist (painters, photographers or writers) or veiled in the eyes of the blindfold fanatics, is in both cases invisible. The Orient is no longer far away enough for the West to see it with exoticism and fantasy. The voices of that identity, the individual expression, is manifest in the recreation of cultural identity, hence the significance of the artistic work in the exhibition, *Dialogue of the Present.* Perhaps Sheherezade was the first feminist of her kind. Women need to be listened to, not looked at. Their artistic expression is *a voice* to be seen. [5]

The Arab world is more cognizant of western culture than the western world is of the Arab. It is more common to meet an Arab who speaks fluent English than an English person who speaks fluent Arabic. The reasons being obvious: colonisation. The Arabic language and Islam have been the two dams that separated the Arab world from the West. For Arab artists to speak to 'the other' and share with him or her their particular experience will be enriching to everyone. The work of these artists is part of that dialogue.

4.6 Sabiha Khemir, *The Djinns Celebrate*, (detail) 1999, 42 x 26cm

Each culture has its idiosyncrasies. Arabic music might sound unmusical to certain western ears — obviously, this does not mean that it is unmusical. I see cultural idiosyncrasies as enriching and losing them as a loss to humanity at large.

As an Arab, I feel it is important for me to define my identity and not create a barrier. Barriers prevent insight which is vital for compassion. I refuse to appoint fear as the guardian of my identity. Each identity tells a different story of humanity. Each difference can be celebrated not as superior but as different, difference as a condition for self-definition. It is a different thread in the tapestry of humanity. Every culture carries life within it.

With my far-reaching memory, I am constantly aware of the possibility of Al-Andalus (especially between the eighth and the 11th centuries), where Muslims, Jews and Christians lived together in peace and where the arts and sciences thrived.[6] Al-Andalus, not as a dream or nostalgia, simply a proof, a promising token of the possibility of positive coexistence and interaction between diverse ethnic

4.7 Ceiling, *Sala de las Dos Hermanas* (Hall of the two Sisters), the Leones Palace Alhambra, Spain, dating from the second reign of Muhammad V (764-94 AH/1362-91 AD), Alhambra, Spain. This *muqarnas* dome constitutes the visual climax within the palace and the most complex ceiling within the history of Islamic architecture. The geometrical pattern decorating the dome departs from a central star and thousands of cells or small niches, domes within a dome transform the solid material into ascending transparence and light. Photo: Sabiha Khemir

4.8 Sabiha Khemir, *Phoenix I* (detail), 1998 drawing, 86 x 41.9cm private collection

groups and religions, and a proof of the enriching civilisational outcome of its happening. (Figure 4.7)

My memory tries to reach to the quintessential in the civilisation of my culture. It is a civilisation that aspires to equality. I believe that I am not simply a carrier of genes but I am a carrier of history too and I have a responsibility towards that. I was given an Arab name and my commitment is to that name. But for the growth of my kaleidoscopic identity, I turn my branches towards the light. I do not bury them with the roots. And as the branches grow so do the roots — they grow too.

I would like to emphasise the simple fact that unlike every European language, Arabic is written from right to left — it is that different.

I carry an Arab name and I am committed to that name. Though personal, my name is a carrier of that greater identity. In English, the whispered H is usually not heard (Sabiha). It is a sound that is not part of the Latin alphabet. Interestingly enough, in transliteration, for phonetic rendering of the word, the H is written with a dot underneath. That dot is not visible when one speaks English. I strive to communicate the invisible and the untranslatable in my cultural identity. I have to keep track of that dot from which everything departed in the Arabic language and script (all letters and words are traditionally believed to be a single form which comes from that point). I aspire to being worthy of my civilisational heritage. (Figure 4.8)

As an Arab the dispossession of the Palestinians is strongly present in my consciousness. But so is Kosovo.

With the advance of technology and the communications revolution there is a constant shift in identities. With the role played by the media, transport and so forth, interaction between different worlds is becoming greater and greater and in one sense they are being brought closer together and in another there is more resistance and a need to reject the other for a definition of oneself.

However, the accretionary phenomenon (the growing together of parts naturally separate) is happening in different areas of life. Music is a good example. Collaborations between musicians of totally different backgrounds are taking place. Cheb Khaled, King of Rai, the Algerian singer whose music cut across boundaries of geographies and cultures is a phenomenon in itself.[7] I was sent a recording of his music from New Delhi before hearing it in New York and Cairo.

Bonds between people of different race, different cultures are evolving and crossing boundaries. They are weaving a cloth that could connect humanity, it is a very slow cloth to weave but that weaving is happening and in that sense, I am optimistic. And the voice of the ninth century Iraqi singer Ziriab, who was an exile in al-Andalus, lives in the Algerian artist Houria Niati and was heard in London, on the day of the opening of the exhibition, *Dialogue of the Present*; cultural identity is more powerful than we think! [8]

We are used to identities being coded in nationalities although, as Mark Twain said, 'Every occupied territory on the earth is stolen.' With immigration, displacement, dual nationalities, the boundaries of identity are more fluid and identities are becoming more kaleidoscopic.

The challenge we Arabs face is to work out how we are going to integrate the Arab experience in the modern consciousness of the world. Arab cultural identity needs to be strongly connected to its civilisation, not to be threatened. Then a claim of that cultural identity becomes unnecessary. Because, as the Nigerian writer Wole Soyinka said, 'A tiger does not proclaim his tigritude.'

The much talked about phenomenon of globalisation, the dramatic changes in the geopolitics of the world which imply changes of position all over the world make one wonder how much is this globalisation a westernisation? Since the end of the Cold War, the occurrence of the Gulf War, enemies are not so readily defined any more. Perhaps hatred is the enemy.

I would like to conclude with a poem by Andrèe Chedid, a Lebanese/Egyptian writer and poet written in French:

Par cette naissance	By this birth
Qui nous dècerne le monde	Which gives us the world
Par cette mort	By this death
Qui l'escamote	Which conjures it away
Par cette vie	By this life
Plus bruissante que tout	More vibrant than one could
l'imaginé	imagine
Toi	You
Qui que tu sois!	Whoever you are!
Je te suis bien plus proche	I am closer to you
qu'étranger	Than I am a stranger

—Andrée Chedid
Poèmes pour un texte (1970—1991)
Paris: Flammarion, 1991; translated by Sabiha Khemir

Notes

1 *From the Heart,* a festival of Irish music and arts held at the Barbican Centre, London, between 27-28 March and 3-5 April 1999.

2 Um Kulthum was born around 1904 in rural Egypt. Her father was a Quran reader who taught her the skills of enunciation when she was a child and sent her to Cairo for voice training when she was still a teenager. She started making records as early as 1926. Her success was immediate and was to dominate the Egyptian music scene throughout the 1940s and 1950s. Her songs were broadcast regularly on the first Thursday of every month and 'Um Kulthum night' became a national institution and her reputation spread throughout the Arabic speaking world. In a style of repetitions and oscillations, her robust, emotionally charged voice had an inebriating effect on raptured audiences. Her death in 1975, after having been an Arab icon for almost 50 years, was received with deep mourning and grief. She left 286 songs and there are plans to set up an Um Kulthum museum in Cairo. See Lloyd, F (ed), *Contemporary Arab Women's Art, Dialogues of the Present*, pp177-179 for Mai Ghoussoub's writing on her sculpture of Um Kulthum, entitled *Diva*, 1998.

3 Review of *Waiting in the Future for The Past to Come* (Quartet Books, 1993), *The Independent*, 7 August 1993.

4 *The Irish Times*, 25 September 1993, review of *Waiting in the Future for The Past to Come* (Quartet Books, 1993), entitled 'Scheherazade' by Dorothy Benson.

5 Night after night, Sheherezade, the storyteller of *The Thousand and One Nights*, held the attention and curiosity of her husband King Shahrayar with her stories. He kept postponing her death (such was the fate of every woman he married the morning after the wedding night), curious to know what came next in the stories within the stories. Sheherezade's creative voice was instrumental in saving her life!

6 Spain was ruled by Muslims (Arabs and Berbers) for over seven hundred years: successively by the Umayyads (711-1031 AD), the Taifa (1031-1086), the Almoravids and the Almohads (1088-1232), and the Nasrids (1238-1492). The new Islamic land was called 'al-Andalus' (the translation of Spania, the Latin name for Spain). The Iberian Peninsula enjoyed a unique culture which included Christians, Jews and Muslims; it was marked at times by extraordinary tolerance, particularly between 711 and 1084 AD. Science, literature, philosophy and the visual arts thrived marking a refined presence in the history of humanity.

7 In Arabic, the name 'Rai' means 'opinion or point of view' and the music that bears this name has long been regarded as a music of rebellion. Rai music emerged in Algeria in the town of Oran about half a century ago when rural women who had immigrated into the city started singing about strife in the big city. Rai remained an underground phenomenon in Algeria for a long time. In the 1970s, with the introduction of the synthesiser, Rai became a 'pop' music sung by Chebs and Chebbas (young men and women). As distinctive syncopated fusion of melody and percussion, mixing Arabic lyrics with a western drumbeat, Rai sings of many subjects which are met with great opposition from the religious fanatics. In Algeria, a country where 75 per cent of the population is under the age of 25, Rai is the music of youth. It has had its role in the assertion of identity in Algeria's postcolonial confusion. On the international scene, it found its place in the growing global music consciousness, the 'world beat' phenomenon. Cheb Khaled, nicknamed the 'King of Rai', was born in Oran in 1960 and now lives in France. He exploded onto the international stage a decade ago and was the first Algerian to establish himself as an international singer. His 1992 hit, *'Didi,'* was the first Arabic language single to crack the top 10 on French pop charts. His singing is marked by a passionate spirit.

8 Ziriab Ibn Nafi was a ninth century composer from Iraq who was forced to live in exile in Islamic Spain (in the town of Cordoba). His music spread from there to Algeria and Morocco through Arabs, Jews and Spaniards who fled the terrors of the Spanish Inquisition. The performances of the painter, Houria Niati — an Algerian living in England — of the Ziriab songs are an integral part of her installation work. Her voice (which on the occasion of the opening of the Exhibition *Dialogue of the Present* had no accompaniment of musical instruments) carried in the depth of its vibration Ziriab's creative act across centuries and a history of exile. The lives of both Ziriab and Niati have been marked by exile.

Our Bodies: Our Orient and Art

Women's bodies in art. Am I entering a sad world or an exciting one? I will not let the discourse take over my gaze and my insights; I will try, in spite of or against the impossible, to allow the image to direct my thoughts and not to let the words triumph over the felt, the seen, and the gaze(s).

Look at *Jeunes Femmes Visitant Une Exposition* (Young Women Visiting an Exhibition, figure 5.1). This is the third time that I have explored this painting, and each time it unfolds new fields of vision and meanings to me. If you know this painting, please do not reveal its origin or the name of its creator. Bear with me for a little while. Women are everywhere in this painting, the oil on its canvas depicts the female figure in different roles, in a variety of postures and fashions. It depicts women as subjects to be looked at as well as viewers, voyeuristic beings — if I can mention a commonly used term nowadays. They are divided into different categories as far as class, geography and the use of colour are concerned. Here the naked bodies of two female figures are offered to the gaze of women; the only males around are either too small or short to look at the nudes (the little boy) or too busy chatting or flirting with a smartly (and very) dressed 'lady' to be bothered by any displayed picture.

The invading gaze is that of the traditionally dressed Arab women. The curiosity and exploration of the naked female bodies depicted in the painting is coming from those who know the female body — at least their own. Is the artist making a point about looking at women's bodies in art as opposed to looking at them in reality? Are these women comparing their own bodies to those of the two models in the painting? Are they conquering and invading these bodies as some radical feminists would put it when arguing against the use of women's nakedness in art?

I am enjoying my so called 'privileged position' as the viewer which allows me to look at the lookers, to read their reading, and my position could be that of a woman controlling the space of these women in the painting. My position could also claim to have the right to do so for I am an Arab and a woman, and I can play an opportunist game and tell a 'western woman' that she cannot see the painting with the same eyes, the same insight, the same histories. But this is exactly what I am not going to do. I am going to play the opposite game and imagine that an Orientalist has painted this work.

What would you say, or what would many who are complaining about the

Facing page
Mai Ghoussoub, *Diva*, 1998, installation detail
iron, aluminium, wool and resin, 200 x 50 x 30cm

invasion of the Arab woman's body, and its representation by the coloniser's brush say? Let us try such a
reading. The group of veiled women is de-humanised
for we only see them as a flock dressed in black! The
naked women are exhibited for the voyeur to fantasise
about: they are on offer for the consumer's eyes to
indulge in seeing them, without being seen. The artist
has relegated the dressed westernised woman to the
side of the painting. Even she has no face, we only see
her body. Veiled, shrouded in black and naked Arab
women. Is this not what we accuse the Orientalists of
having reduced us to in their paintings?

5.1 Omar Onsi, *Jeunes femmes visitant une exposition* (Young
women visiting an exhibition), 1945, oil on canvas, 37 x 45cm,
private collection

Well, the artist is actually an Arab. A Lebanese
artist who painted this work at a time when it was
extremely difficult to exhibit a nude in a Middle Eastern
gallery. His name is Omar Onsi (1901-1969) and this
painting was produced in 1945.

Here, another reading makes more sense to me: it is one of cohabitation, of
the juxtaposition of different eras and values in Lebanon that have made this country
so contradictory. Yes, it is referring to the West and the East but it is a much more
complicated problematic than that of a simple opposition or of the power game in
their relations. Who has power? Who is interested in the exhibited art depicted here?
The traditional or the modern figures?

What I am trying to say is that the analysis of the gaze as a discourse, as a
maker of the Orient through the recurring image of the 'other,' is often reductionist.
There are many layers through which the gaze operates. In order to pursue this
further let us look at another painting which predates Onsi's *Jeunes Femmes*
(figure 5.1). It is the work of the Orientalist Mario Simon, dated 1919. He is obviously

5.2 Mario Simon, *Odalisque,* 1919, gouache, 20 x 26cm, private collection

5.3 Marie Haddad (1895-1973), *The Bedouin,* 1940
oil on canvas, 36 x 27cm, private collection

fascinated by the two veiled women looking at a naked female figure. Could it be that the fully covered women seen next to a naked one is a man's fantasy that knows no East and no West?

Similarly, if we are going to speak of Orientalism, where would we place the famous painting of Marie Haddad (1895-1973), a pioneer woman artist in Lebanon who is renowned for her painting of *The Bedouin* of 1940 (Figure 5.3). Haddad is introduced in the book, *100 years of Plastic Art in the Lebanon* by another Lebanese, Lamia Chahine, as an admirable colourist noted for

"… [her] Bedouin women with their turbans above the full tattooed foreheads, vivacious young nymphs whose perfect oval faces are tanned brown as berry. There are, too, her sprightly little velvet-eyed urchins, their bodies burned to bronze, who resemble 'small wild animals' in the saucy malice and bare-faced impudence of their look."[1]

I have an irresistible desire to add, if a western male critic had written such a comment on an Orientalist painter, we would have screamed and yelled at the making of the East as a body, an exotic subject by a colonising male mind. This is not to mention the use of a wild animal as a metaphorical reference!

Do not misunderstand me. I am not claiming that the Arab East has not been subjugated by the West, that we are not suffering from many prejudices and misrepresentations. What I am trying to emphasise is that as far as the gaze and the image are concerned, we have to look with wider eyes and feel the multitude of layers in the gaze(s). Fantasies are made of too many hidden elements. They are more universal than politics and societal components. Humans are after all more similar, despite the different influences and forms of their socio-economic environments: humans are much more ancient than the particularised societies we witness and study.

Recently I heard an Egyptian academic from Upper Egypt speaking about the Nubians. He stated that they have been seen and depicted through many gazes and that the western one is but one of many — western and Arab, Nubian or those of class and gender. He argued that the need to attack the western gaze solely is a way to avoid looking at our own local prejudices and our distortions of the 'dark Nubians,' their traditions and culture.

Looking at Marie Haddad's paintings and at *Jeunes Femmes*, I do believe him. For I am sure that we need the other as much as we need to invent the other in order to reconcile our fantasies with our social environment. This other is and will always be the product of the encounter of his/her reality with our fantasies and concepts. The other is the prey of our identification and differentiation. Power relations may lie behind our concepts and prejudices but they belong to another category and are not the sole basis for making the other.

However … I am forgetting myself and allowing the discourse, once again, to take over. Let me go back to the images and try to make them speak first before I start speaking for them.

Look at this poster which I recently saw at Georgetown University in America. (Figure 5.4). Are we actually afraid of our own bodies? Afraid of our naked bodies? Is our complaint against the Orientalist's voyeurism into our Arab female bodies a nationalist or a feminist outrage? Are we repeating what 'our' men see as an attack

5.4 Guerrilla Girl Poster, 1999
Georgetown University, United States

on their honour because our bodies should be kept hidden from all eyes but theirs? Or are we just influenced by some feminists' voices whose brand of feminism is puritanical in its essence? Fatima Mernissi once asked if our men had asked us if we wanted our naked bodies to be presented in Orientalist paintings before complaining on our behalf. To be honest, there are numerous images of women that bother me far more than any Orientalist sensual fantasy.

In terms of authenticity, for example, it is revealing to look at the newspaper image of a hostess in an arts centre in Lebanon which celebrates "our traditional arts and crafts," *Muftha al-Sharq* (figure 5.5). If there is a prize to be given to the 'making of a false East' this centre should win the first prize: a woman never wore a fez, tarboush! This one does but cannot resist looking sexy with her hair falling out of it in a very unnatural manner. Similarly, nobody plays the *oud* (the Arab lute) by flattening its chords with their hand! Of course, in reality this woman is a fashion model, she walks around with the *oud* instead of playing it. The sign in Arabic explains that 'here lies the key to the East' *(Muftha al-*

5.5 *'Muftah al-Sharq'*, *Al Hayat Newspaper*, 9 August 1998

Sharq)... I will not go on translating one kitsch cliché after another. In fact, the picture is hardly offensive because of the ridiculousness of it. But why have few people complained about the passive posture of this woman and her representation? Is it because she is not naked? There is a lot to explore in our complaint about the imaging of Arab women's bodies. And let us not search only inside the Orientalist mind and canvas.

Another image that I find fascinating, and which has incurred the wrath of many, is that of *The Great Bath in Bursa* 1885 (Figure 5.6), by the famous (infamous

5.6 Jean-Léon Gérôme, *The Great Bath at Bursa*, 1885
oil on canvas, 70 x 96.5cm, private collection

5.7 Colonial Postcard, *1129 Scenes et Types — Femmes mauresques en Promenade*, Edition des Galeries de France, Algeria

for some) Jean-Léon Gérôme, the Orientalist painter. I find this painting even more fascinating since I visited the Tate Gallery one of the past autumns to see the exhibited works of the Turner Prize nominees. There I saw Tacita Dean's video filmed inside a women's bath in Hungary. This was a great work of art by a woman inside a bath that is not set in the Orient. It was called *Gellert* after the name of the hotel in which the spa is located. The colour of the water through which we could see the ample bodies of the female bathers has the same blue-green quality we see in Gérôme's bath. The women are relaxed, indulging in their bodies in both works. There is one major difference though: the black bodies in Gérôme's work (as well as in many other paintings) are not naked. They are, as is more usual, fully dressed. Why is this so?

Remember Manet's *Olympia*? Is it because the contrast of the positioning of the roles and the identities are symmetrical to the veiled and unveiled in other works? Could it be that the covering of the black bodies is 'more offensive' than the nakedness of the clearer skins? In asking this question I am suggesting that the gaze is never one and unique, and that we should not choose to make it so for the sake of identifying an usurped identity; in so doing, we are more guilty of usurping identities ourselves.

I am sure that there are many who are eager to express their disagreement and would rightly respond by saying that the creation of the East came from the images of fantasised, veiled women and that this is one of the major ways in which the East was misrepresented and created into 'the other,' the hidden and the silent. In this context, Malek Alloula is one of the best exponents of the photographic 'invention of the Arab East.' His book, *The Colonial Harem*, is no doubt erudite and intelligent and, ironically, often enjoyed as an erotic (even pornographic) coffee table book (especially in the original French edition before it was transformed into academia by a university press).[2] Look again at the images he presents. The *Moroccan Women Promenading*, for example (Figure 5.7)

Look honestly and ask yourself: are we not always tempted to discover what

5.8 Mai Ghoussoub, *They Can Still See*, 1986
clay, 20 x 10cm each figure, collection of the artist

lies behind the veil? I am speaking as an Arab woman here. Do we not return frequently to look at the movement of the veil within the group? What is wrong with this curiosity? Moreover, was not the veil invented to mark an impenetrable space between women's bodies, their skins and the male's gaze and public space? Is not the purpose of the veil to keep women's individuality hidden from the public space and confined to her family and husband's recognition? A friend of mine from Saudi Arabia once told me that she did not mind wearing the veil at all, but why was she not allowed to choose its colours? The veil is not only to cover 'women's intimate parts,' but it is also meant to erase her individuality in any public space. Is this the making of the Orientalist postcard? All traditions of dress are linked to some social norms and demands, be it in the East or the West. Fashion is a message, a language, a powerful sign of first encounter in any culture.

In one of my very early sculptures, *They Can Still See* (Figure 5.8), I focused on veiled women. (Forget about the quality of the sculpture, it is one of my first works). In this work I was trying to make the body language speak for these women since their facial expression is hidden. I knew that each one is different from the other; the joyful, the powerful, the older, the timid, all walking together. Could age be betrayed behind the veil? I named my group of women *They Can Still See* in an attempt to explain that the veil is not the end of the world for women. However, it is only when I went to Saudi Arabia, totally veiled like the friends I was with, that I understood that no image can totally create 'the other,' it can merely interpret it. We were in a shop which sold veils and head covers and I saw women spending an hour or more choosing their veil from among the hundreds of very similar veils on offer. They touched the material, looked at the minute differences in the fringes, the finishing of the lining. From afar, and for someone like myself who does not come from a veiled Arab country, these details made no difference. But it did for the women who wore them. People, women, will always seek difference, a mark of individuality in every situation. This is something neither the Orientalist painter, photographer nor the local repression of the fundamentalists could or can change.

5.9 Colonial Postcard, *Femme arabe dans son intérieur*

5.10 *Chemins de Fer du Maroc,* Poster by E Hauville. Printed by Georges Frere, Tourcoing

5.11 Colonial Postcard, *55 Types Algériens, Femme Mauresque*

5.12 Book Cover, *Nizar, The Women's Lover,* written by Ahmad Ziadeh

5.13 Book Cover, *al-Sufur wal Hijab* (Veiling or Unveiling), written by Nazira Zeineddin

5.14 Book Cover, *Palace of Desire,* 1991, written by Naguib Mahfouz

5.15 Book Cover, *Mirage,* written by Naguib Mahfouz

5.16 *Shahr al Tassawok* ('Special offer, the month of sales, come and take a Sri Lankan maid for $1111'), street banner, Beirut, 1998, *Al Hayat newspaper*

In this context, I cannot resist showing the image of a smoking woman from the same Alloula book, entitled *Smoking Girl* (figure 5.9). Invented or not, studio setting or not, this photograph shows a powerful, playful woman that I do not object to seeing either in reality or in an image. In fact, many of the Orientalists' fantasies were not exclusively concerned with the passive naked Arab body (figures 5.10 and 5.11). Some women are depicted as great in their strength, their pride and their postures. Defiant I would say.

Let us now reverse the situation and see how we in the East see the West in our popular imagery. (In this context, I am referring to the postcards which Alloula reproduced as readily available, popular imagery). In order to explore this aspect of our own image-making in the Arab world, I always use illustrated book covers as they circulate widely and are immensely popular. In particular, I love the one depicting the Syrian poet Nizar Kabbani, who died in 1978 (figure 5.12). It is a bad cover both aesthetically and imaginatively. The two women are depicted in a westernised style. There is the blonde and the black haired woman. They are supposed to be sexy and are offered as objects of desire. The cover appears to me to be almost ironical but I am sure that this is not the reason that nobody in the Arab World appears to have found it offensive.

By contrast, the audience of another book, *Al-Sufur wal Hijab*, calling for women's emancipation, written in a very austere and moderate way, appears not to be bothered by the erotic and simplistic image which has been put on its cover (figure 5.13). The woman is chained in a highly suggestive way while her dress is hardly Arab! Her breasts are oozing out of her dress for no good reason. What is the gender of the reader that this cover is trying to address and to attract? Whatever the answer, the result is beyond comment.

Similarly, a number of other covers, printed on serious literary books by the Egyptian novelist Naguib Mahfouz (born 1911), are found all over the Middle East and are extremely popular (figures 5.14 and 5.15). A librarian in Cambridge once asked me if I could find different editions of Mahfouz's novels. His colleagues, who do not read Arabic, thought that he was ordering pornographic books for the prestigious library! Where are the East and the West in these gaze(s)?

I would like to conclude with an image that I find truly offensive (figure 5.16). I will only translate what it advertises. It is of a banner that appeared during the month of the big sales in Beirut a few years ago. It states: "Special offer, the month of sales, come and take a maid from Sri Lanka for a deposit of only $1111." This is the kind of imaging of women that makes me feel like screaming with rage.

Notes

[1] Lamia Chahine. *100 Years of Plastic Art in Lebanon: 1880-1980*, Vol 1 Beirut, Lebanon: Galerie Chahine, 1982, p8.

[2] Malek Alloula. The *Colonial Harem*, trans by Myrna Godzich and Wlad Godzich, Minneapolis and London: University of Minnesota Press, 1986. First published in 1981 as *Le Harem Colonial: Images d'un sous-érotisme*, Editions Slatkine, Genève-Paris.

TINA SHERWELL

Palestinian Art: Imaging the Motherland

He fell passionately on his land, smelling the soil, kissing the trees and grasping the precious pebbles. Like an infant he pressed his cheeks and mouth to the soil, shedding there the pain he had borne for years. He listened to her heart whispering tender reproof:
— You have come back?
— I have, here is my hand.
Here I will remain, here I will die, so prepare my grave.[1]

This quote is taken from the novel *Nida' al ard* (The Call of the Land), by the author Fadwa Tuqan which tells the story of a refugee determined to return to his land. Here the land of Palestine has been imaged as woman in the role of the beloved, the virgin and the mother. Such imaging of women came to occupy a prominent position after the displacement of the Palestinians from their land in 1948. In this essay I want to explore the representations of women in relation to the imaging of the homeland in recent Palestinian art, particularly painting.

The work I will be discussing here has largely been produced by artists who still reside in what was Palestine: the West Bank, the Gaza Strip, Jerusalem and the Arab villages inside Israel. This is significant because the inhabitants of these areas are afforded a special position within the community of Palestinians where they are considered to be 'inside' Palestine, having remained steadfast on the land rather than exposed to a life in exile. As Edward Said explains: "The people of the interior are cherished as Palestinians 'already there,' so to speak, Palestinians who live on the edge, under the gun, inside the barriers and kasabahs, entitling them to a kind of grace denied to the rest of us."[2] A continuing effect of this spotlight on the West Bank and the Gaza Strip since the signing of the Oslo Accords means that the plight of refugees in Lebanon, Jordan, and the diaspora has been largely forgotten by the international community and the negotiators.

Nevertheless, Palestinians on the inside experience a form of displacement which extends beyond the literal consequences of Palestine being a place that has no defined borders (although it is worth noting that Israel became increasingly nervous at the prospect of President Arafat declaring a State on 4 May 1999). It is the experience of displacement of feeling themselves not to be living in what they imagine and desire Palestine to be because Palestine is under foreign occupation.[3] While those in exile hold a more static memory of Palestine, normally centred around the moment of their departure, those on the ground have witnessed the daily transformations and discriminations that have turned them into strangers in their own land. Here I am not speaking of occupation as something that ended with the signing of the peace agreements. Since then the West Bank has been sealed, which has meant that its residents are unable to travel to Israel or to the city of Jerusalem for services or work while Israeli

Facing page
Nabil Anani, *The Palestinian Village*, 1989 (detail, see colour plate 40)

settlement building continues alongside the confiscation of Arab land.[4]

Palestine as a place has come under different successive occupations. As a consequence, the inhabitants have never experienced sovereignty over the terrain and so Palestine, in many ways, has remained a space of imagining while continuing also to be the site of lived experiences for these Palestinians. During the tense years before the war of 1948, Palestinians were already using the iconography of the woman as a way of talking about their homeland. She was described as the bride to struggle for, which is made clear by the following quote by Ajaj Nuwayhid, an essayist from Haifa and a founding member of the Istiqlal party: "We have asked to become engaged to a girl, her bride price is very expensive, but she deserves it. Here is our answer: we will fight for the sake of her eyes."[5]

However, the metaphor of woman became more widespread in literature and painting after the loss of the homeland in 1948. In this context, it is important to note that the practice of creating representations with paint on cloth, stretched over a rectangular frame, was not part of a visual tradition in Palestine. Painting on canvas was imported from Europe, where it had a much longer history of being used as a form of visual expression. Instead, art in Palestine was integral to everyday life and took the form of wall paintings, ceramics, glass and mother-of-pearl work and embroidery, all of which are now defined as handicrafts. Prior to 1948, painters in Palestine mainly produced portraits of prominent individuals or worked as icon painters for the church and the tourist trade. As a consequence of the war that established the State of Israel, much of the history of these arts pre-1948 has been lost. Anyone attempting to piece together the history of Palestinian art prior to 1948, therefore, has to contend with irretrievable gaps which would once have shed light on the development of Palestinian art practices. Art was mainly commissioned for interiors or religious establishments and this evidence was lost as people fled their homes, taking with them only the most essential belongings. Many homes were completely razed to the ground by the Israeli forces when over 350 villages were destroyed and the war of 1948 transformed approximately half the Arab population into refugees, totalling approximately 700,000 people.[6]

The conflict between Palestinians and Israelis centres around the competing claims of two national communities to the same piece of land. However, Palestinians and Israelis are not equally placed in this rivalry as the latter have considerable state apparatus at their disposable. Beginning with the early settlers, the Israelis:

> launched a massive project aimed at revealing an originary historical inscription in the landscape. Their enterprise entailed such activities as using the Bible as a guide for remapping and renaming the territory and organising archaeological digs and hiking expeditions. The Zionist project of uncovering and displaying exclusive Jewish roots had the effect of denying any authentic Arab historicity in Palestine.[7]

Sadly, such projects still continue today.

In the light of these facts it is not surprising that the representation of the landscape occupies a dominant place in the artistic expression of both the Palestinian and Israeli communities. The cultural arena of literature, theatre, cinema, dance and folklore has played a significant role in shaping the vision of the landscape, and has been mobilised by both Palestinians and Israelis as an important site for the articulation and formation of their respective national identities.

The darker side of Israel's projects of rediscovering its identity was the suppression of all forms of expression of Palestinian identity which was interpreted as posing a direct challenge to the founding mythologies of the State of Israel. The suppression of the Palestinians took numerous forms and intervened in every part of daily life: from goods to movement to the building of homes, to water and to the consumption of literary material.[8] Equally, the arena of culture was not free from repression, for culture is one of the spaces in which a nation creates an image of itself, its experiences and its collective identity. Interestingly, within this context, the Palestinians, as Peetet notes, "were not resurrecting traditional culture but rather consciously devising a blend of old and new to form a 'culture of resistance.'"[9]

The popular reception which Palestinian art received from the general public from the mid-1970s to the mid-1980s alarmed the Israeli authorities.[10] Exhibitions were closed and paintings were confiscated for containing political material. Significantly, paintings were classified by military ruling as leaflets and were thus subject to the same censorship regulations as any other printed matter. "Military Order No 101, Article 6" prohibits residents of the West Bank from printing or publishing "any publication, advertisement, proclamation, picture or any other document" which contains any article with "political significance" except after obtaining a license from the Military Commander. "Printing" is defined in the order to include "carving on stone, typing on a typewriter, copying, photographing or any other manner of representation or of communicating expressions, numbers, symbols, maps, painting, decorations or any other similar material."[11]

It was in these conditions that Palestinian art works were censored and in order to hold an exhibition, permission had to be granted by the Israeli military governor which, in most cases, was denied. Exhibitions and artists were also banned from travelling abroad. Artists themselves were victims of discrimination being placed under arrest or restricted by the imposed travel bans. One of the most telling manifestations of the body of this Israeli legislation was the prohibition on the use of the four colours of the Palestinian flag together; red, green, black and white could not be placed in close proximity in any art work.[12]

Artists in the West Bank and Gaza Strip were not only restricted in their creative expression by the repressive environment created by the Israeli authorities but also by the absence of a supporting infrastructure in the occupied territories. To the present day there still does not exist a college for the study of art. Artists who wish to pursue a profession in this field are obliged therefore to either travel abroad for their education, mainly to Egypt or Iraq, or to be educated within the Israeli system. Sliman Mansour (born in Birzeit in 1947), for example, graduated from the Israeli Bezalel Art Academy in Jerusalem, the first art institution established in the country. Others, who have not had the privilege of such opportunities, are self-taught or are taught by other Palestinian painters. Artists are also faced with a lack of museums and this, together with the travel restrictions and the difficulties of touring art exhibitions coming to the occupied territories, means that Palestinian artists have been effectively cut off from contemporary art developments in different parts of the world.

Furthermore, until the early 1990s, no permanent gallery or art centre for the exhibiting of art works existed in the West Bank, the Gaza Strip or Jerusalem. Exhibitions were held in schools or universities, union halls or other make-shift locations. This lack of exhibition spaces has had profound repercussions on the artistic community of Palestine. In particular, it has hampered the development of a purchasing public and, as a consequence, artists struggle to support themselves financially. However, although the public was unable to purchase original art works, visual images circulated and were consumed in other forms, particularly through posters. According to Mansour and Tamari, "people rushed to purchase them treating them with the same protectiveness as valuable museum pieces."[13] Importantly, posters could reach people in the villages and the refugee camps, and were easily affordable.

What I have outlined above is the political context in which the images that I will be discussing were created and received. Within this context, the representation of the landscape comes to occupy an important position in Palestinian art as it is imaged as the locus of identity. Stephen Daniels has suggested that national identities utilise particular landscapes from within the nation as a way of symbolising the terrain of the homeland.[14] In the case of the Palestinians, it is the Palestinian village, its surrounding landscape and the peasantry that has achieved the status of the national signifier. Not surprisingly, this focus on the creating of images of Palestinian villages coincided with a revival of Palestinian heritage and folklore in the late 1970s and throughout the 1980s. As more explicit forms of national expression were denied, the village provided a suitable metaphor for Palestinian identity. By appropriating the village as a signifier of the nation, the image of the village has been moulded into a general stereotype. Often it is not specific villages that are represented but rather all the elements which constitute an ideal type of village. These often include a landscape in full spring bloom, several traditional houses, a woman wearing traditional Palestinian costume with children or engaged in domestic activities such as baking *taboun* bread, grinding wheat or harvesting.

By using images of Palestinian villages and the peasantry, Palestinians could identify themselves as a people who had historical roots in the landscape, as a people who were inhabitants of the land.[15] This way of imaging was not arbitrary. It drew on the fact that the Palestinian population has mainly lived in agricultural communities throughout history.[16] The village and the peasantry were used as a metaphor for the Palestinian nation which enabled the Palestinians to articulate the characteristics of a national identity. The peasant was invested with the symbolism of steadfastness and patience, qualities that Palestinians of the West Bank were adopting in the late 1970s and early 1980s as a political strategy to remain on the land despite all Israeli attempts at making daily life strenuous and indeterminate. This form of resistance relegated activism to those Palestinians on the outside for, as Swedenberg notes, "The chief duty of the Palestinians people 'inside', imagined as peasants, is to continue steadfast (*samid*) on the land and to follow the directives of the leaders — not to undertake their own initiatives."[17] This political strategy continued in the West Bank and Gaza Strip until the outbreak of the Intifada, the grassroots uprising which swept through the Occupied Territories in 1987.

The image of the peasant is used at particular junctions in national discourse when images of continuity with the past and conservative values are required. Yet in the process of valorising the peasantry and transforming them into a national symbol of resistance, historical details and differences are suppressed thereby making the peasantry objects rather than participating agents of historical development.[18] Rarely, for example, are there references to the growing inequalities experienced by peasants during the Ottoman era when the rural surplus became a sought after commodity to trade on the international markets thus increasing the exploitation of the peasantry.[19] On the contrary, the image of the Palestinian village is one of harmony and egalitarianism, of rural utopias which seem to be set in a timeless frame or an ambiguous golden age which gloss over the social transformations that the peasantry has experienced from the changes in the land laws during the late Ottoman era to the present-day confiscation of their land by the Israeli authorities. However, national landscapes function to create a comforting image of the past. Signs of modernity exemplified by the influx of commodity culture and the changes wrought by the Israeli occupation are not represented. Such signs would disturb the comforting image of a homely motherland.

Thus the image of the village and the agricultural community provides a form

6.1 Sliman Mansour, *Olive Pickers*, c1988 (see colour plate 36)

6.2 Saed Hilmi, *Olive Picking*, 1993 (see colour plate 32)

6.3 Sliman Mansour, *The Village Awakens*, 1990 (see colour plate 38)

6.4 Nabil Anani, *The Palestinian Village*, 1979 (see colour plate 39)

for imaging the Palestinian community and Palestinian artists deploy this imagery in a variety of ways. A common subject matter in painting, for example, is the representation of the harvesting of the products of the land. Olive picking is a particularly popular theme evident in the work of the Jerusalem-based artist Sliman Mansour (figure 6.1) and Saed Hilmi (figure 6.2). Hilmi's painting, *Olive Picking* (1993), is filled with women picking olives. All are clothed in traditional dress and placed in a field of endless olive groves which is bathed in a golden light and gives a feeling of the abundance of agricultural produce. Mansour's painting, *The Village Awakens* (1990, figure 6.3) presents an equally idealised scene of an image of community in which each member is engaged in a different activity, harvesting, fruit picking, stone carving and so on, while the men and women march out from the village centre — imaged as the body of a woman — eager to take up their activities.

This painting can be read in a number of ways. Executed during the latter part of the Intifada, the painting can be seen to relate to the spirit of self-reliance that was fostered as part of the uprising.

The Intifada (which means shaking off or an awakening) stands in contrast to the former political strategy of steadfastness which involved consolidating one's position and remaining on the land. However, both policies drew on rural imagery to articulate their position. The Intifada drew a comparison with the peasant rebellion of 1936 in its leaflets. The notion of self-reliance was expressed through the boycotting of Israeli products, the producing of local foodstuffs, and using Arab services. Local committees in each village and town were responsible for the co-ordination of the community and for its welfare.[20] In this context, Mansour's painting is a national allegory. It depicts the village as a microcosm of society, as the ideal community, in which every person is designated a particular role and therefore contributes to the life and productivity of the village. Repeated on a grand scale this system provides a prototype for the nation. Thus, the village provides both a model for the nation and for the familiarity of intimate local communities.

Indeed, the focus on the representation of the Palestinian village and the peasantry has come to contour the very depiction of the landscape which, through these art works, is visualised as a particularly domestic landscape. Rarely does one find paintings representing wide-open panoramas. Instead, landscapes are in the large part populated and centred on the village, agricultural labour or the domestic abode. For example, in an image by Nabil Anani (born 1943)[21] also entitled *Palestinian Village* (1979, figure 6.4), a woman is the main subject of the painting. Her home recedes into the background while she stands motionless watching over children. The colours used by the artist work to blend her body into the landscape. Similarly, it has become customary among Palestinian artists to remove male figures from their representations of the village thus creating a community of women and children. The viewer then comes to occupy a paternalist position interpellated to care for these lone women and children, and their village. Thus, in effect, the viewer is safeguarding Palestine and its future.

The subject of the village and the peasantry has therefore provided a screen onto which artists project their fantasies of past/future Palestine. As such, the representation of the village is subject to different interpretations. It has been used, for example, as a way of depicting an individual privatised image of Palestine that is evident in Nabil Anani's later painting of the *Palestinian Village* (1989, figure 6.5). The subject of the painting is still the village where a family is placed in the foreground. Interestingly, no other members of the village are evident and the figures are posed in a way that recalls a photographic portrait where the sitters' status and property are displayed. In another image, entitled *The Farmer* (1989) by Taleb Dweik (born 1953) [22] (figure 6.6), the peasant is positioned resting underneath a tree with his home in the background. Both these representations offer an image of the landscape as the privatised domain of individual families and the Palestine that is then imagined is one of personal comfort and security.

However, Dweik's image is also a deeply privatised representation of village life which focuses upon one's home and individual space. In a sense one could argue that this project is taking physical form in the contemporary vision of Palestine in which numerous individuals are constructing their ideal landscape/homescape in Palestine. The utopia of Palestine is revealing itself to be a conservative dream of 'my home and garden,' of individualism. The numerous villas that have sprouted up all over the West Bank testify to this ideology in which the architecture is not planned as part of a community but where instead each person is involved in visualising their own personal paradise in Palestine through the form of the domestic abode.

What becomes evident in the paintings I have discussed so far is the centrality of the Palestinian peasant woman. The representation of a peasant woman working in the landscape is the dominant image in numerous paintings. The lone woman gathers olives, wheat, almonds and so forth or bears the products of the land as in the painting by Abdel Muttaleb A' Bayyan (born 1947)[23] of *Harvest* (1990, figure 6.7). Here the presence of the woman inscribes upon the landscape its identity. More than any other member of the community the peasant woman in traditional dress has come to be a marker of national identity. In the aftermath of the loss of the land, the peasant woman's costume, which is unique to every region of Palestine, has come to function as a way of mapping the terrain. The style of the dress indicates the village identity of the woman who wore it through the embroidery and its organisation within the garment and such localised dresses are still worn today.

Similarly, it is mainly artefacts from the peasant home and the woman's sphere, such as cooking utensils, baskets and storage jars, that have been taken up as objects of Palestinian heritage and displayed in museums and people's homes. Meanwhile, embroidery patterns are now reproduced on a host of daily objects such as waistcoats, slippers, headbands, purses, mirrors and cushion covers, thereby expanding the signs of peasantness and enabling this identity to be consumed and displayed as part of everyday modern urban life. The figure of the peasant woman, her surroundings and her belongings has therefore become one of the main spaces through which to signify the homeland.

Women are frequently represented as the privileged bearers of cultural authenticity in the process of articulating national identity.[24] They are perceived as being closer to the land and as maintaining traditions of a past way

6.5 Nabil Anani, *The Palestinian Village*, 1989 (see colour plate 40)

6.6 Taleb Dweik, *The Farmer*, 1989 (see colour plate 41)

6.7 Abdel Muttaleb A'Bayyan, *Harvest*, 1990 (see colour plate 42)

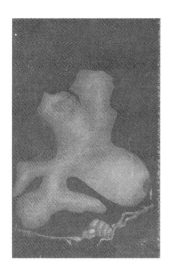

6.8 Ali al Ashab, *In Spite of Pain*, 1984 (see colour plate 43)

6.9 Nabil Anani, *Motherhood*, 1979 (see colour plate 44)

of life through their dress and the cooking of traditional foods. In Palestine women were imaged as unchanging, as if the place of the past was still alive and being continually reproduced. The increasing feminisation of agricultural labour which had taken place in the West Bank as women took over the main responsibility of agricultural labour when the small plots of land could no longer support families and the male members sought other work, served to reinforce the metaphoric association of women, nature and the land.[25] However, as Deniz Kandiyoti argues, although nationalist imagery valorises women by placing them at the centre of nationalist rhetoric and imagery, it also serves to control what roles women actually take up in service of the nation.[26]

Artists, poets and dance troupes have all appropriated the figure of the woman, in most cases the peasant woman, in order to express and elaborate an idea of the Palestinian homeland and, in so doing, they have attributed a gender to the homeland. Becoming female, the homeland is usually imaged as a mother figure and, as Ghassan Hage notes, the use of the mother to signify the nation, distinguishes the qualities of the nation as caring, protective and nurturing: a homeland of bodily comfort and security.[27] In much of the literature that expresses the experience of exile, the love of homeland is eulogised as the love for the mother and it slips at times into a sensuality which perhaps points to the ambiguous relationship to the Mother: for the first exile is exile from the womb and the mother.

In the visual arts similar images are visible. The pain of the severance from the motherland is expressed in very literal terms, for example, in a work entitled *Inspite of Pain* (1984) by Ali al Ashab (born 1956, figure 6.8).[28] The mother's breast has lost its form and it is as though the body has dissolved taking on the outline of a map or a terrain while a hand grasping from below clutches on to a trickle of milk from the breast. In Nabil Anani's painting *Motherhood* from 1979 (figure 6.9), the landscape is reduced to an arch of vines. The peasant woman's dress has shed its specific embroidery (indicating her village identity) and has been exchanged for the main colours of the Palestinian flag. The mother now symbolises and embodies the land of Palestine through both her role as a mother and through the space of her body.

The equally popular theme of the maternal images of mothers with babes in arms can be similarly read as part of a nationalist discourse in which women are seen as responsible for reproducing the nation thereby inscribing women's fertility with political significance and making women's reproductive capabilities a patriotic obligation where women's most productive role in a national struggle is seen as that of child bearers.[29] Women are thus perceived not only as giving birth to a future generation but as also bearing the responsibility of reproducing the boundaries of the nation.[30] In effect, women's bodies are relegated as the site of the nation's purity. Discourses of nationalism are fundamentally conceived upon ideas of exclusion and inclusion and the safeguarding and controlling of women's bodies therefore becomes essential to maintaining the identity and genealogy of the nation.

In addition, women were also given the responsibility of nurturing children with a love of their homeland thereby giving birth to a generation of future fighters and nation builders. Sliman Mansour visualises this division of labour in his painting, *The Village Awakens,* discussed previously (figure 6.3). The Palestinian peasant woman takes on giant proportions blending into the hillside and the village architecture: her legs are spread apart allowing the nation to march forth from her body. She herself occupies a passive role in comparison to the other figures in the painting who are all engaged in some kind of activity. As Nahil Abdo has suggested, the burden of reproducing the nation does not fall equally upon all women as it tends to be the poorer sectors of the community resident in villages and refugee camps who have larger families.[31] It is the sons of these families who make up the casualities and who work for the national struggle. However, large families did not emerge with the birth of nationalism. They have their roots in the social norms of the peasantry for whom the family meant an army of individuals to work the land and to provide an economic resource and a source of security for the older members of the family whom the younger generations would support. During the many years of occupation, when there was no government to protect individuals, the family was once again the main form of security and protection.

6.10 Hashem Klub, *From the Intifada*, 1988
(see colour plate 45)

In recent years, numerous studies of nationalism have concentrated on deconstructing the gendered nature of national discourses and have highlighted, in particular, the politicisation of women's reproductive role where women are called upon to reproduce the nation.[32] As a consequence, women's bodies enter the arena of the conflict often becoming a target for assault because they are perceived as the producers of the next generation of Palestinians. For example, during the Intifada there were instances when Israeli soldiers fired tear gas into confined spaces where pregnant women were present. The effect of tear gas inhalation is known to cause miscarriages.[33] Equally, however, one has to acknowledge the targeting of men's bodies and the injuries they sustained. Men were often subject to numerous forms of torture in Israeli jails, spending many years of their life in prison only to be confronted with the difficulties of assimilating back into the community.[34]

During the Intifada women's domestic work expanded into the public sphere as the division between public and private spaces became more fluid and all aspects of life became a target for the Israeli soldiers. Previously, women's caring work was normally centred on her immediate family. However, with the Intifada, as Carol Bardenstein shows, the definition of the community for whom she catered for was extended.[35] Women became more visible in the public realm, undertaking their 'supportive roles' in dangerous circumstances that frequently led to injury and imprisonment. Women were seen carrying rocks to youths, shielding them from arrest, as in the painting entitled *From the Intifada* (1988) by Hashem Klub (born 1957)[36] (figure 6.10), organising food and health care for communities under curfew and petitioning for the release of prisoners.[37]

6.11 Jawad Al Malhi, *The Beginning and the End*, 1988
(see colour plate 46)

Perhaps one of the few painters who does not glorify the role of motherhood is Jawad Al Malhi, born in 1969 in the Shufhat Camp in Jerusalem.[38] In *The Beginning and the End* of 1988 (figure 6.11) a woman screams with the agony of childbirth which stands in stark contrast to Mansour's monumental woman who emotionlessly produces the nation. During the Intifada mothers took up the role of 'Mothers of All.' All the children were her children, thus women were interpellated as the mother of the nation. This nurturing role is depicted in *The Children of the Camp* (figure 6.12) by Hashem Klub in which the woman is represented protecting all the

6.12 Hashem Klub, *The Children of the Camp*, 1987
(see colour plate 47)

6.13 Fayez al Hassan, *The Martyr's Wedding*, 1992 (see colour plate 48)

6.14 Mohammad Abu Sittah, *The Intifada Bride*, 1989 (see colour plate 49)

6.15 Jawad Al Malhi, *The Bride*, 1990 (see colour plate 50)

6.16 Khalil Rabah, *Womb*, 1997 (see colour plate 51)

children with her clothing and her body. Thus, in many instances, the individual mother-son relationship is subsumed by the collective mother-son relationship which also serves as a way of containing the personal sorrow of losing sons to the national struggle.[39] The highest accolade was given to the 'Mother of the Martyr' who was viewed as having made the ultimate sacrifice of giving up her son for the national cause. Or, as an Intifada communiqué states: "Let the mother of the martyr rejoice she has lifted her voice twice; first on the day of her son's death and again on the day of the declaration of the State."[40]

In the imagery of martyrdom, martyrs are spoken of as bridegrooms and their death as their wedding. The land of Palestine is seen as a virgin, waiting to be inseminated, and it is the blood of the martyr that will give birth to the nation. In this rhetoric women's role as reproducers of the nation is elided. It is male agency which will deliver the nation as the female, symbolised by the land, takes on a passive role. This is particularly evident in a painting by Fayez al Hassan entitled *The Martyr's Wedding* (1992, figure 6.13) where, all in white, it is almost as though the male is being sacrificed to the a giant female figure whose flowing head scarf makes up the lie of the land. Meanwhile, in a work by Mohammed Abu Sittah (born 1954)[41] entitled *The Intifada Bride* (1989, figure 6.14) the bride's body is covered with images of masked youth while her veil is a combination of a black and white kufiyeh[42] and a crown of stones,[43] thus inscribing the space of her body with the emblems of the Intifada. Perhaps she who wears the image of the young men on her body is the virgin land who the martyrs die for?

Martyrdom however is represented in a different light in Jawad Al Malhi's painting of 1990 entitled *The Bride* (figure 6.15). Once again a giant female figure dominates the canvas, however, she is not in traditional dress but in a dark dress and a white headscarf. The camp shrinks into the background as she marches towards us holding up a dead female child in her arms. Her trance-like expression and the dark sockets of her eyes seem to express the grief of a mother. The bride in this case is not a metaphor but a human being, a causality of the national uprising.

Significantly, the imaging of the homeland as a monumental female figure has undergone a dramatic change in recent years. Palestinian painting has witnessed the disappearance of the woman and, more specifically, the mother. The homeland is no longer envisioned as a site of bodily re-unification with the mother or a place of sensual pleasure. This is evident in a recent work by Khalil Rabah (born 1961)[44] entitled *Womb* (1997, figure 6.16), where the organ of the woman's body has taken the shape of an everyday object, a suitcase. The space of nurturing is empty of personal belongings with which to assemble an identity. A chair to rest upon does not even fit into the suitcase and creates an awkward tension. The emptiness of the interior contrasts with our commonly held notion of the womb as a place of comfort and security. Thus, the void one is confronted with intervenes in the conventional comforting representations of the motherland and implies a certain dystopia and disillusionment.

In conclusion I would suggest that the gendered imaging of Palestine is changing. Since the arrival of President Arafat there has been a move towards depicting Arafat as the Father of the nation, the father of all the children. Now that Palestinian rule has been instituted on three per cent of the land that was once Palestine, renamed 'Zone A,' is Palestine shifting to being imaged as a Fatherland?

Notes

[1] Fadwa Tuqan cited in Sulaiman, A. K. *Palestine and Modern Arab Poetry*, London: Zed Books, 1984, p125.

[2] Said, E. *After the Last Sky: Palestinian Lives*, London: Faber and Faber, 1986, p51.

[3] Bowman, G. 'A Country of Words: Conceiving the Palestinian Nation from the Position of Exile' in *The Making of Political Identities*, edited by Laclau, Ernesto. London: Verso, 1994, p139.

[4] A closure of the West Bank and Gaza Strip has been in effect since 1993. It is estimated that since the signing of the Oslo Accords the Israeli government has confiscated 295,000 dunums of land. Some 40,000 dunums of these have been used to create thirty by-pass roads in order to connect Jewish settlements within the West Bank. Cited in *Passia Diary* (The Palestinian Academic Society for the Study of International Affairs), Jerusalem: Passia, 1999, p231.

[5] Ajaj Nuwayhid cited in Katz, S. 'Shahada and Haganah; Politicizing Masculinities in Early Palestinian and Jewish Nationalisms' *Arab Studies Journal*, Fall 1996, p83.

[6] Beinin, J, Hajjar, L and Rabbani, M. 'Palestine and The Arab Israeli Conflict for Beginners' in *Intifada: The Palestinian Uprising against Israeli Occupation*, (eds). Lockman, Zachary and Beinin, Joel. London: I. B. Tauris, 1990, p102.

[7] Swedenberg, T. 'The Palestinian Peasant As National Signifier' *Anthropological Quarterly*, Vol 63, January 1990, p19.

[8] Evidence can be found in the military orders issued under the Israeli Occupation that regulated all areas of life in the Occupied Territories.

[9] Peetet, Julie, 'Authenticity and Gender' in *The Presentation of Culture, Arab Women, Old Boundaries, New Frontiers*, (ed). Tucker, Judith E, Bloomington: Indiana University Press, 1993, p50.

[10] Mansour, S and Tamari, V. Art Under Occupation, 1990, p2.

[11] Shehadeh, R. *Occupier's Law; Israel and the West Bank*, Washington DC: Institute of Palestine Studies, 1985, p57.

[12] Mansour, S and Tamari, V. *Art Under Occupation*, 1990, p2.

[13] Geist, W. 'The Growing Pains of an Art Movement Under Occupation,' *Al Fajr Newspaper*, Jerusalem, 6-12 September 1981, p13.

[14] Daniels, S. *Fields of Vision; Landscape, Imagery and National Identity in England and the United States*, Princeton: Princeton University Press, 1993, p5.

[15] Swedenberg, T. 'The Palestinian Peasant As National Signifier' *Anthropological Quarterly*, Vol 63, January 1990, p24.

[16] Ruedy, J. 'Dynamic of Land Alienation, The Transformation of Palestine' in *Essays on the Origin and Development of the Arab Israeli Conflict*, (ed). Abu-Lughod, Ibrahim, Evanston: Northwestern University Press, 1971, p120.

[17] Swedenberg, T. 'The Palestinian Peasant As National Signifier', *Anthropological Quarterly*, Vol 63, January 1990, p27.

[18] Swedenberg, T. 'The Palestinian Peasant As National Signifier', *Anthropological Quarterly*, Vol 63, January 1990, p25.

[19] Asad, T. 'Class Transformation Under the Mandate'; *MERIP* (Middle Eastern Report) No 53, 1976, p4.

[20] Peretz, Don. *The Intifada Uprising*, Boulder and London: Westview Press, 1990, pp55-57.

[21] Nabil Anani, born in Halhoul, graduated from the Alexandria Fine Arts Institute and is now resident in Ramallah.

[22] Taleb Dweik was born in Jerusalem and received a BA in Art Education from Cairo University, Egypt. He now lives in Jerusalem.

[23] Abdul Muttaleb A' Bayyan, born in Palestine, studied art education at the teacher training college in Gaza and now lives in Gaza.

[24] Kandiyoti, Deniz. 'Identity and its Discontents: Women and the Nation' *Millennium: Journal of International Studies*, Vol 20, No 3, 1991, p431.

[25] Swedenberg, T. 'The Palestinian Peasant As National Signifier' *Anthropological Quarterly*, Vol 63, January 1990, p23.

[26] Kandiyoti, D. 'Identity and its Discontents: Women and the Nation' *Millennium: Journal of International Studies*, Vol 20, No 3, 1991, p433.

[27] Hage, Ghassan, 'The Spatial Imaginary of National Practices: Dwelling-Domesticating/Being-Exterminating' *Environment and Planning; Space and Society*, Vol 14, 1996, p473.

[28] Ali al Ashab, born in Gaza, has a BA in Art Education from Cairo University and lives in Gaza.

[29] Yuval-Davis, Nira and Anthias, Floya (eds). *Woman-Nation-State*, London: Macmillan, 1989, p7.

[30] Ibid.

[31] Abdo, Nahil, 'Women of the Intifada: Gender, Class and National Liberation', *Race and Class*, No 32, 1991, p28.

[32] For example, see the work of Nira Yuval-Davis and Deniz Kandiyoti.

[33] Young, G E. 'A Feminist Politics of Health Care: The Case of Palestinian Women under Israeli Occupation 1979-1982' in Tamar, Mayer (ed). *Women and the Israeli Occupation: The Politics of Change*, London: Routledge, 1994, p186.

[34] *Al Haq*, 'Law in the service of man,' a human rights organisation in Ramallah, has documented the testimonies of Palestinian political prisoners and published these in several of its pamphlets.

[35] Bardenstein, Carol, 'Raped Brides and Steadfast Mothers; Appropriations of Palestinian Motherhood' in *The Politics of Motherhood; Activist Voices from Left to Right*, (ed). Jetter, Alexis *et al*, Hanover and London: University Press of New England, 1997, p175.

[36] Hashem Klub, born 1959 in Jabila Camp, Gaza; studied at the Islamic University in Gaza, resident in Gaza.

[37] Giacaman, R and Johnson, P. 'Palestinian Women; Building Barricades and Breaking Barriers' in *Intifada; The*

Palestinian Uprising Against Israeli Occupation, (eds). Lockman, Zachary and Beinin, Joel, London: I B Tauris, 1989, p9.

[38] Jawad Al Malhi, who has no formal art training continues to live in Jerusalem.

[39] Bardenstein, C. 1997, p177.

[40] Aharoni, R and Mishal, S. *Speaking Stones; Communiqués from the Intifada Underground*, New York: Syracuse University Press, 1994, Communiqué 21.

[41] Mohammad Abu Sittah, born in Khan Yunis, graduated from the Alexandria Fine Arts Institute in Egypt and now lives in Nablus.

[42] The kufiyeh, originally a traditional form of peasant clothing, is the headwear worn by male Palestinians. It has a long history of being used as a symbol of political resistance beginning with the 1936 Arab Rebellion in Palestine. Later, during the 1960s and 1970s, it was adopted by the Palestine Liberation Organisation and worn to show allegiance to the Fateh group within the PLO. During the Intifada the kufiyeh became a popular symbol of Palestinian identity and was worn by young men and women often seen in confrontations with Israeli soldiers.

[43] Significantly, rather than wearing expensive jewellery or a tiara for her wedding, the woman is adorned with a humble crown of stones. Such stones became symbolic during the Intifada as a sign of the Palestinian struggle and of the Palestinian position vis-à-vis the Israeli military's advanced weaponry which was used indiscriminately against them in retaliation for the Intifada Uprising.

[44] Khalil Rabah was born in Jerusalem and graduated with a BA in Fine Arts from Utah University in the United States. He now lives in Ramallah.

HOURIA NIATI

Enacting Vision: A Personal Perspective

I was born in a town called Khemis-Miliana in Algeria, North Africa, about 130 kilometres west of Algiers in 1948. I was born during the time when Algeria was under French colonial rule and it is these circumstances and the experiences that I went through which have informed my work. I have six sisters and one brother who continue to live in Algeria, apart from two sisters who have recently moved to France. There are several events in my life which were extremely vital because in a sense they have made me what I am now.

I was six years old when the war of independence broke out in Algeria in 1954. I did not know what was going on. One day I was playing in the street and my father urged me to get inside the house. It turned out that there was a bomb in the café next door. Khemis-Miliana was like a French town with several Arab areas around it. We could go in and out of the town without any problems. However, nearby was the gendarmerie, the army police station, where the French were overseeing what was going on outside the town, in the countryside. Living so near to the station meant that, literally everyday for several years, I witnessed many horrific things.

At school I was educated in a French system that continued even after Algerian independence was declared in 1962. We were taught about French art and culture which was very much part of my life. My father, Khelifa Niati, was a painter. He never went to art school but he used to paint and draw continually. His inspiration was Cézanne and he always painted landscapes. As a child I always used to ask 'father, father what are you doing?' He used to give me brushes and little bowls and would tell me to paint. So my father was my first teacher. He used to read French and he had a lot of art books at home which I used to copy from incessantly.

At home it was very much an Arab-Islamic world mixed with French culture. Some families were strong practitioners of Islam and others practised it in their own way. At home we observed Ramadan, I knew about Allah and I used to recite the Quran. By contrast, at school I used to learn about Father Christmas, about French history and there were these two things in my life which were absolutely adjusted. They were parallel worlds that went on together. When I went to school it was one thing and then I would go home to another thing. As a little girl I just was taking in what was around me and crossing cultures was not a problem. At home, for example, we used to speak French and Arabic, read French newspapers,

Facing page
Houria Niati, Andalusian Song, 1992-3 (detail of installation, Ziriab…Another Story, 1998)

and listen to French and Arab radio. Of course, this has not changed in Algeria.

The war was something horrific for me. Living near the gendarmerie, I used to see the dead bodies almost everyday. When there was fighting in the mountains the bodies of the dead would be left outside the town for everybody to see and people would go and see if they recognised any of their relatives. It was a horrible sight particularly for a small child.

When the war finished in 1962 it was almost as if another world had started because all the French people seemed to have disappeared. For example, in my class at school there were about 30 pupils but suddenly all the French girls disappeared and the class was made up of the remaining six Algerian girls. By this time I was fourteen years old and I was asking endless questions about death and life. Why do the French people believe in God and why do we believe in Allah? Why? Why? Why?

At that time my father had promised that I could go to art school so I was really looking forward to going to the École des Beaux Arts in Algiers which was then regarded as the most wonderful art school. Many artists wanted to go there, and I was just waiting to reach my 18th year so I could attend.

Unfortunately, my father died when I was 16 years old. He was healthy, he had lived through the war and he was always playing football. He was a great loss to me. The war had finished, a new world seemed to have begun and then, suddenly in 1964, my father died from a heart attack. This idea about death was continually in my mind. Why? Why did my father die and leave us alone? My mother was not working: she could not work and there were eight children. My youngest sister was only eight months old.

My dream of becoming an artist appeared to have been shattered as I became the head of the family. I trained in community arts, specialising in visual arts and music at the Ministry of Youth and Culture National School of Tixeraine in Algiers. It was here that I trained as a singer in the classical Arab-Andalusian tradition which was to be very important for me.[1] Working in education and culture, I was in the privileged position of seeing Algerian culture growing and blossoming. In 1969 a lot of things were going on such as the first Pan-African Festival in Algiers. For the first time I felt that I was part of Africa, too. I used to go to exhibitions in Algiers, and to the cinema and the theatre as often as I could.

7.1 Houria Niati performing at *Dialogue of the Present: The Work of Eighteen Arab Women Artists*, Hot Bath Gallery Bath, England, 16 January 1999

I worked for about six years for the Ministry of Culture and Youth and I was always dreading having to confront myself with the question: 'Why do you not do it?' I wanted to be a painter. I wanted to express things and why was I not doing it?

Finally, one day I explained to my mother that I really wanted to go somewhere just to find out what is going on elsewhere. I was travelling a lot with the Ministry of Youth and Culture, taking groups to France, Poland and Tunisia, for example, and I was witnessing what was going on in the art world. Also, I used to listen to the radio avidly. Although of course my English was very limited but the fact that it was mostly music was helpful! I could listen to Um Kulthum, to the Beatles and so on. I realised that I was born into this mishmash of cultures and I moved easily between them. It was no problem going from one to another.

In 1975 I came to Europe with the idea of travelling around, first in France and then in Britain, just to have a look around basically. I really liked Britain and thought, 'Mm, what a really interesting place to come to.' I had experienced much change and movement and I wanted to be at a place where I could actually breathe and say '...listen to myself.' Is art really part of my life or is it part of my imagination?' So, after my initial visit of a few months, I went back home and I said to my family please allow me to go to Britain to do something with my art. Of course, I was part of the generation that had lived through the 1960s and, while still in Algeria, closely followed what was going on in the arts, cinema, music and politics in Britain, France and the United States.

Eventually, in 1977, I returned to London and it was here that I really started my life as an artist. I did not speak much English and had little money but I felt it was the right time to make the move. During the morning I worked as an au pair, in the afternoon I began taking English classes and in the evening I attended a course on drawing and painting at the Camden Arts Centre. I did this for a year and then I applied to the Croydon College of Art. When I went along for the interview, they said, 'You don't speak English, we cannot take you because you would not be able to write the thesis for your degree.' I said: 'Really, when do I do the thesis?' They said: 'In the third year you have do a thesis.' 'In the third year? I will be able to speak English by then!' Next they asked me how I would pay the fees. Again, I just had to say I will find a way. Just trust me!

I was extremely fortunate to be doing a fine art course at that art college in the early 1980s. The Croydon College of Art had fantastic facilities which meant that I could paint, draw, make prints and work with photography. Also, coming to Britain was important for me in other ways. In many respects I thought I knew very little, but I discovered that I was quite avant-garde in my vision of the world thanks to the reading and research that I did in Algeria when I was working for the Ministry of Youth and Culture. However, I had no strong connection with the Middle East because I did not read Arabic. I did not know what was going on in the art field there, and it was in London that I started to connect with the Middle East, with Japan, with Africa and so forth. It was fantastic for me; it was feeding all this need I had to communicate and to find out what was going on in contemporary art.

7.2 Houria Niati, *No To Torture (After Delacroix's The Women of Algiers),* 1982 (see colour plate 52)

The first exhibition I took part in was in 1983, in London. It was *Five Black Women* at the Africa Centre in Covent Garden and I was really scared.[2] When I started to speak about my work they asked if I was French! I replied that I might speak English with a French accent but I am not French. I am Algerian. When I did that first exhibition it was 'Gosh! Who am I?' Am I Algerian? French? African? Muslim? I felt that I was all of these things and that my work was about myself and about being Algerian. From that moment I started to do performances, in this case, as part of my installation, *No to Torture,* 1982-83 (figure 7.2).[3]

Then in 1984 I was invited by the Riverside Studios in Hammersmith, London, to be their first artist in residence in the borough which was grant-aided by the Greater London Arts Association. Through this I was able to build a body of work and I started to regularly exhibit in museums and galleries in Britain. Interestingly, at this point, I was always exhibited as part of the British art scene in exhibitions on contemporary British art. Then, all of a sudden in the mid-1980s, there was this movement called 'black art' in Britain. I started really searching the field and asking what is black art, what is it like? It was then that I really started connecting. I also became very interested in new image painting through exhibitions such as the *New Figuration* in Bologna, Italy, which showed Sandro Chia and Francesco Clemente, and *La Nouvelle Figuration Libre* in France. In Britain, I saw the 1981 exhibition *A New Spirit in Painting* at the Royal Academy, where I also discovered the American painter Cy Twombly and, of course, Bruce McLean, who had been my tutor at Croydon College.

In 1991 I did a touring exhibition with Eddie Chambers called *Four x 4* which presented the work of black artists in various museums and galleries in Britain.[4] Through such contacts I started feeling more and more sure about myself as an artist and about the nature of my work. It became evident that it was about my life, about identity, about struggle and about much more. Algeria is part of Africa, it is part of the Middle East and it is also part of Europe because of France, so wherever there was a contemporary exhibition that was connected to any of these places I was invited there! Various curators would contact me and we would discuss what the exhibition was concerned with.

These exhibitions were important for so many reasons. In 1994, for example, I was invited to participate in the *Forces of Change* exhibition in the USA which was a most fantastic and enlightening experience for me.[5] Until that point, I did not know about contemporary women's Arab art at all and to see the range of work was extraordinary. It was amazing to discover through being in London what was going on in the Arab world, especially because in Algeria I only really knew what was going on in France. This sounds very bizarre but it was like that! Also, later, in 1997, I took part in *Cross/ing: Time.Space.Movement* in the United States, an exhibition of 10 contemporary African artists, and it was a quite a revelation to see how much African art encompassed. [6] (Figure 7.3)

7.3 Houria Niati, *Bringing Water from the Fountain has Nothing Romantic About It,* 1991 (see colour plate 53)

Of course, Algeria has changed a lot and I have changed a lot too. I go to Algeria quite frequently and on a recent visit I found it a poignant experience to go back to a place that has experienced so much suffering over the years. My hometown, Khemis-Miliana, is situated high up in the mountains and to get there one has to go through very deep valleys. We call one of these valleys 'the valley of death' because of what has happened there in the recent wars in Algeria. Many people were killed there. Although I was advised against it, I went into the valley and went to visit my hometown. You could see the changes so clearly. It is so different from the fighting during the Algerian War when I remember the demonstrations in the streets against the French occupiers. Now the war is between Algerians. People in the same area, in the same place, are fighting each other. Why is this happening? It raised all sorts of questions about how could I help? Should I be there or here in London? All the questions about dying …

In 1985 I had my first exhibition in Algeria. It was the most incredible experience. I was also invited to have an exhibition in my hometown. What was most fantastic about it was that they invited me to choose some of my father's paintings to be put into the exhibition. I was so moved. The first part of the exhibition was of my father's work and the second part was of mine. At the opening there were children singing and orchestral music! That was in 1985. This was followed by another exhibition so I have never had a problem exhibiting in Algeria. I have also never felt the rejection of not being able to exhibit because I was a woman artist.

In a sense though, my work was a way of dealing with some of the suffering; it was a way of exorcising all these fears and indecisions about my life. It was a way of expressing my experiences on canvas and I felt privileged that I was able to do this.

7.4 Houria Niati, *Andalusian Song,* 1992-3. watercolour and ink on paper, 80 x 55cm each, detail of installation, *Ziriab...Another Story,* 1998

7.5 Houria Niati, *Andalusian Song,* 1992-3. watercolour and ink on paper, 80 x 55cm each, detail of installation, *Ziriab...Another Story,* 1998

7.6 Houria Niati, *The Expectation May be Tomorrow,* 1988; oil and pastel, 110 x 80cm

7.7 Houria Niati, *Ziriab...Another Story,* 1998-1999 (detail, see colour plate 54)

7.8 Houria Niati, *Ziriab...Another Story,* 1998 (detail, see colour plate 55)

From about 1984 I did a lot of oil pastels. I loved colours very much and these pastels were like explosions on paper. I just did a series of them. At the time I had only pastel and paper and I had no space to work in. I was travelling and moving around a lot so I worked on paper that was one metre square or even half of that until almost 1993. I also did a lot of watercolours. (Figures 7.4 and 7.5)

You can see all the things that inspired me — from the work of the Post Impressionists, ancient Algerian rock paintings, to children's art. Gradually the works got bigger but they were still done quickly and I never corrected them. However, sometimes they did present problems. For example, Princess Wijdan Ali, who was organising an exhibition at the Barbican in London, had read some articles about my work and visited me in my studio. At the time, one of my sisters was pregnant and, wanting to do a work about the future, I did *The Expectation May be Tomorrow,* 1988, which showed a pregnant nude female (figure 7.6). Wijdan Ali had to explain that the content was not suitable for a gallery in the Middle East but, because she liked the work, she bought it along with two other works. These were included as the *Triptych* in Contemporary *Art from the Islamic World* in the Concourse Gallery at the Barbican in 1989.[7] Subsequently, they were also shown at the Jordan National Gallery.

Recently, I have concentrated on the installation and performance work in *Ziriab...Another Story,* which enables me to bring all of my concerns into the gallery space. (Figures 7.7 and 7.8)

Notes

[1] Trained by Smain Henni in Algeria, Niati performs the songs of Ziriab in ninth century classical Arabic.

[2] *Five Black Women*, Africa Centre, London (September - October 1983) was important for foregrounding the work of black women artists in Britain and included Sonia Boyce, Lubaina Himid, Claudette Johnson and Veronica Ryan. Niati was also one of the 15 artists included in *Black Women Time Now*, organised by Himid at Battersea Arts Centre, London (29 November - 4 December 1983). See Rozsika Parker and Griselda Pollock (eds). *Framing Feminism: Art and the Women's Movement 1970-1985*, London: Pandora, 1987, pp64-68 and pp258-259.

[3] For a fuller discussion of Niati's installations and performances see: Hassan, Salah M, 'The Installations of Houria Niati,' *NKA, Journal of Contemporary African Art*, Fall/Winter, 1995, pp50-55; Todd Porterfield, 'Western Views of Oriental Women in Modern Painting and Photography' in Nashashibi, Salwa Mikdadi (ed). *Forces of Change, Artists of the Arab World*, 1994, pp58-71; Lloyd, Fran (ed). *Contemporary Arab Women's Art: Dialogues of the Present*, 1999 and Lloyd, Fran, 'Contemporary Algerian Art: Embodiment and Performing the 'Self': Houria Niati and Zineb Sedira,' *Journal of Algerian Studies*, London, March 2000.

[4] *Four x 4* brought together the installations of 16 artists in groups of four in different gallery spaces. Niati exhibited with Shaheen Merali, Sher Rajah and Lesley Sanderson at the Harris Museum, Preston, 8 September - 17 October 1991.

[5] This ground-breaking exhibition, organised by Salwa Mikdadi Nashashibi, included the work of over 70 Arab women artists drawn from 21 countries. *Forces of Change: Women Artists of the Arab World*, opened in February 1993 at The National Museum of Women in the Arts, Washington and toured the United States until May 1995.

[6] Curated by Olu Oguibe, *Cross/ing: Time.Space.Movement* opened at the Contemporary Art Museum, Florida, in September 1997 and subsequently travelled to Santa Monica, California in 1998, and Indianapolis Museum of Art, Indiana in 1999.

[7] See Ali, Wijdan. *Contemporary Art from the Islamic World*. London: Scorpion Publication Ltd, Amman: The Royal Society of Fine Arts, 1989.

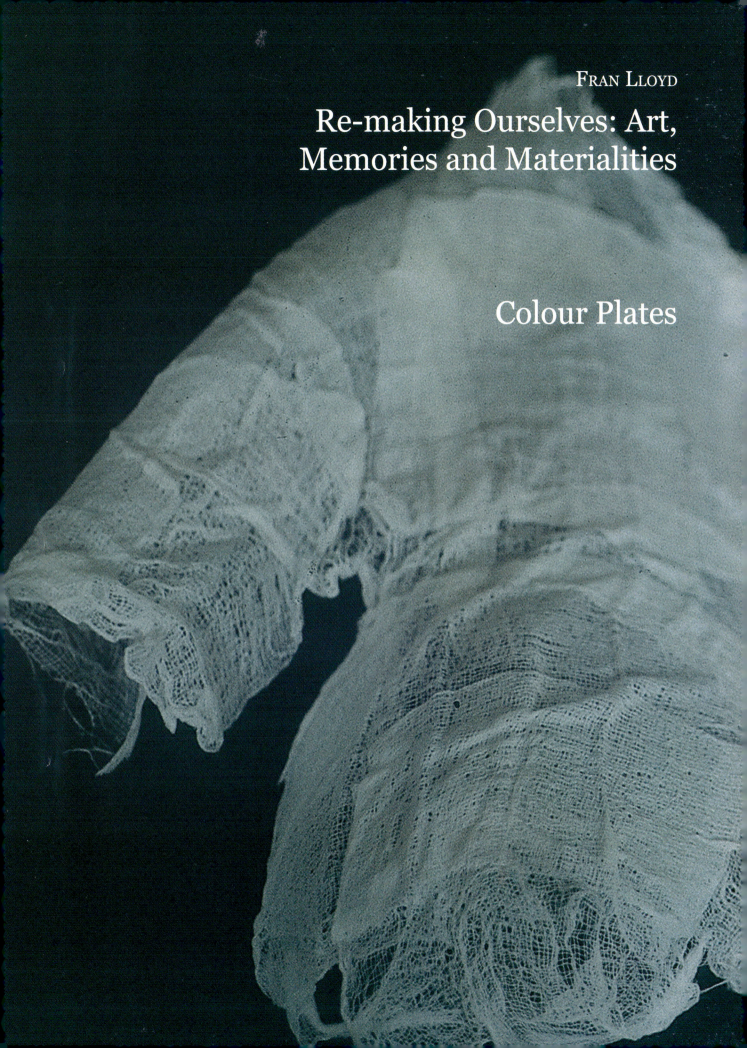

FRAN LLOYD

Re-making Ourselves: Art, Memories and Materialities

Colour Plates

Overleaf and on this page

Saadeh George, *Today I Shed My Skin:
Dismembered and Remembered,* 1998
detail of installation, life size

1 Liliane Karnouk, *Black and Green*, 1992
mixed media on canvas, 75 x 69cm

2 Liliane Karnouk, *Untitled*, 1998
acrylic on canvas, 1 of 3 panels, each 168 X 61cm

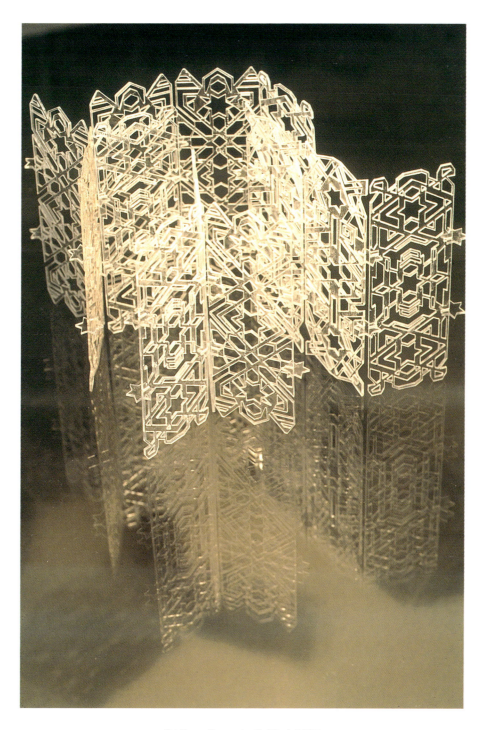

3 Liliane Karnouk, *Untitled*, 1998
glass, 180 X 360cm
model for public sculpture

4 Doris Bittar, *Watching Jacob*, 1992
oil on 3 canvas 150 x 455cm

5 Ghada Jamal, *Music Series: The Traveller*, No 34, 1998
mixed media on wood, 30 x 30cm

6 Ghada Jamal, *Music Series: The Traveller*, No 25, 1998
mixed media on wood, 30 x 30cm

7 Ghada Jamal, *Music Series: The Traveller*, No 29, 1998
mixed media on wood, 30 x 30cm

8 Kamala Ibrahim Ishaq, *Reflection at the Dinner Table*, 1998
acrylic and coloured ink on paper, 50 x 40cm

9 Kamala Ibrahim Ishaq, *Images in Crystal Balls*, 1998
oil on canvas, 175 x 175cm

"The large oil paintings are usually figurative abstractions which are inspired from old African stories that I used to hear when I was young ... The African story telling tradition has been important to my work and African mythology is an important source..." [1]

Kamala Ibrahim Ishaq, born 1939, from Sudan

10 Batool al-Fekaiki, *Closed City*, 1997
oil on canvas, 80 x 70cm

11 Batool al-Fekaiki, *Ishtar*, 1998
oil on canvas, 120cm x 100cm

"For over thirty years I have tried to produce works of art which give material form to
my personal and artistic views of the world around me...
My art is concerned with desire and loss, with distance and nearness and with
memories and hopes." [2]

Batool al-Fekaiki, born 1942, from Iraq

12 Batool al-Fekaiki, *Children of the Future,* 1999 installation of painted stone and gravel, from *Dialogue of the Present:* S*ite and Performance*, Pitshanger Manor and Gallery, London, July - August 1999

13 Batool al-Fekaiki, *Children of the Future*, 1999 (detail)

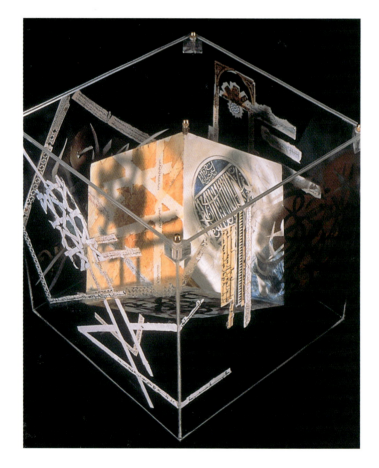

14 Leila Kawash, *Hexahedron 11*, 1997
mixed media; acrylic, collage and enamel on constructed wood and
plexiglass 43 x 43 x 43cm

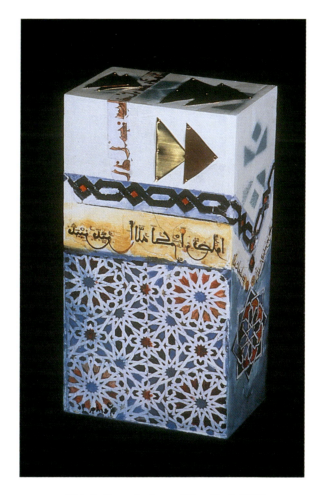

15 Leila Kawash, *Seven Pillars No 3*, 1997

acrylic, collage and enamel on constructed wood, 30 x15 x 10cm

"Using many layers of paint, fragments of collage, heavy textures and light washes, I have tried to piece together different time periods; to find a place where the past and present overlap, where countries shed their boundaries and distances. The canvas is simply the merging point of these things..." [3]

Leila Kawash, born 1945, from Iraq

16 Saadeh George, *Today I Shed My Skin: Dismembered and Remembered*, 1998
detail of installation, life size

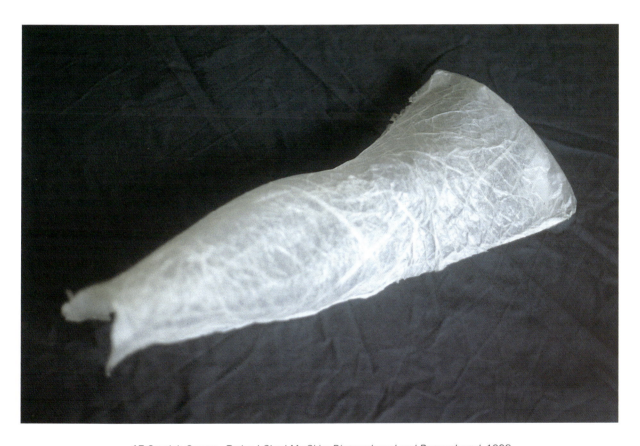

17 Saadeh George, *Today I Shed My Skin: Dismembered and Remembered*, 1998
detail of installation, life size

"My work is a homage to all those who experience the painful state of being an 'other'; those caught up in a conflict of identity/ies; those who experience loss and alienation...The origins of my work lie within my own personal journey ...coming ...practicing ...assuming..."[4]

Saadeh George, born 1950 in Iraq, brought up in Lebanon

18 Laila al-Shawa, *Children of Peace*, 1992-95
silkscreen, 100 x 230cm
part of *The Walls of Gaza* installation of 10 silkscreens

19 Laila al-Shawa, *Children of War*, 1992-95
silkscreen, 100 x 230cm
part of *The Walls of Gaza* installation of 10 silkscreens

"The land and the body are linked and both bear the scars of different forms of invasion." [5]

Laila al-Shawa, born 1940 in Gaza, Palestine

20 Thuraya al-Baqsami, *Blue Dreams,* 1998
acrylic and masking glue on canvas, 120 x 160cm each

"My identity as a woman from an Arab country, especially as a woman artist in Kuwait, and my cultural heritage are important to me ...particularly given the recent debates about the freedom of women. Opinions on what women should do or be are rife." [6]

Thuraya al-Baqsami, born 1952, from Kuwait

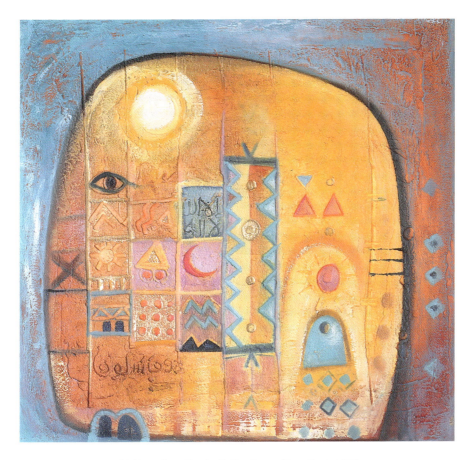

21 Maysaloun Faraj, *Civilisations...Unearthed*, 1993
mixed media on canvas, 60 x 60cm

22 Maysaloun Faraj, *Pots of Baraka*, 1994
white earthenware with onglaze and gold enamel, height 30cm

"To record or preserve a piece of my history and indeed world history …I create and recreate…" [7]

Maysaloun Faraj, born 1955 California, US, educated Iraq

23 Rima Farah, *Blue and Gold*, 1997
carborundum etching, 55 x 55cm

24 Rima Farah, *Jigsaw*, 1994
etching, 67.5 x 67.5cm

"My childhood vision of letters saw them as incomprehensible, cut into stone, punched onto leather, gilded, waxed, or inked onto paper, parchment or silk. I felt the need to recapture these elusive memories ...this process of rediscovery in progress..." [8]

Rima Farah, born 1955, in Jordan

25 Najat Maki, *Untitled 1*, 1998
mixed media and oil on paper, 128 x 95cm

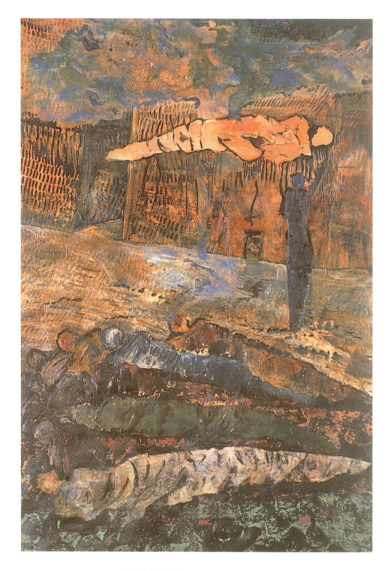

26 Najat Maki, *Untitled 2*, 1998
mixed media and oil on paper, 128 x 95cm

"These materials [saffron and henna] together with their fragrances are
intimately linked with memories of my childhood..." [9]

Najat Maki, born 1956, Dubai, UAE, trained in Egypt

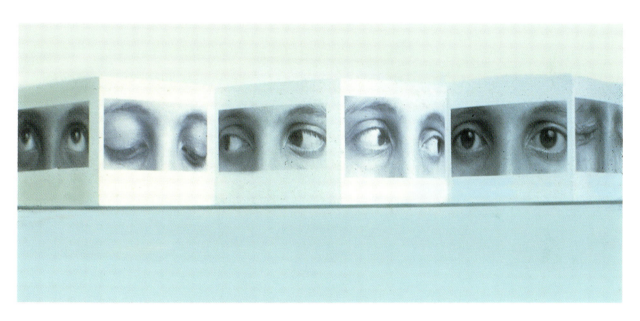

27 Zineb Sedira, *Silent Witness*, 1995
black-and-white photographs stitched together, 40 x 180cm

28 Zineb Sedira, *Don't Do To Her What You Did To Me*, No 2 (detail), 1996
installation of colour photographs, scarf made and worn by the artist
The Gallery of Modern Art, Glasgow

"It is through perception then, where memory surfaces, that my individuality is continuously affirmed and I renegotiate my presence in French contemporary society and yet again in my migration to Britain. By making this process visible new strategies towards selfhood are recorded through images, reflections, illusions and words." [10]

Zineb Sedira, born 1963, French Algerian

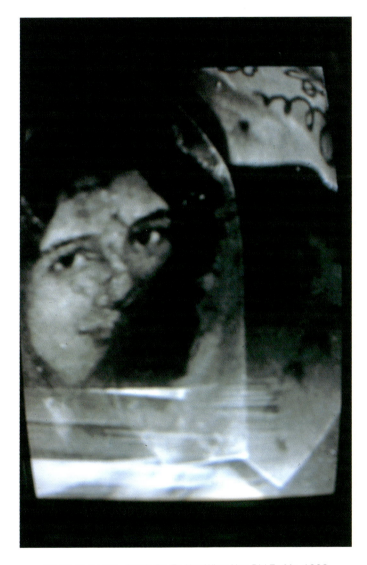

29 Zineb Sedira, *Don't Do To Her What You Did To Me*, 1998
video stills

30 Jananne Al-Ani, *After Eden*, 1995
installation (detail)

"My interest in Orientalism was the beginning of a long
process of re-examining my Arab cultural background which
I had rejected out of hand on arrival in Britain. In 1991 the
war in the Gulf brought me face to face with the issue of
my own cultural identity with a great jolt." [11]

Jananne Al-Ani, born 1966 in Iraq of Irish mother

31 Jananne Al-Ani, *Untitled (Veils Project)*, 1997
black-and-white photograph, second of a pair, each 180 x 120cm

32 Jananne Al-Ani, *Chinese Whispers*, 1998

video stills

33 Mai Ghoussoub, *Diva*, 1999
installation, variable dimensions

34 Mai Ghoussoub, *Diva*, 1999
installation, variable dimensions

35 Wafaa El Houdaybi, *Meknés 1*, 1998 mixed media; thread and paint on stretched leather, 65cm diameter

"I started working with simple, ordinary things which are part of the daily life of Morocco including wrapping paper, clothes pegs, threads of wool and wax …We are always wrapping things up, hanging things out or being warmed by the individual threads of our bed covers which are usually hidden from view …The threads are like the threads of society which unfold in time but they also veil and unveil this history."[12]

Wafaa El Houdaybi, born 1966 in Morocco

36 Sliman Mansour, *Olive Pickers*, c1988
oil on canvas, 100 x 80cm

37 Saed Hilmi, *Olive Picking*, 1993
oil on canvas, 170 x 150cm

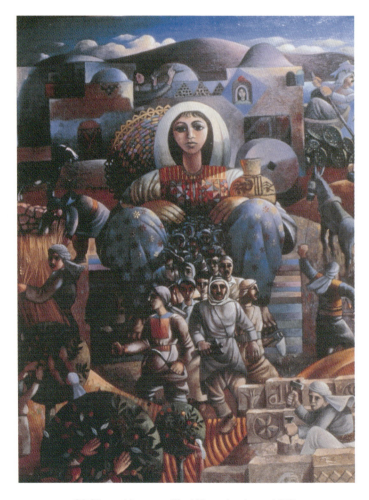

38 Sliman Mansour, *The Village Awakens*, 1990
oil on canvas, 110 x 80cm

39 Nabil Anani, *The Palestinian Village*, 1979
oil on canvas, 80 x 80cm

40 Nabil Anani, *The Palestinian Village*, 1989
gouache, 60 x 40cm

41 Taleb Dweik, *The Farmer*, 1989
mixed media, 80 x 100cm

42 Abdel Muttaleb A'Bayyan, *Harvest*, 1990
oil on canvas, 100 x 80cm

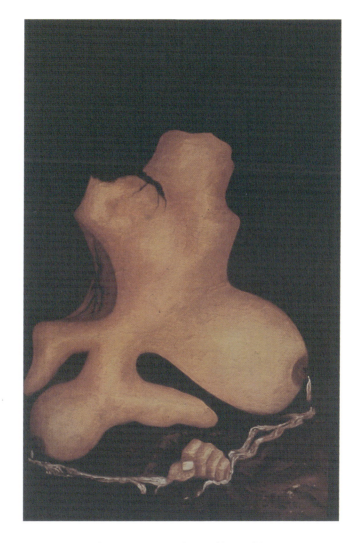

43 Ali al Ashab, *In Spite of Pain*, 1984
oil on canvas, 50 x 70cm

44 Nabil Anani, *Motherhood,* 1979
oil on canvas, 100 x 80cm

45 Hashem Klub, *From the Intifada*, 1988
oil on canvas, 100 x 70cm

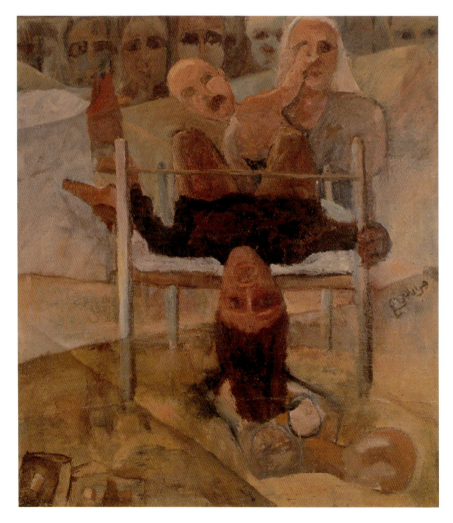

46 Jawad Al Malhi, *The Beginning of the End*, 1988
oil on canvas, 300 x 120cm

47 Hashem Klub
The Children of the Camp, 1987
oil on canvas, 100 x 70cm

48 Fayez al Hassan, *The Martyr's Wedding*, 1992
oil on canvas, 54 x 70cm

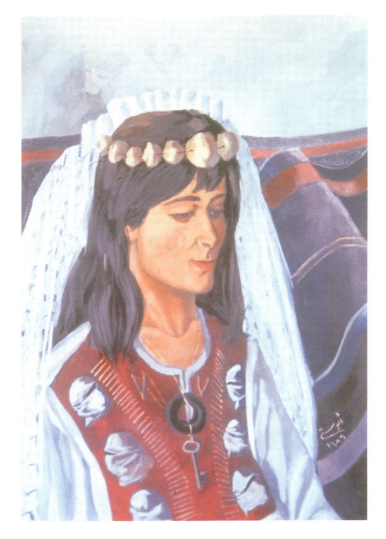

49 Mohammad Abu Sittah, *The Intifada Bride*, 1989
oil on canvas, 55 x 74cm

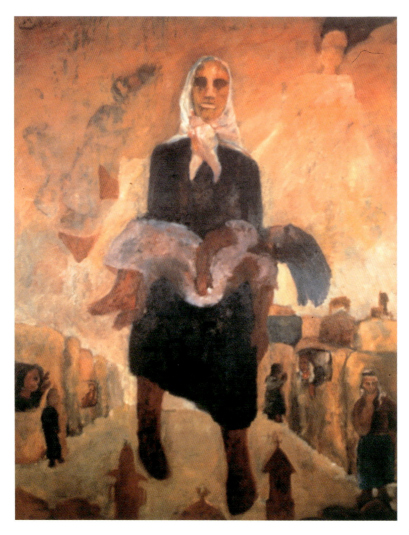

50 Jawad Al Malhi, *The Bride*, 1990
mixed media, 180 x 140cm

51 Khalil Rabah, *Womb*, 1997
mixed media, suitcase, chair and band aids, 120cm

52 Houria Niati, *No To Torture* (After Delacroix's *The Women of Algiers*), 1982
oil on canvas, 188 x 270cm, part of *No to Torture* installation, 1982-93

53 Houria Niati, *Bringing Water from the Fountain has Nothing Romantic About It*, 1991
installation: paint on paper, enlargements of colonial postcards, water pitchers and sound track
dimensions variable

54 Houria Niati, *Ziriab…Another Story* (detail), 1998-1999

installation at *Dialogue of the Present: Site and Performance*, Pitshanger Museum and Gallery, London, 13 July 1999

55 Houria Niati, *Ziriab...Another Story* (detail), 1998-1999
installation at *Dialogue of the Present: Site and Performance*, Pitshanger Museum and Gallery, London, 13 July 1999

FRAN LLOYD

Re-making Ourselves: Art, Memories and Materialities

The words and images on the preceding pages are those of five generations of Arab women artists, from eight different countries and three continents: from different generations and different geographies. They signal difference and yet they all touch upon identity: identity as cultural belonging, as place, identity as gender, identity as artist, as displaced, as absent; identity as a process of negotiation and renegotiation and, crucially, identity as something always changing. In effect, they are characterised by a continual creation and recreation of identities, whether in Arab countries or/and in the diaspora.

Central to these words and images is the importance of memory: memory as personal and cultural history, memory of objects and memory as part of a process of making meaning in the work. Perhaps this is not surprising given that it is through memory that we locate ourselves, through our histories and experiences at both a personal and collective level. In this essay I want to consider the art work as a site of the renegotiation of identity, of a coming into being, and the importance of memory and materiality in this renegotiation, both for the maker and the audience. By placing memories alongside materialities — or in the same space — I also want to examine the way memories, like identities, have bodies. Memories, I will argue, are embodied and engendered through the active subject of the artist in their work and, in quite different and unexpected ways, in the active subject of the spectator through engagement with the work.

My approach has been informed by much recent writing on embodied subjectivities and identities, drawn from a wide range of disciplines and approaches, and my own long-held concerns with how meaning is negotiated in relation to works of art and by whom.[13] Central to this concern is the interactive nature of the process of engagement between the work and the artist, and the work and the spectator or reading audience at any given moment. Meaning, or rather meanings, are therefore not waiting in the work to be discovered but are produced as part of this engagement (or intersubjectivity): they are not fixed nor are they universal objective truths. Instead, meanings are made (and remade) by the embodied subjects who make them and the embodied subjects who view them — embodied through the complex intersections of gender, class, race, sexuality and geographies — at specific historical moments in particular locations. Memory,

Facing Page
Kamala Ibrahim Ishaq,
installation detail, *Dialogue of
the Present: Site and
Performance,* Pitshanger Manor
and Gallery, 1999

and all that it entails, is a crucial part of these intersubjective and performative acts of making meaning.[14]

The basis for this essay came from re-looking at the work shown in *Dialogue of the Present* at the Brunei Gallery in the light of what I had previously written on contemporary Arab women's art, and what I knew already about the artists. In looking again, I was struck (as the quotes accompanying the colour plates show) by how important memory was to many of the artists and of how important it had become to me in a quite different way as part of the process of engaging with the works. Memory, far from dealing with the past, was a living thing, part of the dynamics of perception, of multiple points of identifications and the on-going process of making meaning. Furthermore, it became apparent that the entire project of exhibiting the works and providing a framework for them was also part of an interconnected memory project; of bringing into view what is forgotten or repressed or stereotyped, particularly within a western art context and a postcolonial Britain.

In the course of writing this essay I realise that I am touching on an area of enquiry that is simultaneously immense in scope and yet elusive. Although the terminology varies, every discipline and culture has something different to say about memory. Yet, memory itself is an immaterial thing which is always manifested through an object, through an image or through embodied subjectivity and constantly subject to change. It is very real to us when we experience it but it never stands alone. Embedded in a complex web of changing mental and physical formations, memory is part of the process of living and locating ourselves in the world. It is intricately bound up with perception, the way we view ourselves and others as embodied subjects, both consciously and unconsciously, our desires and fears and, by extension, our view of history and the present in time and space.

In the new millennium questions about memory and forgetting have become of paramount importance. Much recent writing has concentrated, for example, on the issues surrounding various forms of public and private memory, national and group memory (particularly in relationship to the traumatic effects of the Holocaust), the effects of new technologies on human memory and the fractured experiences associated with contemporary life.[15] Equally, questions about how memory operates in relationship to material objects in the public and private spaces of the museum and the home have begun to be asked and it is within this emergent body of research that I want to focus more specifically on how art works, as particular forms of material objects, may affect us as embodied subjects.[16]

As Marius Kwint notes the growing interest in memory apparent in the arts, humanities and social sciences, "owes much to post-modernist criticism of the very notion of history that has traditionally underpinned Western thought."[17]

No longer generally regarded as an impartial, objective record of the past, the making of history has been shown to be partial, selective and subjective, and previously totalising or universalising theories of history have fractured along the often intersecting lines of race, class, gender, sexuality or geography.[18] The resultant emphasis on the specificities of located experience, articulated through memory, has provided a powerful means of recovering, rediscovering and of reclaiming historical visibility on both a personal and collective level for previously marginalised or disenfranchised groups.[19] Indeed, for the German-Jewish writer, Walter Benjamin, who has influenced much recent thinking in this area, "To articulate the past historically …means to seize hold of a memory as it flashes up at a moment of danger."[20]

The recent histories of the black diaspora and/or of women show clearly how a rediscovery of the historical past through, for example, a repositioning of once denigrated oral traditions or autobiographical writing, has enabled individuals and groups to become active subjects in culture rather than objects subjected to omissions and absence.[21] As previously noted, this rewriting of and into history is also part of the project of engaging with Arab women's art, given that the histories and experience of Arab women as active subjects in the contemporary world as women and artists both in Arab countries and in the diaspora, have to a large extent been denied. However, before discussing the specificities of the ways in which these Arab women artists might embody and perform identities in their work and the role memory may play, I want to dwell for a while on memory. (Figure 8.1)

What do we mean when we talk of memory and what does it mean to remember? Usually, I think that we associate memory with the past and with a linear concept of time which divides the past from the present and the present from the future. And yet, if we ask in what time does memory occur, we find it always occurs as embodied in the present. Although linked to the past, memories arise in the present in response to, and against the experiences and events of the present or the dominant discourses which surround us. In other words, memories which are a crucial part of our cultural identities are not static things located in the past which we discover and reproduce. Memories are actively produced in the present as part of our continual negotiation of our contradictory identities in lived experience.

Memory is also generally associated with the mind, with a mental process that has, until recently, been split from the materiality of the body: a common manifestation of the Western mind/body duality. Yet again, the experience of memory is quite other to this. Memory can possess

8.1 Houria Niati, *Ziriab…Another Story* (detail), 1998-1999
Installation at *Dialogue of the Present: Site and Performance*, Pitshanger Museum and Gallery, London, 13 July 1999

a materiality of body which arises with it and which cannot be separated from it. Memory is rarely a straightforward moment of thought but includes sight, sound, feeling, touch, taste and smell in varying combinations. In fact, memory may be 'triggered' (as we commonly say) through these senses rather than through thought, which implies that memories may be both non-verbal and verbal. They may be embedded in the body as well as in mental processes.[22]

It is this 'presentness' of memory which operates both across and through time and space (through the locations of history), and the complex physical and mental interconnections which constitute it, that have made the reconsidering of memory as part of our embodied subjectivities so timely and necessary. For, in spite of all that has been written recently about the fragmented and contingent nature of postmodern subjectivity and identity, we locate ourselves and are located, however temporarily, through our particular histories, our identities and our embodied and often contradictory experiences in the world, and it is memory that links these together in different ways at different times. Crucially, as Victor Burgin notes, "An identity implies not only a location but a duration, a history. A lost identity is lost not only in space but in time."[23]

However, memory (like the identities it helps to form) is multiple, continuous and discontinuous. On a day-to-day level memory is clearly an intrinsic part of our lives. It enables us to hold together the simplest of conversations or perform actions in time and it allows us to recall and reflect on certain past events, objects, people and feelings at will. It is also part of our everyday life in the sense that previous memories (conscious or unconscious) colour the way in which we perceive and respond to feelings and objects in the present moment. Henri Bergson put this beautifully in his great tome on *Matter and Memory* when he wrote "there is no perception which is not full of memories. With the immediate and present data of our senses, we mingle a thousand details out of our past experience." [24]

In addition, there is a more volatile form of memory where past events or experiences are remembered seemingly suddenly, with an immediacy, a resonance or a materiality in the present. Unlike nostalgia, 'the memory of old times,' which is generally characterised by a continual revisiting or replaying of the past that has often lost any direct contact with this past, these 'involuntary' rememberings are direct and unpredictable.[25] They are not habitualised re-workings of 'old memories' or of times lost but rethinkings or re-seeings which enable us to reclaim a past and, sometimes, to change our experience of it in the present.

While stressing the complexity of memory, I am not seeing it as a return to a safe space of a singular wholeness or associating it with the golden glow of nostalgia, although these may all be part of what we commonly call memory. Instead, I am arguing that memory is a crucial (if particularly slippery and amorphous) part of the way we perceive the world, our knowledge of it, our subjectivities and our identities. These identities are not pre-made things that we rediscover but are always in process and continually changing. They are perpetually created and re-created. Furthermore, if cultural identities are, to cite Stuart Hall, "not the rediscovery but the production of identity. Not an identity grounded in the archaeology, but in the retelling of the past,"[26] then memories are at the heart of this production and retelling. Of necessity, these memories will be partial, multi-sited and intricately linked to forgetting, but what is important is what is retold or remembered at a given time and in a specific context.

In order to show how memories and materialities are crucial elements in the act of producing identities grounded in the present and not in the past, and how art works are a site for this active renegotiation and performative act of the making and inscribing of identities, I want to revisit some of the works imaged at the beginning of this essay. Coming from different locations within the Arab world, the artists I will focus on now live in the diaspora of London and work in a range of media including painting, photography, installation, sculpture and video. Re-looking at these works through the specificities of the artists' histories and experiences as embodied subjects in the contemporary world, I will concentrate primarily on the materialities of memory rather than using psychoanalytical models, which are the more common tool for describing memory as part of a psychic process. In effect, following the process of memory, my method starts with the art work in the present and works through this to a broader understanding of memory and being. While discussing the diverse and contradictory ways in which memory operates in these works, I also want to suggest how "the texture of memory" can impact upon the spectator who is equally a part of the negotiation and making of meaning in the present.[27]

Locating Memories

For the Iraqi-born artists Batool al-Fekaiki and Saadeh George, both now living in the Arab diaspora of Britain, the need to maintain their contact with their histories and thereby their cultural identities is strong. Their works focus on displacement and difference; al-Fekaiki through the experience of physical exile and George through the experience of exile both 'from within' and, later, through geographical displacement. Both use memory as a central part of their work.

Al-Fekaiki's work *Closed City* (figure 8.2), for example, focuses on Baghdad,

8.2 Batool al-Fekaiki, *Closed City*, 1997
(see colour plate 10)

once the capital of the Islamic east, and her place of birth and education. It is a complex and contradictory painting. At first sight, we may see it as a romanticised image of the Orient which identifies Baghdad as the oriental other and references its rich decorative tradition, the warm colours of the east and the conscious evocation of an atmosphere of desire through the bodies and the tactile surface. However, on closer examination we see that this is no romantic image of an imagined past. Contemporary Baghdad is represented as a closed city, boarded up through war and the continuing of sanctions. The crudely nailed planks and the impenetrable door prevent entry and the city is closed both to those represented within its gates and those without. Despite the unifying colours and the sliding forms, the surface is fragmented and divided. The sense of loss and exile are uppermost.

As Edward Said eloquently writes: "Exile is strangely compelling to think about but terrible to experience. It is the unhealable rift forced between a human being and a native place, between the self and its true home: its essential sadness can never be surmounted."[28] Although one might query the 'true home' philosophically, the experience of this division and rupture is real for many artists now living in other Arab countries, and al-Fekaiki images this forcibly in *Closed City*.

From al-Fekaiki's present location in the Arab diaspora, the work can be seen to present her embodied memories of the now geographically distant Baghdad she once knew. Yet, curiously, as Benjamin notes (following Freud's ideas) such memory traces, often associated with place, have "the appearance of closeness, however distant the thing is which left it behind."[29] They have a richness of proximity known through the senses, through touch, sight, smell and so on. I am proposing that this disruption of habitualised spatial and temporal patterns is given visual form in the painting in a number of ways: the soft focus effect of the outer figures which suggest filmic devices that are often used to signify memory as the past; the sudden shift to the careful detailing of the architectural motifs; and the materiality of the nailed wood which emphasise the closeness of the present. Through such visual devices that play with space and textures, the past and the present, distance and nearness, absence and presence, the hallmarks of memory are brought together in one place in the physicality of the painting. These contradictory juxtapositions suppress a narrative reading, force the rupture of linear time, and echo the embodied effect of moments of remembering.

Furthermore, the work is also connected with memory in other ways. For, if the art work is, as I am arguing, a place of inscribing the embodied subjectivities of the artist through the making of meaning in the present, the work can also be understood as an active negotiation of the past in the act of making in the present. Produced by an Iraqi woman artist, *Closed City* can be seen therefore as a simultaneous negotiation of this past and the accompanying stereotypical views which dominate it both within and outside the Arab world. For example, it is commonly held that Arab art is always abstract, that the body cannot be shown and that Arab women are not an active part of this artistic tradition. Seen against these histories, *Closed City* images and questions these interconnecting stereotypes of gender, race and sexuality while refusing to be fixed by any of them. In effect, al-Fekaiki is claiming a series of multiple identifications as an Arab woman artist which works against stereotypes, and creates a space for herself that is frequently denied both in the West and in the East. Importantly, this space (which includes memories of the past through events of the present) does not set up modernity against tradition but presents them as existing side by side.[30] It is at this further interstice of histories, in the present, that the artist locates her presence, a presence further marked by the prominence of her signature.

This insertion into history is a critical one particularly within a pervasive art system that validates works of art through systems of classification which work to separate along the lines of tradition (the past) versus modernity (the present), the universal rather than the particular, and overarching categories that suppress the vested interests of the present in the construction of this history and thus deny the complexities of multiple points of identifications and differences through gender, race, sexuality and geographies.[31]

If the performativity of the embodied artist is located in the present (against and through the arising of personal and collective memory) the performativity of the embodied spectator in the making of meaning will be necessarily different both from that of the artist and from other spectators according to the specificities of their locatedness through the multiple intersections of race, gender, class, sexuality and/or geography. However, given that we experience artworks as physical objects, I would suggest that, as embodied spectators, we are also drawn into the vicinity of memory through perception, in the operation of our senses and the way we view ourselves and others. While this approach has major repercussions for the way we make meaning (which I will discuss later) it raises questions here about how specific art works affect us.

This has been a problematical area, particularly for western-based art historical writing since the 1960s. Discussion of the material qualities of the work have tended to be associated with either the privileging of a formalistic, disembodied mastery of sight characteristic of a supposedly dominant Modernist form of writing which denied differences of embodied subjectivities or with equally disembodied, universalising theories of aesthetics.[32] In reaction to this, most writing of the 1970s and 1980s (influenced by semiotic and/or psychoanalytical concerns and Marxist-derived methods) has focused more on the politics of representation, on what is represented, by whom and who does the looking. Such approaches have equally tended to privilege sight (the gaze) over the other senses and emphasised conceptual meaning which overlook the physical impact of the works as material objects, especially in relation to the older, hierarchical forms of painting and sculpture associated with modernism.[33] Although there are complicated and important historical reasons for this suppression of the materiality of art works (particularly linked to the much needed critique of Modernism by feminist writers) the result is still a negation of the physicality of objects.[34] However, as noted earlier, an intersubjective approach, closer to a phenomenological one, admits the possibility of an embodied spectator who as 'flesh in the world' is affected by the materiality of the work through all of the senses, including that of the mind.[35]

While I am not proposing that meaning is inherent in the form of the work, I am suggesting that the materiality of specific modes of presentation affect us and are part of the visual strategies used by artists to produce meaning. These meanings are not singular, fixed or overdetermining but they are necessarily a part of the process of making, of discovery and of visual communication against and through existing cultural conventions and the located histories of the engendered spectator.[36]

Thus, with specific reference to *Closed City*, I am suggesting that the physicality of the painting and its size, together with the devices of closeness and distancing discussed earlier, evoke the body through touch as well as through sight, and in bringing touch and sight into close proximity the work addresses the embodied subjectivity of the spectator. The particular meanings of the image will differ according to the spectator's own memories and associations with loss and fragmentation, for example, but the materiality of the work is an important part of

8.3 Batool al-Fekaiki, *Children of the Future,* 1999
(see colour plates 12 and 13)

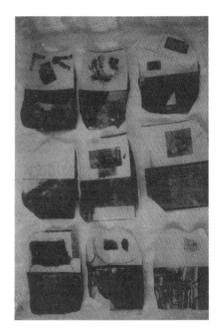

8.4 Saadeh George, *Windows,* 1997
installation

this process of the recognition of the embodied specta-tors' engagement (through identification or disavowal) in the act of looking. Furthermore, this engagement, based upon the complex intersections of gender, class, race and sexuality, is part of what Amelia Jones and Andrew Stephenson have recently referred to as "the performing of the text" where "viewers/interpreters are caught up within the complex and fraught operations of representation—entangled in intersubjective spaces of desire, projection and identification." [37]

Significantly, in her more recent work, al-Fekaiki uses three-dimensional forms, which the audience has to physically negotiate within the gallery space in order to heighten the sense of materiality of place and the located bodies of memory. *The Children of the Future* (figure 8.3), exhibited in 1999 at the Pitshanger Gallery in London, was made in response to the site and is situated underneath Sir John Soane's dome.[38] Enclosed within a circle of gravel, the intricately painted stone heads invite the spectator to move closer to engage in the work. From this perspective their richly decorated and alluring surfaces are transformed as the facial details are variously erased, distorted and mutilated. The work refers to both the past and present effects of the Gulf War and, through the title, their effects on the future generation. In the context of Britain's portrayal of the war, they provide a different perspective on the physical reality of this destruction in the present and its continuing effects in history. For the artist it addresses the silences or amnesia associated with these specific histories where the heads may be seen to double-up as memorials or silent witnesses/victims of loss or destruction; but the forms are open to other meanings that the spectator may link with other places and people.

Saadeh George's installations similarly deal with the negotiation of displacement, war and exile through the connecting threads of memory. Born in Iraq to a Palestinian Christian father and a Lebanese Druze mother, George was brought up and trained as a doctor in Beirut, in Lebanon, the artistic centre of the Middle East in the 1970s renowned for its cultural and religious diversity. The war in Beirut changed this in 1975. Beirut became internally divided by borders and restricted areas: a difficult terrain for those who crossed the boundaries of cultural identities. These experiences, of coming from a mixed marriage and of working as a doctor in a divided, war-torn Lebanon, are an important part of the work which George produced after coming to Britain in 1984 and subsequently studying fine art.

Initially, George's work focused on the involuntary memories or momen-tary flashes of imagery frequently associated with geographical displacement. *Windows* (1997, figure 8.4), for example, is a hanging installation made up of a series of translucent resin plates. Each contains a photograph and a photo etching on thin paper: tangible records of her life in Beirut. Like fragments encased in resin and frozen in time, these fragile objects act simultaneously as frames of the mind and x-ray plates. They poignantly recall the windows and balconies of a once vibrant Lebanon, an image brought about by the experience of being in another place, in London, watching the windows of a tube carriage flash by. Such an experience is common to many of us but, as Said observes, this may be more acute for those who are exiled:

> Most people are principally aware of one culture, one setting, one home; exiles are aware of at least two, and this plurality of vision gives rise to an awareness of simultaneous dimensions ... where expression or activity in the new environment inevitably occurs against the memory of these things in another environment. Thus both the new and the old environments are vivid, actual, occurring together contrapuntally.[39]

For Benjamin, also writing in exile, such moments are decidedly image-based and are characterised by a sudden realisation of one's positioning vis-à-vis the past and the present where "an image is that in which the has-been comes together in a flash with the Now to form a constellation...the image in the Now of cognizability, bears to the highest degree the stamp of the critical, dangerous moment which is the basis of all reading." [40]

Echoing the vividness and actuality of Said and Benjamin's cognizability of the past in the present, I am proposing that works such as George's *Windows* and *Echoes* (figures 8.4 and 8.5) which use the evocative image of fading photographs and emphasise tactile experience, are more than a recollection of images of the past. They represent an integration of both the physical and mental experiences which constitute memories in the present and, as such, they are part of the crucial need, whether conscious or unconscious, to articulate an embodied identity in the present. While such acts of performativity are part of our everyday modes of identification, they become particularly important in moments of danger where our identities are disrupted, marginalized, forgotten or suppressed, in this case through exile and displacement.

Noticeably, in recent installations George has moved away from using remembered objects to evoke her embodied subjectivity and explores instead the complexities of time, place and memory through the use of her own body. *Today I Shed My Skin: Dismembered and Remembered,* 1998 (colour plates 16 and 17) consists of life-size casts, suspended and distributed in different parts of the gallery space. Rather than presenting the images of memory, George focuses here on the embodiment of memory: the detailed casts of her gendered body literally embody the traces of place, of history as time and experience in their surfaces. Equally, the processes and materials involved draw attention to the specificities of her medical knowledge and the experience of attempting to repair the body and its tissues through the wrapping of wounds, the setting of limbs and surgery stitching.

8.5 Saadeh George, *Echoes*, 1997 (detail)

Viewing these works through the artist's history, I would agree with Homi Bhabha that the act of "Remembering is never a quiet act of introspection. It is a painful re-membering, a putting together of the dismembered past to make sense of the trauma of the present."[41] The work can be seen as a coming to terms with the past in the present, as the title suggests, through remembering. However, the multiple and contradictory experiences and effects of this past are evidenced in the work where, as George notes, "The materials I use are translucent media: tissue paper, muslin and gauze. They reflect the fragility of life but also the arbitrary landmarks attached to identity...because of religion, race and colour."[42] George refuses this fixity by shedding the skin, the "epidermal schema" of Frantz Fanon which operates as one of the prime signifiers of difference and discrimination.[43] Thus, while the performing of the body is a coming into being that overcomes the silences of the recent past, these memories are only recorded through the traces left on the gauze during a particular period of time. The body which made these impressions (and was made through them and by them) is absent; it has already changed in the act of making the work. What is left behind is an imprinted gendered skin, no longer fixed by race, religion, geography or ethnicity.

Although George's images are of loss and trauma, an important point here is the act of agency, of recreating and performing these multiple and ambivalent identities within the conditions of the present. Or, to put it another way, of operating on the past in the present, not by reproducing past memories, but by remaking the past in the present.[44] Interestingly, Adrienne Rich, the American feminist writer, calls this remaking a "re-vision — the act of looking back, of seeing with fresh eyes" which she argues is more than just a question of cultural identity for women but a necessary act of survival in a culture of omission and silence.[45]

Curiously, drawing upon Freud and Benjamin, Kaja Silverman touches upon a similar view of memory in *The Threshold of the Visible World* in her discussion of film when she writes:

> And implicit in this transformation or rewriting of our recollections is the possibility of also constantly reconfiguring the screen. To remember perfectly would be forever to inhabit the same cultural order. However, to remember imperfectly is to bring images from the past into an ever new and dynamic relation to those through which we experience the present, and in the process ceaselessly to shift the contours and significance not only of the past, but also of the present.[46]

Like Silverman, I am arguing that we constantly reconfigure the screen and that memories, which are part of our cultural identities, are not static things, located in the past to be discovered and reproduced. They are actively produced in the present and are a crucial part of the process of continuous constructing and reconstructing of our identities. The function of memory therefore, can also be seen to transform, not simply to reproduce. In the context of Hall's definition of diasporic identities as "those which are constantly producing and reproducing themselves anew, through transformations and difference," memory clearly plays an important role.[47]

As Rosemary Betterton has shown, a central issue within contemporary art practice has been the mapping of a new space for female postcolonial subjectivity where "themes of exile, separation and return have provided a powerful means of exploring the self as an ongoing construction in time and space through the operation of memory ... and in the articulation of loss and desire."[48] For many women artists this has involved the assertion of the specificities of "this body, the particularity of this history against prevailing gender and racial stereotypes."[49] If stereotypes seek to fix and to contain in singular prescribed identities, the work I have been discussing seeks to unfix and to re-present a deliberately multi-sited image of what Arab women artists are and to articulate their situated experience.[50]

This is particularly evident in the work of Zineb Sedira where these specificities are directly imaged through a performing of the self in her photographically based installations and video pieces. Born in 1963 Sedira was brought up in the Parisian suburb of Gennevilliers in the diaspora of France in the aftermath of the Algerian war where "intense political and racial animosity towards the Algerian community" was evident.[51] Coming from an Algerian Arab speaking family and educated in French Catholic schools, Sedira was acutely aware of being a 'beurette' (the less than complimentary colloquial expression for females born of North African immigrant parents) which signified "difference, a particular history and context, and a sign of cultural ambiguity."[52] (Figure 8.6)

Sedira moved to London in 1986 and, in common with many of the artists mentioned here, the move to another place provided the conditions for reflection and another space in which to explore and negotiate the issues surrounding locatedness and personal memory. She subsequently trained in fine art at Central St Martin's School of Art (1992-95) and at the Slade School of Art (1995-1997) in London. Since the mid 1990s Sedira's work has centred on the issues surrounding the veil, which has come to be one of the most visible and much debated external signs of racial and gendered difference, of exclusion/inclusion, and a complex symbol that carries a multiplicity of frequently shifting and often contradictory meanings, particularly in the context of Algerian history.[53] For Sedira, however, the effects of veiling extend beyond the physical veil (which she rarely images directly) but to what she calls "the concept of veiling the mind" which "is a metaphor for censorship and self-censorship and permeates through all my work... I never had to wear the physical veil, but I definitely wore the mental veil."[54]

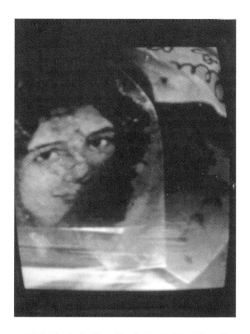

8.6 Zineb Sedira, *Don't Do To Her What You Did To Me*, 1998
video stills

The veiling of the mind for Sedira is a complex affair. It involves both an exploration of her social and historical positioning through personal memory and the negotiation of its often contradictory effects in the present. Through a series of performative acts where she uses her own body as the basis for the work, Sedira draws upon her experiences of being brought up in two different cultures to question and disrupt the received history of Arab women and the accompanying stereotypes. She also explores the difficult area of how such histories subtly condition behaviour at a psychological level.

In the large black and white photographic work, such as *Silent Witness* of 1995 (colour plate 27) it is the eyes of the artist, confined or framed by the slit-like opening which evokes an invisible veil, that dramatically confront the spectator. The public scale of the work and its directness is challenging. It suggests the different ways in which Arab women are usually framed by western audiences as anonymous, veiled woman, as submissive objects or as objects of fantasy (particularly through photographs). The concentration on the eyes (in this case ever moving) foregrounds the specificities of the female Arab gaze as opposed to the male gaze which has, until recently, dominated cultural discourse, particularly in writing on colonialism and the Orient. However, the title and the disembodied eyes also carry the weight of internalised policing where one is witness rather than active subject. In the context of the gallery (a space designed for the looking at objects) *Silent Witness* refers directly to the performative act of looking and being seen, and the accompanying contradictory play of subject and object.

8.7 Zineb Sedira, *My Sister's Scarf*, 1996 (detail)

Similarly, in *Don't Do To Her What You Did To Me, No 2*, 1996 (colour plate 28) Sedira is both subject and object, while the powerful adversarial title addresses the spectator more directly through the use of the first and second person. The over life-size installation, made up of a series of colour photographs set against a gold background, present the artist veiling and unveiling herself with a *hijab* or scarf. The averted gaze of the artist suggests an image of subjugation, but on further looking it becomes evident that the scarf (which was made by Sedira) is a "patchwork of

8.8 Zineb Sedira, *Silent Sight (Self-portrait)*, 1999, three computer generated photographic images, back-lit, 100 x 45 cm overall

photographs of the artist's sister unveiled with her hair down."[55] (Figure 8.7)

While the installation effectively works as a disruption of stereotypical views of Muslim women and problematises the continual negotiation of the boundaries between being veiled/unveiled or subject/object which has preoccupied the West, it is simultaneously a physical enactment of the awareness that the subject has 'veiled' herself, through the painful process of being othered.[56]

Sedira returns to this question of the veil in her recent self-portrait, entitled *Silent Sight,* 1999 (figure 8.8) where, unusually, she presents three colour photographs of herself wearing a full-length white veil. Set against a white background and backlit, the images appear shroud-like, almost as dematerialised forms where all colour has been drained from them except for the eyes, which defiantly stare out. The work is deeply embedded in personal and collective memory. The Muslim veil and 'voilette' (the small white covering for the bottom of the face) belonged to the artist's mother who, now living in Algeria, is no longer required to wear it because of age, while the use of the triptych form (usually associated with Christianity) and the veiling (which is simultaneously reminiscent of the Virgin Mary and a nun's habit) recalls the in-between buerette culture of Sedira's youth where the icons and rituals of French Catholicism co-existed with those of Islam and an Algerian history. In this context, the images can be seen to focus, through a re-looking at the specificities of the past, on the complex relationships between age, power and visibility, and the differing way in which women's bodies are always subject to cultural coding and regulated across different geographies whether in the name of religion, nation, revolution or tradition.[57] Here the presentational mode of the light boxes, in which the images are set and framed, intimate this closure and become a powerful metaphor of the female figure being simultaneously both absent and present, veiled and unveiled through the process of making the work and viewing it.

Finally, I want to re-look at Sedira's video work, *Don't Do To Her What You Did To Me,* 1998 (colour plate 29), which is particularly important in terms of memory and its negotiation in the process of making. It brings together a series of events

8.9 and **8.10** Zineb Sedira, *Don't Do To Her What You Did To Me*, 1998
video stills (see colour plate 29)

and experiences associated with Sedira's youth in Paris. These memories are powerfully evoked by the black and white format where the materialities of the photographic images slip in and out of view. Using the initial framing or veiling device of a glass being filled with water, the viewer is presented with the imagery and sound of running water and the film of a hand writing. Black ink drops into still, clear water: unfurling, veil-like and staining (Figures 8.9 and 8.10). This is followed by photographs of a young Arab woman and glimpses of hand-written text which fall through the water and are slowly mixed together and then spun until they dissolve into a pulp. Evoking the senses and the materialities of photographs as a "class of objects formed specifically to remember,"[58] the images are powerful reminders of loss, absence and death. Sedira explains the particularities of the work in the following way:

> The talisman subverted in the video is one I remember I was forced to drink, in order to become a good girl, a good Muslim. A *taleb*, a priest would write verses of the Quran on a piece of paper that would subsequently be carried or swallowed by whomever needed the help of God. The piece is a homage to a girl who died through the conflicts of her mixed identity, when I was sixteen. I used the girl's last words in the talisman to exorcise the sacrifice of the deceased woman, to release her from the racism and pressure of French culture.[59]

Here it becomes clear that the making of the work is itself an act of performativity. Through the act of remembering and giving form to these painful events of the past, the work becomes an act of embodiment in the present which restores the presence of the dead woman and enables a re-looking at a suppressed past. In confronting the complex and horrific consequences of the specific intersections of race, gender, sexuality and religion, the artist is actively renegotiating identity through and against these memories, feelings and events. Thus the work is a dual site of enquiry. It is both the site of what Hall concisely calls "the production of identity" through a negotiation of the past in the present through memory and locatedness, and at the same time it is an act of discovery and articulation in which a new awareness of identities and their consequences is formed. (Figure 8.11)

Such articulations and inscriptions are important to us all. They are particularly important in circumstances where one is constructed as the other through

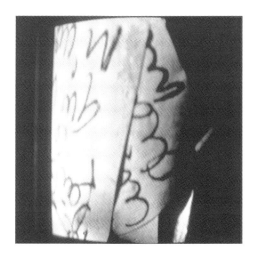

8.11 Zineb Sedira, *Don't Do To Her What You Did To Me*, 1998 (detail)

video stills

class, gender and/or race, or where, as Fanon describes it, one is made to "experience ourselves as 'Other'."[60] For Arab women artists the foregrounding and contestation of perceived identities gives presence and self-image to what has frequently been the triply 'othered' body in the western art world—the body of the female, the female artist and the non-normative Arab body. As such, these works become an intervention not only in the cultural politics of representation but also in the systems of categorisation which ignore the presence of Arab women artists as active subjects in the contemporary art world.

Certainly for all of these artists working within the diaspora, where they have come from and moved to has played an important part in their making of their identities and their inscriptions in the present. Aware of multiple positionings and of cultural codings, their work is particularly concerned with the way different histories have been written and can be rewritten. Sedira expresses this eloquently in relationship to the history of the self: "A lived life it seems is not a collection of unchangeable facts that might be objectively recorded, looked at from different perspectives, it is varied and inexpressibly volatile."[61] It is this volatility, this unexpectedness of returning, renegotiating and remaking the past through memory which is one of the strategies that the artists employ in their work to destabilise and disrupt preconceptions about what they should be as women, artists or Arabs while simultaneously asserting a sense of locatedness, however contradictory or multiple this may be.

Equally, these acts of performativity imply that the making of art is not necessarily a representation of the already known which is put in to the work or transcribed onto the surface but that it can be an act of discovery through the process of making in the present, through the handling of materials, through re-membering, re-thinking or re-looking. Catherine de Zegher aptly refers to this as a "coming-into-language from a space of uncertainty" where the emphasis is on process and becoming rather than a mastery of predetermined meanings.[62] Thus, while recognising the complexities and the weight of social and historical positioning, such an approach offers the possibility of creating anew, of remaking identities and imaging change which can produce new conditions for the future.

In this context, therefore, by concentrating on the diverse ways that these artists have employed memory as part of an active process of making new meanings, as acts of performativity, I am suggesting that it is the very process of remembering as a specifically located and embodied, sensate being, that enables this remaking of meaning in the present to take place. The implications of this are far-reaching, according to what is remembered. Not least, it provides a much needed balance between the effects of being conditioned and the effects of individual agency in a changing present. In terms of the making and viewing of visual objects, memory implies, as Kaja Silverman perceptively notes, "the possibility of effecting change at the level of representation."[63] For these artists, as I have shown, this has meant the disruption of fixed stereotypical and normative representations of Arab women and the imaging of more complex and dynamic, multiple points of identifications and difference which are part of their embodied subjectivities.

Furthermore, as I have suggested, memories and their materialities are equally as critical to us as embodied spectators in the process of looking, engaging and interpreting. Looking is mediated in complex ways by our embodied subjectivities, our perceptions, experiences, and the cultural representations which surround us.

8.12 Dialogue of the Present: Site and Performance, Pitshanger Manor and Gallery, 1999

Memory and remembering (as noted at the beginning of the essay) play multiple roles in the way we transform the past through the present and, by the same logic, what we view in the present has immediate effects for future moments of perception. Again Silverman is helpful in theorising this process when she argues that: "To look is to embed an image within a constantly shifting matrix of unconscious memories. When a new perception is brought into the vicinity of these memories which matter most to us at an unconscious level, it too is 'lit up' or irradiated, regardless of its status within normative representation."[64] Thus, although images usually confirm dominant values, she identifies memory (part also of perception) as one of the keys to 'productive looking' where images, (embedded in the unconscious) may at some future point be remembered and make us reassess the way we look at ourselves and others.

Equally, as I have stressed, when we engage with a work of art our subjectivities are part of the process through which and against which we continually make meaning anew and, as recent writing has stressed, we need to be aware of the "cultural identities being assumed as well as projected in the process of interpretation."[65] Memory as located histories in all of its various forms, is central to this self-reflective awareness.

Finally, I want to briefly consider the materiality of the work discussed here in terms of place or the 'politics of location.' Often the disembodied eye of aesthetics is separated from the action of politics, but in looking at the work in *Dialogue of the Present* (figure 8.12) I see the exhibition as a collective action to contest and transform dominant cultural meanings and to reclaim personal and collective agency within the spaces of a contemporary art system that is resistant to change. Working against commonly held assumptions about non-western art (and therefore about western art), I have stressed the work as the site of an active process of negotiating memory and of agency in the present through embodied subjectivities which are not reducible to a singular sameness or to a singular difference. Equally, memory is not a 'narrative of retrieval' based on a consensual past now lost, nor a reinstatement of the traditional or ethnic against the modern: it is part of the present where identities and locatedness are continually made.

Through acknowledging the working of memory in the act of making meanings for the artist and the spectator, the works of art neither create a singular female Arab identity nor do they remove us from the 'vulgar flux of life' of the present in order to transport us to another place or time as certain forms of modernist writing would suggest. We are not left with timeless values, removed from the present. By engaging with the materialities of the works we engage with the present. Our subjectivities are not fixed at the point from where we came or where we are now; they are continually being constructed again and again, in this case through an engagement with works which use memory to focus on the experience of exile, displacement, war, the effects of distinctions made along the interconnected lines of gender, race, sexuality and class, and the act of making as an act of embodied discovery.

In conclusion, what this essay has shown through the enmeshed threads of memory, the specificities of the works and the performative acts of making meaning, is that memories are always embodied in the present and that it is only by being fully aware of our histories and our locations by being fully embodied, that we have the chance to change the linear conditioning of our past and future and the accompanying distinctions between self and others. Remembering is the difference between absence and presence and the much needed point of recognition of difference in sameness and sameness in difference. Remembering is also inextricably linked to forgetting and the numerous acts of amnesia which we perform at a personal, group or collective level.

Notes

[1] All quotes are from the artists' statements produced for the exhibition, *Dialogue of the Present*, and published in Lloyd, Fran (ed). *Contemporary Arab Women's Art*, 1999, p187.

[2] *Ibid*, p170.

[3] *Ibid*, p192.

[4] *Ibid*, p173.

[5] *Ibid*, p219.

[6] *Ibid*, p159.

[7] *Ibid*, p167.

[8] *Ibid*, p162.

[9] *Ibid*, p199.

[10] *Ibid*, p213.

[11] *Ibid*, p154.

[12] *Ibid*, p183.

[13] Recent poststructuralist theories of identity and embodied subjectivities emphasise the interactive processes of identities which are constructed, negotiated and embodied through and against the specificities of gender, race, sexuality and geographies. See Stuart Hall, 'Cultural Identity and Diaspora,' 1990. First published in *Identity, Community, Culture, Difference* edited by Jonathan Rutherford, 1990, pp222-37. Reproduced in Williams, Patrick and Chrisman, Laura (eds). *Colonial Discourse and Post-Colonial Theory, A Reader*, 1993 pp393-403; Jones, Amelia, *Body Art/Performing the Subject*, 1998; Betterton, Rosemary, *An Intimate Distance: Women, Artists and the Body*, 1996; Butler, Judith *Bodies that Matter: On the Discursive Limits of 'Sex,'* London & New York: Routledge, 1993; Zegher, Catherine M de (ed). *Inside The Visible, An Elliptical Traverse of 20th Century Art*, 1996. On questions of perception and subject/object see Maurice Merleau-Ponty *The Phenomenology of Perception*, trans Colin Smith, London and Henley: Routledge, Kegan and Paul, 1962; and Vasseleu, Cathryn *Textures of Light: Vision & Touch in Irigaray, Levinas and Merleau-Ponty*, 1998.

[14] For a rethinking of performativity in relation to recent art and the performative nature of interpretation see Jones, A and Stephenson, A (eds), *Performing the Body: Performing the Text*, 1999 which was published just as this essay was being completed.

[15] See, for example, Jay Winter, *Sites of Mourning, Sites of Memory: The Great War in European Cultural History*, Cambridge, 1995; Simon Schama, *Landscape and Memory*, London, 1991; Andreas Huyssen, *Twilight Memories: Marking time in a Culture of Amnesia*, London, 1995; James E Young, *The Texture of Memory: Holocaust Memorials and Meaning*, New Haven and London, 1993; D Middleton and D Edwards (eds), *Collective Remembering*, London, 1990. For a perceptive study of Walter Benjamin's memory work see Sigrid Weigel, *Body-and Image-space: Re-reading Walter Benjamin*, London and New York: Routledge, 1996.

[16] See, for example, on collecting, Susan Stewart, *On Longing: Narratives of the Miniature, the Gigantic, the Souvenir, the Collection*, Baltimore: John Hopkins University Press, 1984; on design objects and photographs, Marius Kwint, Christopher Breward and Jeremy Aynsley (eds), *Material Memories: Design and Evocation*, 1999; Chapman, Helen C. *Memory in Perspective: Women Photographers' Encounters with History*, 1997; and, for a psychoanalytical approach, Victor Burgin, *In/Different Spaces: Place and Memory*

in Visual Culture, 1996. My thanks to Brenda Martin for bringing the Kwint book to my attention.

[17] Marius Kwint 'Introduction: The Physical Past' in Kwint, Breward and Aynsley (eds), 1999, p1.

[18] Key works include Roland Barthes, *Mythologies* (1957) trans from French, London, Paladin, 1973; Jean Baudrillard, *The Illusion of the End*, trans by Charles Turner, Cambridge: Polity Press, 1994; Michel Foucault, *The Order of Thing: An Archaeology of the Human Sciences* (1966), trans from French, New York: Vintage, 1973. See also Robert Young, *White Mythologies: Writing History and the West*, 1990 and Keith Jenkins, *Re-thinking History*, London, 1991.

[19] See, for example, Toni Morrison *Beloved*, New York: Plume, 1987; Cheryl A Wall (ed), *Changing Our Own Words: Essays on Criticism, Theory and Writing by Black Women*, New Brunswick and London: Rutgers University Press, 1989; Russell Ferguson (ed) *et al*, *Out There: Marginalization and Contemporary Cultures*, 1990. For further discussion on issues of writing the self see Wolff, Janet, *Resident Alien, Feminist Cultural Criticism*, 1995; hooks, bell, 'Critical Genealogies Writing Black Art' in *Art on My Mind: Visual Politics*, 1995.

[20] Walter Benjamin, *Illuminations*, edited by Hannah Arendt, translated by Harry Zohn, Collins/Fontana Books: London, 1973, p257.

[21] For specific studies on Arab culture see Abu-Lughod, Lila, *Writing Women's Worlds: Bedouin Stories*, (1993); Badran, Margot and Cooke, Miriam (eds), *Opening the Gates: A Century of Arab Feminist Writing*, 1990; Baker, Alison, Voices *of Resistance: Oral Histories of Moroccan Women*, 1998; Nashat, Guity and Tucker, Judith E. *Restoring Women to History: Women in the Middle East and North Africa*, 1999. Ostle, Robin, de Moor, Edo and Wild, Stefan (eds). *Writing the Self: Autobiographical Writing in Modern Arabic Literature*. London: Al Saqi Books, 1998.

[22] There is no better example of this than the writing of Marcel Proust (1871-1922), whose ideas of 'involuntary' memory had a major impact on Benjamin. See Proust *A la Recherche du Temps Perdu In Search of Lost Time*, trans C K Scott Moncrieff and Terence Kilmartin, revised D J Enright, 6 vols, London, 1966. For Benjamin's writing on Proust see *Charles Baudelaire: A Lyric Poet in the Era of High Capitalism*, translated by Harry Zohn, London: NLB, 1973. On memory and embodiment see Vasseleu, Cathryn *Textures of Light*, 1998.

[23] Burgin, Victor, *In/Different Spaces: Place and Memory in Visual Culture*, 1996 p36.

[24] Bergson, Henri, *Matter and Memory*, (1908) New York 1988. p33. Cited by Susan Stewart 'Prologue: From the Museum of Touch' in Kwint *et al*, 1999, p17. This echoes the phenomenological approach of the neuropsychologist Magda B Arnold, *Memory and the Brain*, New Jersey and London: Lawrence Erlbaum Associates, 1984. By contrast, memory as mindfulness has long been central to understanding the mind-body processes in Buddhist philosophy.

[25] Interestingly, Benjamin views nostalgia as a form of 'voluntary memory': "a registry, which classifies the object with a number, behind which the object disappears. 'We must have been here.' (That was an experience)." Cited by Esther Leslie in a perceptive discussion of the souvenir as pre-packaged intentional experience, 'Souvenirs & Forgetting: Walter Benjamin's Memory-work' in Kwint *et al*, 1999, p107.

[26] Stuart Hall, 'Cultural Identity and Diaspora' in Williams, P and Chrisman, L (eds). 1993, p393.

[27] Young, James E, 1993.

[28] Edward Said, 'Reflections on Exile,' *Granta*, Vol 13, 1984, pp159-172. Reprinted in Ferguson *et al*, *Out There*, 1990, pp357-366, p357.

[29] Cited in Weigel, Sigrid, 1996, p120. Helen Chapman argues that it is through place that memories emerge for Benjamin, *Memory in Perspective*, 1997, pp29-31.

[30] For further discussion of modernity, tradition and diaspora identities see Paul Gilroy, *The Black Atlantic: Modernity and Double Consciousness*, 1993.

[31] In his incisive critique of the founding principles of museology and art history, Donald Preziosi refers to these as "instrumental ways of distributing the space of memory...Where...the illusion that the past exists in and of itself, somehow immune from the projections and desires of the present is sustained." 'Performing Modernity: The Art of Art History' in Jones, A and Stephenson, A, 1999, pp34. See also Coombes, Annie E. 'Inventing the 'Postcolonial: Hybridity and Constituency in Contemporary Curating' in *The Art of Art History: A Critical Anthology*, edited by Donald Preziosi, 1998, pp486-497.

[32] In particular, the formalist writings of the British critic Roger Fry, and the later American critic, Clement Greenberg, which privileged art as a pure, aesthetic experience (gender free and universal). See the following for an interesting discussion of the history of the senses in western philosophy: Susan Stewart 'Prologue: From the Museum of touch' in Kwint *et al*, 1999, pp17-36.

[33] Within British art history, John Berger's *Ways of Seeing*, London: Penguin, 1972 and Laura Mulvey's 1975 essay on 'Visual Pleasure and Narrative Cinema,' *Screen*, were influential texts which provided alternative models.

[34] For a detailed analysis of these conditions and their effects on subsequent postmodernist writing see Amelia Jones (ed), *Sexual Politics: Judy Chicago's Dinner Party in Feminist Art History*, California: UCLA, 1996 and the opening chapters of Amelia Jones, *Body Art/Performing the Subject*, Minneapolis and London: University of Minnesota Press, 1998.

[35] Merleau-Ponty's later unfinished writing, including the essay, 'The Interwining—The Chiasm,' published posthumously as part of *The Visible and the Invisible*, trans Alphonso Lingis, Evanston, Illinois: Northwestern University Press, 1968, are particularly important here. For Merleau-Ponty, perception is a creative act rather than a passive receiving of impressions and it is inseparable from its corporeality as 'flesh in the world.' For a critical discussion of Merleau-Ponty's ideas of corporeal subjectivity and their significance for recent writers see Vasseleu, Cathryn *Textures of Light: Vision and Touch in Irigaray, Levinas and Merleau-Ponty*, 1998.

[36] Hilary Robinson proposes that the presence of the embodied artist can be seen at the level of mark making where traces of the gendered body reside, through the use of materials, the subject matter and, finally, the effect of these on the body of the viewer. See 'Border crossings: womanliness, body, representation' in Pollock, Griselda (ed), *Generations and Geographies*, 1996, pp138-146.

[37] Jones, A and Stephenson, A, 1999, p1.

[38] *Site and Performance*, part of the touring exhibition, *Dialogue of the Present*, included the paintings of Kamala Ibrahim Ishaq and Laila al-Shawa, and installation work by Batool al-Fekaiki, Saadeh George, Mai Ghoussoub, Houria Niati and Zineb Sedira. Pitshanger Gallery and Museum, 14 July - 14 August 1999.

[39] Said, Edward, 'Reflections on Exile' in Ferguson *et al*, *Out There*, 1990, p366.

[40] Cited in Weigel, Sigrid, *Body-and Image-space: Re-reading Walter Benjamin*, 1996, p155.

[41] Bhabha, Homi K, *The Location of Culture*, 1994, p63.

[42] Artist's statement in Lloyd, Fran (ed), 1999, p173.

[43] Frantz Fanon, *Black Skins, White Masks*, London: Pluto Press, 1986, p112. (first published in French, 1952).

[44] This performative view of remembering parallels Benjamin's famous statement that "To articulate the past historically does not mean to recognize it 'the way it was' (Ranke)." Walter Benjamin, Illuminations, edited by Hannah Arendt, 1973, p257.

[45] Adrienne Rich, 'When We Dead Awaken: Writing as Re-vision' in *On Lies, Secrets and Silence: Selected Prose 1966-1978*, London: Virago, 1979.

[46] Kaja Silverman, *The Threshold of the Visible World*, 1996, p189. I am thankful to Gilly Booth for suggesting that I read Silverman's writing.

[47] Stuart Hall, 'Cultural Identity and Diaspora' in Williams, P and Chrisman, L (eds), 1993, p402.

[48] Rosemary Betterton, *An Intimate Distance: Women, Artists and the Body*, 1996, p162.

[49] *Ibid*, p162.

[50] For an extended discussion of stereotypes see Homi K Bhabha 'The Other Question: Difference, Discrimination and the Discourse of Colonialism' in Ferguson *et al*, *Out There*, 1990, pp71-87.

[51] Pasquier, Edith Marie, 'Zineb Sedira: The Oblique Gaze' in Lloyd, F (ed), 1999, p215.

[52] *Ibid*, p216.

[53] For an incisive account of the role of veiling in Algeria see Hélie-Lucas in Margot Badran and Miriam Cooke (eds), *Opening the Gates: A Century of Arab Feminist Writing*, 1990, pp108-113.

[54] Unpublished interview with the artist by Edith Marie Pasquier, 1997.

[55] Tina Sherwell, 'Bodies in Representation: Contemporary Arab Women Artists' in Lloyd, F (ed), 1999, p67.

[56] In her recent book Meyda Yeğenoğlu argues that "If veiling is a specific practice of situating the body within the prevailing exigencies of power, so is unveiling.... Not-to-veil is also another way of turning flesh into a particular type of body. However, the body that is not veiled is taken as the norm for specifying a general, cross-culturally valid notion of what a feminine body is and must be." Yeğenoğlu, Meyda, *Colonial Fantasies: Towards a Feminist Reading of Orientalism*, 1998, p115. I am grateful to Tina Sherwell for bringing this thought-provoking book to my attention.

[57] For the linking of women and nation see Deniz Kandiyoti 'Identity and its Discontents: Women and the Nation' in *Millennium: Journal of International Studies*, Vol 20, No 3, 1991: pp429-43.

[58] Elizabeth Edwards, 'Photographs as Objects of Memory' in Kwint *et al*, 1999, p222.

[59] Unpublished interview with the artist by Edith Marie Pasquier, 1997.

[60] Frantz Fanon, *Black Skins, White Masks*, London: Pluto Press, 1986 (1st published in French, 1952), cited by Hall, 'Cultural Identity and Diaspora' in Williams, P and Chrisman, L (eds). 1993, p394.

[61] Unpublished interview with the artist by Edith Marie Pasquier, 1997.

[62] Catherine de Zegher, (ed), *Inside The Visible, an Elliptical Traverse of 20th Century Art*, 1996, p27.

[63] Silverman, K. *The Threshold of the Visible World*, 1996, p190.

[64] *Ibid*, p4.

[65] Jones, A and Stephenson, A (ed), 1999, p3.

Artists' Biographies

FIRYAL AL-ADHAMY

MEDIUM Acrylic, gold and watercolour on canvas and paper
BORN Baghdad, Iraq; lives in Bahrain and the UK
EDUCATION Baghdad University

Selected Solo Exhibitions

1990 Kufa Gallery, London
1988 Intercontinental Hotel, Bahrain

Selected Group Exhibitions

1999-2000 *Dialogue of the Present, the Work of 18 Arab Women Artists,* Hot Bath
    Gallery, Bath; Plymouth Arts Centre, Plymouth; Brunei Gallery, University of
    London; University of Brighton Gallery, Brighton
1996 *Women Artists of the Islamic World*, Islington Museum Gallery, London
1995 *Arab Women Artists in London,* Saidy Gallery, London
— *The World's Women on-line Electronic Ballet*, Internet Exhibition, UN Conference,
    Beijing, China
— *Arab Fine Art Exhibition*, Arab-British Chamber of Commerce, London
1994 Al Abbar Gallery, Dubai, UAE
— Aramco, Inmaa Gallery, Saudi Arabia
1993 *Exhibition of International Artists*, Imperial College, London organised by
    Eastern Art Report
— *Iraqi Artists' Society*, Gallery 4, London
1992 *Iraqi Women's Festival of Culture*, Kufa Gallery, London
— *Iraqi Artists' Society*, Camden Town Lock, London
— *Arab Women Artists* (The General Union of Palestinian Women), Kufa Gallery,
    London
1991 *Iraqi Artists*, Kufa Gallery, London
— *Iraqi Artists' Society*, Gallery 4, London
1988 *Bahrain Art Society Annual Exhibition*, Bahrain
— Alfan Gallery, Bahrain
1987 *Bahrain Art Society Annual Exhibition*, Bahrain

Facing page

Rima Farah, *Jigsaw,* 1994
(detail, see colour plate 24)

MALIKA AGUEZNAY

MEDIUM Oil on canvas: etchings
BORN Marrakesh, Morocco; lives in Casablanca, Morocco
EDUCATION
1966-1970 Ecole des Beaux-Arts, Casablanca

Selected Solo Exhibitions

1997 The Spanish Cultural Centre, Cervantes Institute, Casablanca
1996 The National Gallery of Bab Rouah, Rabat, Morocco
1993 Alif Ba Gallery, Casablanca
1987 The French Cultural Centre, Casablanca
1983 Nadar Gallery, Casablanca

Selected Group Exhibitions

1999-2000 *Dialogue of the Present, the Work of 18 Arab Women Artists,* Hot Bath
       Gallery, Bath; Plymouth Arts Centre, Plymouth; Brunei Gallery, University of
       London; University of Brighton Gallery, Brighton
1998 *Le Face ˆ Face des '8' de Casablanca*, the Spanish Cultural Centre, Cervantes
       Institute, Casablanca
1997 *Art and Dialogue*, National Gallery of Bab Rouah, Rabat
1996 *Three Moroccan Painters*, National Museum of Women In the Arts, Washington
       DC, USA
— *18th Exhibition of Drawings*, Kanagawa Kenmin Gallery, Kanagawa, Japan
— *Plasticiens de Maroc*, Museum of Marrakesh, Morocco
1995 Al Manar Gallery, Morocco, Syria, Tunisia
— Contemporary Art Gallery, Marsam
1994 Anfa Cultural Centre (Alif Ba Gallery), the occasion of the Economic Summit of
       North Africa and the Middle East *Women and Peace*, Marrakesh, Morocco
1993 Galerie Espace Ligne, Rabat
— Unesco Exhibition, Paris, France
— *1st International Biennale of Engravings*, Maastricht, Holland
1992 National Gallery of Bab Rouah, Rabat
1991 Grand Palais, Paris, France
1990 *Triennial of Cracow*, Poland
1989 *Contemporary Moroccan Painting*, Del Conde Duque Cultural Centre, Madrid,
       Spain
— Anfa Cultural Centre and French Cultural Centre, Casablanca
1988 *2nd Biennale of International Art*, Baghdad, Iraq
— Anfa Cultural Centre, Maarif Cultural Centre, Casablanca
1986 *Exposition des Anciens de l'Ecole des Beaux-Arts de Casablanca*, Ecole des
       Beaux-Arts Gallery, Casablanca

JANANNE AL-ANI

MEDIUM Video installation and photographs
BORN 1966, Kirkuk, Iraq: lives in London, UK
EDUCATION
1986-89 Byam Shaw School of Art
1991-95 University of Westminster, BA in Arabic
1995-97 Royal College of Art, MA in Photography

Selected Solo Exhibitions

1998 Margaret Harvey Gallery, St Albans, UK
1997 Harriet Green Gallery, London

Selected Group Exhibitions

1999-2000 *Dialogue of the Present, the Work of 18 Arab Women Artists,* Hot Bath
Gallery, Bath; Plymouth Arts Centre, Plymouth; Brunei Gallery, University of
London; University of Brighton Gallery, Brighton
1997 *20/20*, Kingsgate Gallery, London
— *Ruch*, GI Gallery, Zilona Gora, Poland
1996-7 *John Kobal Photographic Portrait Award* (1st prize winner), National Portrait
Gallery, London
1996 *Contemporary Art from the Museum's Collection*, Imperial War Museum,
London
— *After Eden*, Garden Galleries, Yoxall, Staffordshire
1995 *Natural Settings*, The Chelsea Physic Garden, London
— *Art History Representation*, The Concourse Gallery, London
1994 *Who's Looking at the Family?* Barbican Art Gallery, London
1993 *No more heroes any more*, The Royal Scottish Academy, Edinburgh
— *Declarations of War*, *Contemporary Art from the Collection of the Imperial War
Museum*, Kettle's Yard, Cambridge
1992 *Fine Material for a Dream: A Reappraisal of Orientalism*, Harris Museum and
Art Gallery, Preston, touring to Ferens Museum and Art Gallery, Hull, and
Oldham Art Gallery, Oldham
— *The Whitechapel Open*, The Whitechapel Gallery, London
1991 *Contact*, Royal Festival Hall, London
— *Sign of the Times*, Camerawork, London
— *Guernica Revisited: Artists' Response to the Gulf War,* Kufa Gallery, London
1989-90 *The Whitechapel Open*, The Whitechapel Gallery, London
1987 *Women in View*, Brixton Art Gallery, London

THURAYA AL-BAQSAMI

MEDIUM Acrylic, oil on canvas and monoprints
BORN 1952, Kuwait; lives in Hawalli, Kuwait
EDUCATION
1972-73 College of Fine Arts, Cairo
1974-81 Arts Institute, Surikov, Moscow, MA in Graphic Book Illustration and Design

Selected Solo Exhibitions

1999 Omani Society of Fine Arts, Muscat, Oman
— Taj-Marhaba Hotel, Soussa, Tunisia
— German Foreign Office, Bonn, Ippendorf, Germany
— Ajanta Art Gallery, New Delhi, India
1998 Central University for Nationalities, Beijing, China
— Gallery Via Larga, Florence, Italy
1997 Dar Al Kuth, Sana'a, Republic of Yemen
— Cultural Foundation, Abu Dhabi, UAE
— Casa Di Italia, Asmara, Eritrea
— Arabic Cultural Centre, Damascus, Syria
— Arts Gallery, Dahiyat Abdullah Al-Salem, Kuwait
1996 Museum of Applied Arts, Budapest, Hungary
— Art Connoisseur Gallery, London
1995 Ahmed Al-Adwani Gallery, Kuwait
1994 Art Centre, National Museum of Bahrain
— National Museum of Scopje, Macedonia
— Opera House, Cairo, Egypt
— Ghadir Gallery, Kuwait
1992 Ghadir Gallery, Kuwait
— Athens College Theatre, Athens, Greece
1991 Ghadir Gallery, Kuwait
— Alpine Gallery, London
— Kiklos Gallery, Paphos, Cyprus
1990 Ghadir Gallery, Kuwait
1988 Ghadir Gallery, Kuwait
1986 Kuwaiti Journalists' Association, Kuwait
1979 Free Art Gallery, Kuwait
1971 National Museum of Kuwait

Selected Group Exhibitions

1999-2000 *Dialogue of the Present, the Work of 18 Arab Women Artists,* Hot Bath
        Gallery, Bath; Plymouth Arts Centre, Plymouth; Brunei Gallery, University of
        London; University of Brighton Gallery, Brighton
1999 *4th Sharjah Arts Biennal,* Sharjah, UAE
1998 *Al Qorin Cultural Festival,* Arts Gallery, Kuwait
— United Nations Development Program, Mishrif Theatre, Kuwait
1997 *Al Qorin Cultural Festival,* Kuwait
1996 *Al Qorin Cultural Festival,* Kuwait
— *Arabic Artists' Exhibition,* Egyptian Cultural Centre, London
— *Kuwait Cultural Week,* Beirut, Lebanon
— *Arabic Women Artists' Exhibition,* Baladna Gallery, Amman, Jordan
1995 *Kuwait Cultural Week,* Casablanca, Morocco
— *Al Qorin Cultural Festival (2),* Ahmed Al-Adwani Gallery, Kuwait
— *Biennal of Latakia,* Syria
— *Sharjah Arts Biennal,* Sharjah, UAE
— National Museum of Bahrain, State of Bahrain, Manama

1994 *Al Qorin Cultural Festival*, Ahmed Al-Adwani Gallery, Kuwait

— *Kuwait Association of Human Rights Exhibition*, Graduates Society, Kuwait

1994-95 *Forces of Change*, travelling exhibition, The National Museum of Women in the Arts, Washington DC; Chicago; Miami; S Atlanta, USA

1993 *International Triennial of Graphic Arts*, Cairo, Egypt

— *Kuwaiti Association for Human Rights*, Ghadir Gallery, Kuwait

— Albert Gallery, London

1989 *International Exhibition of Children's Illustrations*, Bratislava, Slovakia

1988 *International Festival for Formative Arts*, Baghdad

1985 *Exhibition of the Contest Square*, Kuwait Municipality

DORIS BITTAR

MEDIUM Oil on canvas
BORN Lebanese, in Baghdad, brought up in Lebanon and later New York; lives in
    San Diego, California
EDUCATION
1981 State University of New York at Purchase, BA. Fine Art
1993 University of California, San Diego, MA Fine Art
1995-96 Whitney Museum of American Art Independent Study Program

Selected Solo Exhibitions

1999 *Lebanese Linen, Doris Bittar*, David Zapf Gallery, San Diego, California
1997 *Doris Bittar*, Hyde Gallery, Grossmont College, El Cajon, California
1996 *In the Seasons of Heat and Cold*, John R. Steppling Gallery, San Diego State
    University, Imperial Campus, Calexico, California
1995 *People of the Book*, David Zapf Gallery, San Diego, California
1994 *Ornamental Subjects*, Boehm Gallery, Palomar College, San Marcos, California
— *Under the Sun of the West*, The Alternative Museum, New York
1994 *Looking at Delacroix*, New Visual Arts Complex, University of California, San
    Diego, La Jolla, California
1988 *Trees and Roots*, San Diego Art Institute, San Diego, California

Selected Group Exhibitions

1999 *Museum of Contemporary Art, San Diego Art Auction '99*, Museum of Contem-
    porary Art, La Jolla, California
1996 *Substituting 'Rasquachismo' for 'Mimesis': Doris Bittar, Mariam Ishaque,
    Fatimah Tuggar*, spot, New York
— *Whitney 1995-96 Independent Study Program Exhibition*, Whltney Museum of
    American Art, New York
— *Houna wa Hounak, Update: Copenhagen '96*, Copenhagen, Denmark
1995 *San Diego Artists 1995*, David Zapf Gallery, San Diego, California
— *Artists' View: the Arab World*, University Gallery, Willemette University, Salem,
    Oregon
— *Black & White & Color 111*, David Zapf Gallery, San Diego, California
— *Gallery Artists: Insite 94*, David Zapf Gallery, San Diego, California
1994 *Colective Binacional 2 en !*, Centro Cultural Tijuana, Tijuana BC, Mexico and
    Centro Cultural Mexicali, BC, Mexico
1990 *Doris Bittar: Paintings*, sponsored by the American Arab Anti-Discrimination
    Committee, Los Angeles, California
1989 *N. H. I. (No Humans Involved)*, a collaborative project, Flor y Canto Gallery,
    San Diego State University, San Diego, California
— *San Diego Artists Guild Juried Exhibit*, San Diego Museum of Art, San Diego,
    Califomia
1983 *Yale on Trial*, 22 Wooster Gallery, 22 Wooster St. New York

RIMA FARAH

MEDIUM Etching and monoprint
BORN 1955, Amman, Jordan; lives in London, UK
EDUCATION
1977 Cambridge School of Art, UK

Selected Solo Exhibitions

1995 Atassi Gallery, Damascus, Syria
— Gallery 50 x 70, Beirut, Lebanon
1993 Aphrodie, Izmir, Turkey
1992 AlIf Gallery, Zamalek, Cairo, Egypt
1991 Tanjer Flandria Art Gallery, Tangiers, Morocco
— Plum Gallery, Tokyo, Japan
1989 Sultan Gallery, Kuwait
1987 Sultan Gallery, Kuwait
1986 Van Wagner, Ankara, Turkey
1986 The Gallery, Amman, Jordan
1984 The Graffiti Gallery, London

Selected Group Exhibitions

1999-2000 *Dialogue of the Present, the Work of 18 Arab Women Artists,* Hot Bath
     Gallery, Bath; Plymouth Arts Centre, Plymouth; Brunei Gallery, University of
     London; University of Brighton Gallery, Brighton
1995 Aphrodie, Izmir, Turkey
— ODA Gallery, Istanbul, Turkey
1994-95 *Forces of Change*, travelling exhibition, The National Museum of Women in
     the Arts, Washington DC; Chicago; Miami; S. Atlanta, USA
1994 The American College, London
1992 Alif Gallery, Washington DC, USA
— Von Cranch, Cologne
1991 Studio 5, Seibu, Ikeburkuro, Japan
1990 Majlis Gallery, Dubai, UAE
1989 Egee Art, London
1988-91 *It's Possible*, travelling exhibition, USA and Europe
1987 ICCP Geneva, Switzerland
1986 *The Bordeaux Collection*, Royal Academy, London
— The Mall Gallery, London
— Falcon Gallery, Riyadh, Saudi Arabia
1985 Arab Heritage Gallery, Al Khobar, Saudi Arabia
— The Islamic Cultural Centre, London
1984 *Arab Artists*, Graffiti Gallery, London

MAYSALOUN FARAJ

MEDIUM Ceramics; mixed media on board and canvas
BORN 1955 to Iraqi parents in California, USA; lives in London, UK
EDUCATION
1973-78 Baghdad University, Architecture B.Sc.

Selected Solo Exhibitions

1995 *Once upon...a Culture*, SOAS, University of London, London
1994 *Oriental Delight*, Trocadero Centre, London
1993 *Vibrations from my Past*, Oakshire Gallery, Texas, USA
1992 *Sisters in...Harmony*, River Gardens, London
1990 *Ya Rab*, Rochan Gallery, London
— *Faith*, Argile Gallery, London
1989 *Home Sweet Home*, Baghdad, Iraq
1985 *Longing, Espace 2000*, Paris, France

Selected Group Exhibitions

2001 International Print Portfolio: Artists for Human Rights, touring exhibition launched in Durban, South Africa
2000 pARTicipation, Eu-man (European Union-Migrant Artists, Helsinki, Finland), Kaapelitehdas Puvistamo, Helsinki;
        Gallery Shambala, Copenhagen; Dockland Gallery, London
1999-2000 *Dialogue of the Present, the Work of 18 Arab Women Artists,* touring the UK: Hot Bath Gallery, Bath,
        Plymouth Arts Centre, Brunei Gallery, University of London, University of Brighton Gallery
1998 *20th Anniversary*, Soni Gallery and Egee Art, London
1997 *Homage to Jewad Selim*, Kufa Gallery, London
— Riverside Open Studios, London
— Museum of Mankind, Museum of Women's Art, London
1996 *Eastern & Icelandic Art, The Inspiration for William Morris*, Merton Arts Festival, Merton, London
1995 Arabian Eyes, Ministry of Culture and Information, Sharjah, UAE
— *Visions of East and West*, Sayde Interiors, London
— *Arab Artist Fine Arts*, Arab-British Chamber of Commerce, London
1994-95*Forces of Change*, travelling exhibition, The National Museum of Women in the Arts, Washington DC;
        Chicago; Miami; S. Atlanta, USA
— *Culture and Continuity*, Midlands Art Centre, Birmingham
1993 Gallery 4, London
— *Our Home Land and Us*, Imperial College, London
1992 *Iraqi Cultural Festival*, Camden Lock, London
— *Arab Women Artists Festival*, (General Union of Palestinian Women) Kufa Gallery, London
— *Iraqi Women's Art Celebration*, Kufa Gallery, London
1991 Kufa Gallery, London
— *Contemporary Collectors*, Artizana Gallery, Manchester
1989 *Baghdad Biennial International Art Festival*, Baghdad
— Orfali Gallery, Baghdad
— *International Women's Week*, Brazil Gallery, Brazil
1988 *ILEA Grand Exhibition*, Chelsea School of Art, London
— *Contemporary Artists and Calligraphy*, Egee Art Consultancy, London
— *Arab Women Artists in the UK*, Kufa Gallery, London

BATOOL AL-FEKAIKI

MEDIUM Oil on canvas and drawing
BORN 1942, Baghdad, Iraq; lives in London, UK
EDUCATION
1963 Institute of Baghdad, BA

Selected Solo Exhibitions

1988 Dr Christian Hyden Hall, Traunstein, Munich, Germany
1997 Beledna Gallery, Amman, Jordan
1994 Sayda Interiors, London

Selected Group Exhibitions

1999-2000 *Dialogue of the Present, the Work of 18 Arab Women Artists,* Hot Bath
        Gallery, Bath; Plymouth Arts Centre, Plymouth; Brunei Gallery, University of
        London; University of Brighton Gallery, Brighton
1998 *11th International Exhibition of Fine Art,* Al Mahras, Tunisia
1997 *International Exhibition of Fine Art,* Al-Mahras, Tunisia
1996 *The Palestinian Child Exhibition,* Dubai
1995 *Arab Artists Exhibition,* Arab-British Chamber of Commerce, London
1993 Orfali Gallery, Baghdad
1992 *Iraqi Modern Art Exhibition,* The Royal Cultural Centre, Jordan
1991 *Joint Exhibition with Ibrahim Al Abdali,* The Royal Cultural Centre, Jordan
— *Iraqi Modern Art Exhibition,* Iraqi Artists' Union, Italy
1990 *Iraqi Women Artists Exhibition,* Brazil
1989 *The Second International Festival,* Al-Benali, Baghdad
1988 *Victory and Peace Exhibition,* Baghdad
1987 *Martyrs Exhibition,* Baghdad
1986 *The First International Baghdad Exhibition,* Al-Benali, Baghdad
1985 *Annual Exhibition,* Orfali Gallery, Baghdad
1984 *Graphics Exhibition,* Rewaaq Gallery, Baghdad
1981 *Iraqi Modern Art Exhibition,* Amman, Jordan
1980 *National Arab Women Artists Exhibition,* Baghdad
1979 *Art and Revolution Exhibition,* Thawra Newspaper, Baghdad
1976 *Iraqi Modern Art Exhibition,* Paris, Bonn, London
1975 *Iraqi Women Artists Exhibition,* Kuwait, Madrid, Vienna, Italy
1974 *Mobile Iraqi Art Exhibition,* Paris, Damascus, Kuwait
1973 *Al Wasti Festival,* The National Museum of Modern Art, Baghdad

SAADEH GEORGE

MEDIUM Mixed, installation, sculpture, prints and photographs
BORN 1950, Iraq, brought up in Lebanon; lives in London, UK
EDUCATION
1971-76 Trained as a doctor
1997 Central St Martin's College of Art and Design, BA
1995 Artist in Residence, Small Mansions Art Centre, London

Selected Solo Exhibitions

1998 Grapevine Gallery, Ealing, London
1995 Questors, Theatre Foyer Gallery, London

Selected Group Exhibitions

1999-2000 *Dialogue of the Present, the Work of 18 Arab Women Artists,* Hot Bath
      Gallery, Bath; Plymouth Arts Centre, Plymouth; Brunei Gallery, University of
      London; University of Brighton Gallery, Brighton
1996 *International Art Exhibition*, Paris
— *Cultural Aid for a United Bosnia*, Covent Garden, London
— *Oleum*, Academia Italiana; Italian Trade Centre, London
1995 *Arab Artists in Britain*, Arab-British Chamber of Commerce, London
— *Seeing … Believing*, Waterman's Art Centre, London
— *Faulkner's Fine Papers*, Lethaby Gallery, London
1994 *Hard Space*, Waterman's Art Centre, London
1993 *Mono 93*, Small Mansions Art Centre, London
1992 Emerald Centre, London
— *Art Themes*, Obelisque Gallery, Richmond, Surrey
1989 *Roots*, Bristol
1978 *Rue Makhoul Festival of Arts*, Beirut, Lebanon
1976 *Rue Bliss Festival of Arts*, Beirut, Lebanon

MAI GHOUSSOUB

MEDIUM Sculpture, installation, performance
BORN 1952, Lebanon; lives in London, UK
EDUCATION
1971-74 The American University of Beirut, BA
1971-75 Lebanese University, French Literature
1988-92 Morley College, London, Sculpture

Selected Solo Exhibitions

1995 *Metal Blues*, Argile Gallery, London
1993 *Theatrical Performance with Sculptures*, Kufa Gallery, London

Selected Group Exhibitions

1999-2000 *Dialogue of the Present, the Work of 18 Arab Women Artists,* Hot Bath
    Gallery, Bath; Plymouth Arts Centre, Plymouth; Brunei Gallery, University of
    London; University of Brighton Gallery, Brighton
1998 *Displaces*, installation on theme of refugees, Shoreditch Town Hall, London
— Installation, Stoke Newington Library Gallery, London
1996 *Under Different Skies*, Copenhagen
1994 Gallery 23, London
1993 Kufa Gallery, London
1993 *The Witching Hour and a Half*, ICA, London
1985 Holland Park Orangerie, London

WAFAA EL HOUDAYBI

MEDIUM Mixed, painting, thread on leather
BORN 1966, Asilah, Morocco; lives in Asilah
EDUCATION Asilah and Tangiers, Morocco and Lisbon, Portugal

Selected Solo Exhibitions

1997 The Cultural Foundation, Abu Dhabi, UAE
1993-94 Henry Kissingser Office, Rabat, Morocco
1993 Arts Centre, Manama, Bahrain
— Al Manzah Hotel, Tangiers, Morocco
1992 Conference Palace, Marrakesh, Morocco
— Museum Al Batha'a, Fes, Morocco
— Al Wadaia Museum, Rabat, Morocco
1985 The Spanish Cultural Centre, Tangiers, Morocco
1984 Qudama' Al Iman Al Aseely Association, Asilah, Morocco

Selected Group Exhibitions

1999-2000 *Dialogue of the Present, the Work of 18 Arab Women Artists,* Hot Bath
        Gallery, Bath; Plymouth Arts Centre, Plymouth; Brunei Gallery, University of
        London; University of Brighton Gallery, Brighton
1998 Museum Dakar, Senegal
1997 *Hallamash*, Gallerie Sur, Vienna, Austria
— *3rd International Arts Biennial*, Sharjah, UAE
1996 Al Hassan II Centre, Asilah, Morocco
— Conference Palace, Marrakesh, Morocco
1995 *2nd International Arts Biennial*, Sharjah, UAE
1995 *Pottery Festival*, Bahrain
1994 Arts Centre, Manama, Bahrain
— *Homage to Tshikaya Otomsee*, International Cultural Festival, Asilah, Morocco
1992 Jerusalem Hall - Fes, Morocco
1989 French Cultural Centre, Casablanca, Morocco
1986-8 Al Hassan II Centre (Asilah Seasons), Asilah
1988 *The African Conference* (about the family),
— Hayat Regency Hotel, Casablanca. Morocco
1986 The Association of Qudama'a Al Iman Al Asilee, Asilah
1984 The Culture Palace, Asilah, Morocco
1983 Da'ar El Shabab, Tangier, Morocco
1982 Da'ar El Shabab, Asilah, Morocco
1981 Al Borj Hall, Asilah, Morocco

KAMALA IBRAHIM ISHAQ

MEDIUM Oil on canvas, acrylic on paper
BORN 1939, Omdurman, Sudan; lives in Muscat, Oman
EDUCATION
1959-63 College of Fine and Applied Art, Khartoum
1964-66 Royal College of Art, London (mural painting)
1968-69 Royal College of Art, London (lithography, typography, illustration)

Selected Solo Exhibitions

1970 Ikhnaton Art Gallery, Cairo, Egypt

Selected Group Exhibitions

1999-2000 *Dialogue of the Present, the Work of 18 Arab Women Artists,* Hot Bath
    Gallery, Bath; Plymouth Arts Centre, Plymouth; Brunei Gallery, University of
    London; University of Brighton Gallery, Brighton
1997 *Transafrican Art*, Orlando Museum of Art, USA
1996 *Arab Artists*, Jordan, Amman
1995 *Arab Women In the Arts/Arab Eyes*, Sharjah, UAE
Seven Stories from Africa, Whitechapel Art Gallery, London
1994-95 *Forces of Change*, travelling exhibition, The National Museum of Women in
    the Arts, Washington DC; Chicago; Miami; S. Atlanta, USA
1986 *Ten Women Artists from the World*, Carolyn Hill Gallery, New York, USA
1982 *Biennial*, Sudan Pavilion, Alexandria, Egypt
1977 *Contemporary African Art*, Howard University, Washington DC
1973 *African Festival*, Tunis
1970 *Biennal*, Sudan Pavilion, Festac, Nigeria
1969 *Contemporary African Art*, Camden Arts Centre, London
1963-8 *Winter Exhibitions*, Association of Fine Artists In Khartoum, Sudan
1963-4 Harmon Foundation, New York, USA
1963 *Biennal*, Sao Paolo, Sudan Pavilion, Brazil
1962 *World Fair*, Sudan Pavilion, New York, USA

GHADA JAMAL

MEDIUM Mixed media on paper and wood
BORN 1955, Beirut, Lebanon: lives in Los Angeles, California, USA
EDUCATION
1984 Beirut University College, Lebanon, BA Liberal Studies
1991 California State University, Long Beach, California, MA Drawing and Painting

Selected Solo Exhibitions

1997 Agial Gallery, Beirut, Lebanon
— *Paintings by Ghada Jamal*, Plaza Club, Broummana, Lebanon
1990 *Lebanon- Cityscapes*, California State University, Long Beach
— *Lebanese Landscapes*, California State University, Long Beach

Selected Group Exhibitions

1997 *LAU Alumni Artists*, Sheikh Zayed Gallery, Lebanese American University,
     Beirut, Lebanon
— *Five Artists from Lebanon*, Hammurabi Art Gallery, Amman, Jordan
— *'97 Art Festival: Landscape and Cityscape in Lebanese Art*, International College,
     Beirut, Lebanon
— *Books as Art: 10th Anniversary Exhibition*, The National Museum of Women in the
     Arts Library and Research Centre, Washington, DC
— *Summer Festival '97'*, Darat Al Funun, Abdul Hameed Shoman Foundation,
     Amman, Jordan
1996 *Summer '96'*, Darat Al Funun, Abdul Hameed Shoman Foundation, Amman,
     Jordan
— *XXe Salon D'Automne 1996*, Mus+e Nicolos Sursock, Beirut, Lebanon
— *Friends of the Foundry*, Foundry Gallery, Washington, DC
— *Contemporary Urban Landscape*, Long Beach Arts, Long Beach, California
— *Paradox and Perception: Leon Caraco, Ron Libbrecht, Ghada Jamal, Carolyn Buck
     Vosburgh*, Ark Gallery, Long Beach, California
— *Small Wonders II*, Brand Gallery, Santa Ana, California
1995 *Surroundings: Jamal and Minorus*, Brand Gallery, Santa Ana
— *Restless Voices: Abstraction from Los Angeles*, Schick Gallery, Skidmore College,
     Saratoga Springs, New York
1994 *Ghada Jamal, Carolyn Buck Vosburgh, Janice M. Arnold*, Sacred Grounds, San
     Pedro, California
— *Women In the Arts*, Grand National Bank, Santa Ana, California
1993 *Four Arab Artists from the United States*, Abdul Hameed Shoman Foundation,
     Amman, Jordan
— *Shaken Realities: Ruth Eyrich, Ghada Jamal, Rhoda Weiseman*, Joslyn Fine Arts
     Gallery, Torrance, California
— *Art of the Small: Paintings by Five Los Angeles Artists*, Palladio Gallery, Los
     Angeles, California
— *Structure and Content*, Michael Folonis and Associates, Santa Monica, California
— *Still Life in Lebanese Art*, Sheikh Zayed Gallery, Lebanese American University,
     Beirut, Lebanon
1992 *LA Abstract Artists: Works on Paper*, Gallery X, Exeter, England
— *World News,* Muckenthaler Cultural Center, Fullerton, California
1991 *Angel's Gate Cultural Center Members Exhibition*, San Pedro, California
— *World News*, Beyond Baroque, Venice, CA and The Onyx, Los Angeles, California
1990 *Long Beach Art Expedition*, Printworks Gallery, Long Beach, California
— *Group 390*, California State University, Long Beach, California
— *WAM*, Downey Museum of Art, Downey, California
1989 *Group 89*, California State University, Long Beech
— *Group II 89*, California State University, Long Beach

— 1988 *Alumni Exhibition*, Beirut University College, Lebanon
— *Beit-Aiddean Annual Exhibition*, Beit-Alddean Palace, Lebanon (Lebanese Association for Painting and Sculpture)
— *X11 Salon 1986 D'automne*, Mus+e Sursock, Beirut, Lebanon (Lebanese Association for Painting and Sculpture)
1985 *Three Beirut University Graduates*, Sheikh Zayed Gallery, Lebanese American University, Beirut, Lebanon

LILIANE KARNOUK

MEDIUM Mixed media: oil and acrylic on canvas, glass
BORN 1944, Cairo, Egypt: lives in British Columbia, Canada
EDUCATION
1966 Academy of Fine Arts, Rome
1972 University of British Columbia, Vancouver, MA in Art Education

Selected Solo Exhibitions

1993 *Retrospective 88-93*, Alif Gallery, Cairo, Egypt
1992 *Ibrahim*, Centre d'Expositions de la Gare, L'Annonciation, Quebec
— *Black-Green*, Goethe Institute Gallery, Cairo, Egypt
1991 *Eastern Desert*, Gallerie La part Du Sable, Cairo, Egypt
1988 *Hautungen*, Ifa Gallery, Bonn, Germany
— *Sabra and Shatilla*, Goethe Institute Gallery, Cairo, Egypt
1987 *Flying Carpets*, Gallery of the Italian Cultural Centre, Cairo, Egypt
1985 *Miniatures and Books*, Goethe Institute Gallery, Cairo; Ostracca Gallery,
    Alexandria, Egypt
1983-4 *Desertscapes*, The National Art Centre, Main Gallery, Cairo; Gallery Samia
    Zeytoun, Meadi; Goethe Institute Gallery, Alexandria

Selected Group Exhibitions

2000 National Museum of Civilization, Ottawa,
1997 *6th International Sculpture Exhibition*, Fine Arts Gallery, University of Hawaii
— *Rhythm and Form, Visual Reflections on Arab Poetry*, Fine Arts Gallery, University
    of Arkansas; Fine Arts Gallery, University of California in Berkeley
1995 *Artist's View, The Arab World*, Willamette Arts Gallery, Willamette University,
    Salem, Oregon, USA
1994-95*Forces of Change*, travelling exhibition, The National Museum of Women in
    the Arts, Washington DC; Chicago; Miami; S Atlanta, USA
1994 *Time Machine*, Main Hall of Egyptian Antiquities, British Museum, London
1993 L'Annonciation, Quebec; KIO Kunstnersenteret, Lillehammer, Norway
— *Aesthetica Diffusa 4. Natural-Cultura*, Centro Sociale, Salerno, Italy; Centre
    International Multimedia, Sint-Baafs-Vigve, Belgium
1991 *Papier-Parallel*, Neuer Kunstverein, Aschaffenbourg, Germany
1992 *Ecart, Boreal Multimedia*, Centre d'Exposition de la Gare,

1990-91 *Acht Kunstler aus Agypten*, Gallerie der Kongresshalle, Augsburg; Gallerie
    der Kongresshalle, Rosenheim. Germany
— *Storie Naturale*, Museo di Genoa, Italy
1986 *First International Biennale of Paper*, Leopold Hoech, Museum, Duren, Ger-
    many
1982 *Biennale of Alexandria*, Museum of Modern Art, Alexandria, Egypt

LEILA KUBBA KAWASH

MEDIUM Mixed media, oil on canvas
BORN 1945, Baghdad, Iraq; lives in Washington
EDUCATION
1966 Manchester School of Art and Architecture
1992 Corcoran School of Art, Washington DC

Selected Solo Exhibitions

1997 *Dawns and Invocations,* Magna Art Gallery, Athens
1996 Academias Cultural Centre, Athens, Greece
— Abu Dhabi Cultural Centre
1994 *Crossings*, Royal Cultural Centre, Amman, Jordan
1993 ADC Convention, Washington DC, USA
1991 *Words, Echoes and Images*, Alif Gallery, Georgetown, Washington DC, USA
1987 *Movements and Traditions*, Hilton Hotel, Athens, Greece
1986 International Monetary Fund, Washington DC, USA

Selected Group Exhibitions

1999-2000 *Dialogue of the Present, the Work of 18 Arab Women Artists,* Hot Bath
    Gallery, Bath; Plymouth Arts Centre, Plymouth; Brunei Gallery, University of
    London; University of Brighton Gallery, Brighton
1995 *Artist's View, The ArabWorld*, Willamette Arts Gallery, Willamette University,
    Salem, Oregon, USA
1995 *Jerusalem Cultural Show,* Cultural Foundation, Abu Dhabi
1994-95 *Forces of Change*, travelling exhibition, The National Museum of Women in
    the Arts, Washington DC; Chicago; Miami; S Atlanta, USA
1993 *Interpretations in Texture*, Michael Stone Gallery, Washington DC, USA
1992 Corcoran White Walls Gallery, Washington DC, USA
1989 Alif Gallery, Washington DC, USA
— Braathen Nusseibeh Gallery, New York City, USA
1984-6*Through Arab Eyes*, touring Middle States of America

SABIHA KHEMIR

MEDIUM Drawing, book illustration
BORN 1959, Tunisia; lives in London, UK
EDUCATION
1986 London University, School of Oriental and African Studies, MA (with distinction)
in Islamic Art and Archaeology
1990 University of London , PhD
University of Pennsylvania, Philadelphia, USA, Post Doctoral Fellow in the History of
Art Department

Illustrative Work

1994 *The Island of Animals*, Quartet, London
1978 *Le Nuage Amoureux*, Maspero, Paris
1975 *L'Ogresse*, Maspero, Paris

BOOK COVERS INCLUDE
Respected Sir, Naguib Mahfouz
Tiger on the Tenth Day, Zakaria Tamer
Distant View of a Minaret, Alifa Rifaat

Selected Group Exhibitions

1999-2000 *Dialogue of the Present, the Work of 18 Arab Women Artists,* Hot Bath
Gallery, Bath; Plymouth Arts Centre, Plymouth; Brunei Gallery, University of
London; University of Brighton Gallery, Brighton
1998 The School of Oriental and African Studies, London University, London
— The Ismaili Centre, London
1994-5 *Forces of Change*, travelling exhibition, The National Museum of Women in
the Arts, Washington DC; Chicago; Miami; S Atlanta, USA
1993 Kufa Gallery, London
1988 Kufa Gallery, London
1987 Kufa Gallery, London
1986 The Islamic Centre, London
1979 The Beaubourg Pompidou Centre, Paris, France

First novel, *Waiting in the Future for the Past to Come,* was published by Quartet
(London) in 1993

NAJAT MAKI

MEDIUM Mixed media on paper
BORN 1956, Dubai, UAE; lives in Dubai, UAE and Cairo, Egypt
EDUCATION
1981 College of Fine Art, Cairo, Egypt (Sculpture and relief sculpture)
1997 MA, College of Fine Art, Cairo, Egypt

Selected Solo Exhibitions

1997 Sharjah Art Museum, Sharjah, UAE
— Writers and Artists Atelier, Cairo, Egypt
1986 Al Wasti Club, Dubai

Selected Group Exhibitions

1999-2000 *Dialogue of the Present, the Work of 18 Arab Women Artists,* Hot Bath
        Gallery, Bath; Plymouth Arts Centre, Plymouth; Brunei Gallery, University of
        London; University of Brighton Gallery, Brighton
1997 *Third Sharjah International Biennial*, Sharjah, UAE
1996 *International Arts Festival Biennial*, Cairo, Egypt
1996-93 Numerous shows in the UAE, Egypt, Sudan, Musqat, Qatar, Jordan, Syria,
        Cairo, Turkey, Germany, USA, Spain, Italy, Moscow, Japan and France
1995 *2nd Sharjah International Biennial*, Sharjah, UAE

HOURIA NIATI

MEDIUM Mixed, installation, performance, painting and drawing
BORN 1948, Khemis-Miliana, Algeria; lives in London, UK
EDUCATION
1969 National School of Tixeraine, Algiers. Dipolma Community Arts
1979-82 Croydon College of Art and Design, Surrey, Dip. Fine Art
1984 First Artist in Residence, Riverside Studios, London

Selected Solo Exhibitions

1992-95 *Open Studios*, ACAVA, London
1990 Rochan Gallery, London
— Small Mansion Arts Centre, London
1988-9 *Mystery and Metaphor*, Ikon Gallery, Birmingham
1988 Africa Centre, London
1987 Maison de la Culture, Courbevoie, Paris, France
1985 Khelifa et Houria Niati, Festival Culturel, Khemis-Miliana, Algeria
1984 *Delirium*, Africa Centre, London
— Smith's Gallery, London
— *Métaphores*, Galerie du CCWA, Algiers
— *Répercussions*, Maison de la Culture Tizi-Ouzou, Algiers

Selected Group Exhibitions

1999-2000 *Dialogue of the Present, the Work of 18 Arab Women Artists,* Hot Bath
   Gallery, Bath; Plymouth Arts Centre, Plymouth; Brunei Gallery, University of
   London; University of Brighton Gallery, Brighton
1997-9 *Cross/ing, Time.Space.Movement.* Contemporary Art Museum, Florida:
   University of South Florida, touring USA
1998 mediterranea, Contemporary Art of the Mediterranean Countries, Brussels
1997 *Gendered Visions, The Art of Contemporary Africana Women,* Cornell University, New York State
3rd Sharjah International Biennal, Sharjah, UAE
1995 *New Visions*: Recent Works by Six African Artists, Zora Neale Hurston National
   Museum of Fine Arts, Florida, USA
1994-5 *Forces of Change*, travelling exhibition, The National Museum of Women in
   the Arts, Washington DC; Chicago; Miami; S. Atlanta, USA
1991 *Four x 4*, Harris Museum, Preston, Britain
1989 *Forms of Intuition*, Cartwright Hall Museum, Bradford
— *Contemporary Art from the Islamic World*, Concourse Gallery, Barbican Centre,
   London
1986 *From Two Worlds*, Whitechapel Gallery, London and Fruitmarket Gallery,
   Edinburgh
1984 Riverside Studios, London
— *Into the Open*, Mappin Art Gallery, Sheffield and Castle Museum, Nottingham
1983 *Five African Artists*, Africa Centre, Covent Garden, London
— *Black Women's Time Now*, Battersea Arts Centre, London

AZZA AL-QASIMI

MEDIUM Mixed, collage, prints and oil on canvas
BORN 1974, Sharjah, UAE; lives in Sharjah, UAE
EDUCATION Higher Diploma in Banking and Finance, UAE

Selected Group Exhibitions

1999-2000 *Dialogue of the Present, the Work of 18 Arab Women Artists,* Hot Bath
   Gallery, Bath; Plymouth Arts Centre, Plymouth; Brunei Gallery, University of
   London; University of Brighton Gallery, Brighton
1998 *17th Annual Fine Arts Exhibition*, Sharjah, UAE
1997 *Third Sharjah International Arts Biennal*, UAE
— *GCC Exhibition*, China
— *Members Exhibition*, Dubai International Art Centre, UAE
— *The Emirates Artists' Exhibition*, Paris, France
— *The Emirates Artists' Exhibition*, Sharjah, UAE
— *16th Annual Fine Arts Exhibition*, Sharjah, UAE
1996-7 *Sharjah Women's Club Art Exhibition*, Sharjah, UAE
1996 *Members Exhibition*, Dubai International Art Centre, UAE
— *The Feminine Touch*, Dubai
— *Emirates Fine Arts Society*, Al Hanajer Centre, Egypt
— *15th Annual Fine Arts Exhibition*, Sharjah, UAE
— *Jarash International Art Festival*, Jordan
— *Cairo International Arts Biennal,* UAE

ZINEB SEDIRA

MEDIUM Video installation, photographs
BORN 1963, Gennevilliers, France: lives in London, UK
EDUCATION
1992-95 Central St. Martin's School of Art, London. B.A. Hons.
1995-97 Slade School of Art, London. M.A. in Media and Fine Art
1998 Royal College of Art, M.Phil. Photography

Selected Solo Exhibitions

1999 *MosaÀques,* The French Institute, London
Where Are You From? BM Contemporary Art Center, Istanbul, Turkey

Selected Group Exhibitions

2000 April *We're Not in Kansas Anymore*, Poplar Baths, East End, London
— *Home: Sweet: Home*, Beirut
2000 Feb. *Fresh Masala*, Mead Gallery, Warwick
2000 Jan. *Genealogies, Miscegenations, Missed Generations*, William Benton
    Museum of Art in Connecticut, USA (touring exhibition)
1999-2000 *Dialogue of the Present, the Work of 18 Arab Women Artists,* touring the
    UK: Hot Bath Gallery, Bath, Plymouth Arts Centre, Brunei Gallery, University of
    London, University of Brighton Gallery
1999 *Shoe Shop*, Istanbul, Turkey
— *The Order of Things*, Bluecoat Gallery, Liverpool
1998 *Showgirls Billboard Project*, Women's Art Factory, Sheffield
— *Return of the Showgirls*, Women's Art Factory, Sheffield
— *Interim*, Henry Moore Gallery, Royal College of Art, London
— *Stream TV*, ICA, London
— *Is Art Beneath You*, site specific project, Serpentine Gallery, London
1997 *Point of Entry*, Cable Street Gallery, London
— *Out of the Blue*, Gallery of Modern Art, Glasgow, Scotland
— *Une Génération de Femmes, Silent Sight*, MA Degree Show, Slade School of Art,
    London
1996 *Bound*, Commercial Too Gallery, London
1995 *Untitled* (3 screens/video installation), BA Degree Show, Central St. Martin's,
    School of Art, London
1994 *Cite Dortolr*, 198 Gallery, London
1993 *Espoir* (outdoor sculptures), Skoki Centre, Poland
— *Topology of the Veil*, Lethaby Gallery, London

LAILA AL-SHAWA

MEDIUM Silk screen, oil on canvas, sculpture
BORN 1940, Gaza, Palestine: lives in Gaza and London
EDUCATION
1957-58 Leonardo da Vinci School of Art, Cairo, Egypt
1958-64 Academia de Belle Arte Rome, Italy, BA Hons. Fine Art
1960-64 Academia St. Giaccomo, Rome, Italy, Diploma in Plastic Decorative Arts

Selected Solo Exhibitions

1996 Mermaid Theatre Gallery, London, UK
1992 The Gallery, London
1990 The National Art Gallery, Amman, Jordan
1976 Sultan Gallery, Kuwait

Selected Group Exhibitions

1999-2000 *The Transvangarde*, October Gallery, London
— *Dialogue of the Present, the Work of 18 Arab Women Artists,* Hot Bath Gallery,
    Bath; Plymouth Arts Centre, Plymouth; Brunei Gallery, University of London;
    University of Brighton Gallery, Brighton
— 1998 *mediterranea, Contemporary Art of the Mediterranean Countries*, Brussels
1996 *Transvangarde*, October Gallery, London
— *The Right to Write*, from the Collection of the National Art Gallery, Jordan, Agnes
    Scott College, Atlanta, Georgia
— The World Bank Gallery, World Bank, Washington DC
— *The Winter Exhibition*, October Gallery, London
1995-7 *The Right to Hope, One World Art*, World touring exhibition
1995 *Contemporary Arab Artists*, Darat Al-Funun, Amman, Jordan
— *Contemporary Arab Artists*, Riwaq Al Balq'a Gallery, Jordan
— *Artist's View, The Arab World,* Willamette Arts Gallery, Willamette University,
    Salem, Oregon, USA
— *Contemporary Middle Eastern Art*, John Addis Gallery, British Museum, London.
    (Recent acquisitions)
1994-5 *Forces of Change*, travelling exhibition, The National Museum of Women in
    the Arts, Washington DC; Chicago; Miami; S. Atlanta, USA
1994 *From Exile to Jerusalem*, Al-Wasiti Art Centre, Jerusalem
— *Shawa and Wijdan*, October Gallery, London
1993 *Saga*, Salon de L'éstampe et de L'édition d'art a Tirage Limité, Grand Palais,
    Paris, France
1992 *Three Artists from Gaza*, The Shoman Foundation, Jordan
1990 *Malaysian Experience*, National Art Gallery, Kuala Lumpur, Malaysia
1989 *Contemporary Art from the Islamic World*, Barbican Centre, London
1988 *The Baghdad Biennale*, the Saddam Centre, Baghdad
1987 *Arab Women Artists in the UK*, Kufa Gallery, London

MARY BAHJAH TUMA

MEDIUM Mixed media: installation
BORN America: lives in Charlotte, North Carolina, USA
EDUCATION
1994 MA Fine Art: Fibers, University of Arizona, Tuscon, Arizona

Selected Solo Exhibitions

1998-9 *Topographia: Passages Between Worlds*, Charlotte International Airport,
    Charlotte, NC
1994 *Shapeshifters*, MFA Thesis Exhibition University of Arizona Museum of Art,
    Tucson, Arizona
1993 *Memory and Loss*, Local 803 Gallery, Tucson, Arizona

Selected Group Exhibitions

2000 *Seventh International Shoebox Sculpture Exhibition*, University of Honolulu Art
    Gallery, Honolulu
1999 *Fiberrat International '99*, Pittsburgh Center for the Arts, Pittsburgh, PA
— *17th Annual September Competition Exhibition*, Alexandria Museum of Art,
    Alexandria, LA
— *Stitches*, Woman Made Gallery, Chicago, Illinois
— *Stitching Outside the Lines*, Three person exhibition, Rowe Arts Main Gallery, The
    University of North Carolina at Charlotte, Charlotte, NC
— *Loss and Grief*, Woman Made Gallery, Chicago, IL
1998 Faculty Exhibition, Rowe Arts Gallery, University of North Carolina, Charlotte
1997 *International Icarus '97*, Ghost Fleet Gallery, Nags Head, North Carolina
— *10th Annual Fiber Art Exhibition*, BASF Fibers and Creative Arts Guild, Dalton,
    Georgia
— *Phoenix Exhibition*, Phantom Galleries, Sacramento, CA
1996 *Texas National '96*, Stephen F Austin State University Gallery, Nacogdoches,
    Texas
1995 *Dinnerware's 13th Biennial Invitational*, Dinnerware Contemporary Art Gallery,
    Tucson, Arizona
67th Annual Juried Exhibition, Art Association of Harrisburg School and Gallery,
    Harrisburg, PA
1994 *ParticipArt*, National Juried Exhibition, Galeria Mesa, Mesa, Arizona. Juror's
    Award.
— *Encompassing Women: Perspectives on Process*, Central Arts Collective, Tucson,
    Arizona
Intuition: The Direction in Craft, Pan-American Juried Exhibition, Gallery of Artifacts
    and Treasures, Daytona Beach, Florida
— *University of Arizona 1994 Faculty Exhibition*, University of Arizona Museum of Art,
    Tucson, Arizona
— *Paper/Fiber XVII*, Iowa City/Johnson County Arts Center, Iowa City.
— *Reclining Woman: Constructed Installation*, Sixth Congress Gallery, Tucson,
    Arizona
— *Women and Madness*, Congress Street Gallery, Tucson, Arizona

Artists' Bibliographies

FIRYAL AL-ADHAMY

Bahrain This Month, March 1998.

Greenan, Althea. 'Dialogue of the Present,' *Visiting Arts*, No 37, Summer 1998, pp22-23.

Issa, Rosa. *New Horizon*, September 1990.

Jalal, A. *This is London*, October 1990, London.

Khoury, Anton. *Al Hayat*, 3 July 1992.

Lloyd, Fran (ed). *Contemporary Arab Women's Art: Dialogues of the Present*. London: Women's Art Library and IB Tauris, 1999.

MALIKA AGUEZNAY

Galerie Bab Rouah. *Malika Agueznay, Les Mots Magiques*, Rabat, Morocco, essays by Toni Mariani and Mostafa Nissabouri, 1996.

Greenan, Althea. 'Dialogue of the Present,' *Visiting Arts*, No 37, Summer 1998, pp22-23.

Lloyd, Fran (ed). *Contemporary Arab Women's Art: Dialogues of the Present*. London: Women's Art Library and IB Tauris, 1999.

JANANNE AL-ANI

Barbican Art Gallery. *Who's Looking at the Family?* essay by Val Williams, London: Barbican Centre, 1994.

Greenan, Althea. 'Dialogue of the Present,' *Visiting Arts*, No 37, Summer 1998, pp22-23.

Harris Museum and Art Gallery. *Fine Material for a Dream...?* essay by Emma Anderson, Preston, UK, 1992.

John Kobal Photographic Portrait Award. Catalogue, Zelda Cheatle Press, 1996.

Lloyd, Fran (ed). *Contemporary Arab Women's Art: Dialogues of the Present*. London: Women's Art Library and I B Tauris, 1999.

Raftery, Alison. *Opening Lines*. London Arts Board, 1997.

Williams, Val. *Modern Narrative, the Domestic and The Social*. Artsway Gallery, UK, 1997.

THURAYA AL-BAQSAMI

Al-Baqsami. 'An Artist's View of Kuwait,' *Kuwait Bulletin*, Issue No 28, August 1996, London, pp4-5.

Ali, Wijdan. *Contemporary Art from the Islamic World*. London: Scorpion Books, 1989.

Ali, Wijdan. *Modern Islamic Art, Development and Continuity*. Florida: University Press of Florida, 1997.

Greenan, Althea. 'Dialogue of the Present,' *Visiting Arts*, No 37, Summer 1998, pp22-23.

Lloyd, Fran (ed). *Contemporary Arab Women's Art: Dialogues of the Present*. London: Women's Art Library and I B Tauris, 1999.

Nashashibi, Salwa Mikdadi. *Forces of Change, Artists of the Arab World*. Lafayette, California: International Council for Women in the Arts, 1994.

2nd Sharjah International Arts Biennial. Sharjah, UAE: Department of Culture, 1995.

4th Sharjah International Arts Biennial. April 1999, Sharjah, UAE: Department of Culture, 1999.

DORIS BITTAR

Al Jadid, March cover featuring *Jiddo's Roses Visit France*, 1997.

Batchen, Geoffrey. *Oriental Subjects*. Catalogue. The Alternative Museum New York, New York, September, 1993.

Epstein, Benjamin. '3 Hour Tour: Doris Bittar's Ornamental Subjects,' *Los Angeles Times*, 30 March 1995.

Pincus, Robert L. 'Contraptions and Canvases,' *San Diego Union Tribune*, 11 February 1999.

Pincus, Robert L. 'The Subject Was Roses,' *San Diego Union Tribune*, 17 August 1995.

Salem Times, 'Art Focuses on Arab Struggle,' 1 September 1995.

'SDSU Gallery Features Doris Bittar Exhibit,' *Imperial Valley Press*, 10 October 1996.

Zubaldl, Khayria. 'The Paintings of Doris Bittar,' *Shenouq*, October 1995.

Zuhur, Sherifa. *Performance, Art, Image and Gender in the Modern Middle East*. American University of Cairo Press and University of Florida Press, l995.

RIMA FARAH

Arts and the Islamic World, July 1983.

Arts Review, July 1983; December 1984; September 1986; January 1990.

Arts Review Year Book, 1987.

Bahechar, S. *Le Journal de Tanger*, July 1991.

Egee, Dale, *Eastern Art Report*, August 1991.

Greenan, Althea. 'Dialogue of the Present,' *Visiting Arts*, No 37, Summer 1998, pp22-23.

Lloyd, Fran (ed). *Contemporary Arab Women's Art: Dialogues of the Present*. London: Women's Art Library and I B Tauris, 1999.

Nashashibi, Salwa Mikdadi. *Forces of Change, Artists of The Arab World*. Lafayette, California: International Council for Women in the Arts, 1994.

Washington Post, April 1986.

MAYSALOUN FARAJ

Artists for Human Rights: International Prints Portfolio, Durban, South Africa, December 1999.

Faraj, Maysaloun. 'Strokes of Genius... Contemporary Iraqi Art,' *Visiting Arts*, No 37, Summer 1998, ppl8-19.

Greenan, Althea. 'Dialogue of the Present,' *Visiting Arts*, No 37, Summer 1998, pp22-23.

Lloyd, Fran (ed). *Contemporary Arab Women's Art: Dialogues of the Present*. London: Women's Art Library and I B Tauris, 1999.

Nashashibi, Salwa Mikdadi. *Forces of Change, Artists of the Arab World*. Lafayette, California: International Council for Women in the Arts, 1994.

Parmelee, Terry. 'Forces of Change,' *Washington Review*, Vol XIX, No 6, April-May, 1994.

pARTicipation, EU-MAN (European Union-Migrant Artists Network) Helsinki, Finland, January 2000.

Rinaldi, Therese. 'Maysaloun Faraj,' *Arts and the Islamic World*, No 29, Autumn 1996, pp49-51.

BATOOL AL-FEKAIKI

Alray Newspapers. (Arabic), Amman, Jordan, 17 October 1996.

Amir, Ah Abdul. *Al Quds Al Arabi*, (Arabic), London, 17 October 1996. Berlin Cultural Centre. *Contemporary Iraqi Arts*, Berlin, 1979.

Greenan, Althea. 'Dialogue of the Present,' *Visiting Arts*, No 37, Summer 1998, pp22-23.

Al-Habib, Kifah. *Al Ayyam Newspaper* (Arabic), 29 September 1996.

Hamdan, Munther. 'Myths of Heart and Home,' *The Star*, Jordan, 1997.

Al-Matbiey, Hameed. *Encyclopaedia of Well Known People in Iraq*, Baghdad: Ministry of Culture, 1995.

Lloyd, Fran (ed). *Contemporary Arab Women's Art: Dialogues of the Present*. London: Women's Art Library and I B Tauris, 1999.

Morgenroth, Gabriele. 'Batool al-Fekaiki,' *Traunsteiner Wochenblatt*, (German), 20 December 1997.

MAI GHOUSSOUB

Al Hayat, No 13218, Monday 17 May 1999, p23.

Asharq Al-Awsat, Issue 7541, 22 July 1999, p23.

Ghoussoub, Mai. *Comprendre le Liban*, Paris, 1976.

Ghoussoub, Mai. *Women and The Male Nature of Authenticity* (Arabic). London, 1991.

Ghoussoub, Mai. *Postmodernism, Arabs in a Video Clip*, (Arabic), Beirut, 1994.

Ghoussoub, Mai. *Leaving Beirut, Women and the Wars Within*. London, 1998.

Ghoussoub, Mai. ' 'La Culture': The Problem of the Definite Article,' *Prince Claus Fund Journal*, Vol 2, June 1999, pp61-64.

Lloyd, Fran (ed). *Contemporary Arab Women's Art: Dialogues of the Present*. London: Women's Art Library and I B Tauris, 1999.

Merali, Shaheen. 'Displaces: Topography of Unbelonging,' *Third Text*, Vol 39, Summer 1997, pp103-5.

WAFAA EL HOUDAYBI

Faiza, M. 'La Rupture avec la norme artistique,' *Le Matin du Sahara*, 14 February 1998.

Greenan, Althea. 'Dialogue of the Present,' *Visiting Arts*, No 37, Summer 1998, pp22-23.

Haouzir, Malika. 'Réussir sa vie professionelle,' *Nouvelles du Nord*, 6 March 1998.

Lloyd, Fran (ed). *Contemporary Arab Women's Art: Dialogues of the Present*. London: Women's Art Library and I B Tauris, 1999.

2nd Sharjah international Arts Biennial. 11-22 April 1995, Sharjah, UAE: Department of Culture, 1995.

3rd Sharjah International Arts Biennial. April 1997, Sharjah, UAE: Department of Culture, 1997.

'Wafaa El Houdaybi expose aux Oudayas,' *Le Matin du Sahara et du Maghreb*, 10 January 1992.

KAMALA IBRAHIM ISHAQ

Ali Wijdan. *Contemporary Art from The Islamic World*. London: Scorpion Books, 1989.

Ali, Wijdan. *Modern Islamic Art, Development and Continuity*. Florida: University Press of Florida, 1997.

Greenan, Althea. 'Dialogue of the Present,' *Visiting Arts*, No 37, Summer 1998, pp22-23.

Hevesi, J. 'The paintings of Kamala Ishaq,' *Studio International*, 1969, p276.

Kennedy, J. *New Currents Ancient Rivers, Contemporary African Artists in a Generation of Change*. Washington: Smithsonian Institution Press, 1992.

Lloyd, Fran (ed). *Contemporary Arab Women's Art: Dialogues of the Present*. London: Women's Art Library and I B Tauris, 1999.

Nashashibi, Salwa Mikdadi. *Forces of Change, Artists of The Arab World*. Lafayette, California: International Council for Women in the Arts, 1994.

Whitechapel Art Gallery. *Seven Stories About Modern Art in Africa*. London: Flammarion, 1995.

GHADA JAMAL

Al Amirieh, Mohamad. 'Experimentation Intergrates the Traditional with the Contemporary,' *Al-Distour*, 23 April 1997, Beirut, Lebanon.

Al Hayek, Nohad. 'Forces of Change in Art for Arab Women,' *Al Majal*, March 1994.

Book as Art: 10th Anniversary Exhibition. The National Museum of Women in the Arts Library and Research Center, 1997.

Bowen, Dorothy, 'Sheherezade's Stories: Arab Women Show 'Devastation of War,' *Contra Costa Sun*, 14 June 1995.

Dagher, Shirbil. Exhibition of Lebanese Artist Ghada Jamal,' *Al-Hayat*, 21 March 1997.

Dasi, Hussein. 'Collection of Contemporary Art from Lebanon,' *Al-Raleh*, 14 April 1997, Amman, Jordan.

Dasi, Hussein. 'Paintings of Contemporary Artist Ghada Jamal Spread Light and Color,' *Al-Raleh*, 21 April 1997, Amman, Jordan.

'Editor's Choice,' *Crain's Chicago Business*, 31 October 1994.

Ghanem, Zuhare. 'In Gallery Agial: Artist Ghada Jamal,' 6 March 1997. Ghreib, Lor. 'Escape from Reality,' *Al-Nahar*, 28 February 1997.

Khal, Helen. 'Inviting Interior of Soft Light,' *Daily Star*, 7 March 1997.

Kohen, Helen L. 'A surprising and engaging Forces of Change,' Miami *Herald*, 28 January 1995.

Lebanese American University Alumni Artists. Exhibition catalogue. The Alumni Association of LAU, Beirut, Lebanon. 1997.

L' Orient-Le Jour, 19 May 1987, p4.

Malouf, Nabila. 'Nature as Teacher: Jamal's Studio View,' *Campus Magazine*, February 1997, Beirut.

Mosalli, Irene. "Un Coup de Force Signe Salwa M. Nashashibi,' *L' Orient-Le Jour*, 31 March 1994.

Mufti, Mahmoud J. 'Rendezvous with Art: Collective Exhibition of 50 Arab Artists Keeping Admiration Alive,' *Jordan Times*, 4 July 1996.

Nashashibi, Salwa Mikdadi. *Forces of Change, Artists of The Arab World*, Lafayette, California: International Council for Women in the Arts, 1994.

Restless Voices: Abstraction from Los Angeles. Schick Art Gallery, Skidmore College, Saratoga Springs, New York, 1995.

Saleh, Mustata. 'Daret Al Funun Presents 50 Arab Artists,' *Al Distour*, 1 July 1996.

Still Life in Lebanese Art. Alumni Association, Beirut College, Lebanon. 1993.

The Artist's View: Two Hundred Years of Lebanese Painting. The British Lebanese Association. Beirut and London: Quartet Books, Ltd. 1990.

WORLD NEWS: Artists Respond to World Events. Catalogue. Muckenthaler Cultural Center, Fullerton, California, 1992.

Zalzal, Zena. 'Artist Ghada Jamal a La Galerie Agial,' *L'Orient - Le Jour*, 28 February 1997.

'97 Art Festival, International College, Beirut, Lebanon. 1997.

LILIANE KARNOUK

Black and Green ein kunstinstallation. Cairo: Goethe Institute, 1992.

Claus, Elizabeth and Toufel, Helmut (eds). *Papier-Kunst Forum Aschaffenbourg 1.* Aschaffenbourg: Neuer Kunstvorein, 1991.

Easthetica Diffusa: Natura- Mater. Text by Sergio Tagulli and Giancarlo Cavallo. Andre Demedtshuis, Belgium, 1991.

Hautungen: Papierobjekte. Text by Dr. Dorothea Eimert. Das Institut fur Auslandsbezichungen zeigt die Ausstellung. Bonn: IPA Gallery, 1988.

International Bienrurale Der Papierkunst Handgeschopftes. Prefaced by J. Vosen and Dr H Lentz. Leopold-Hoosch Museum, Duren, 1986.

Karnouk, Liliane. *Contemporary Egyptian Art.* Cairo, Egypt: American University, Cairo, 1995.

Karnouk, Liliane. *Modern Egyptian Art, The Emergence of a National Style.* Cairo, Egypt: American University in Cairo, 1988.

Liliane Karnouk. Ministry of Culture. National Centre for the Arts, Akhnaton Gallery, Cairo, 1979.

Nashashibi, Salwa Mikdadi (ed). *Forces of Change, Artists of The Arab World.* Lafayette, California: International Council for Women in the Arts, 1994.

Nashashibi, Salwa Mikdadi (ed). *Rhythm and Form: Visual Reflection on Arabic Poetry.* Berkeley, California: Cultural and Visual Arts Resource Division of the International Council for Woman in the Arts, 1997.

Putnam, James and Davis, W. Vivien (eds). *Time Machine: Ancient Egyptian and Contemporary Art.* London: Trustees of the British Museum and Institute of Contemporary Art, 1994.

Ruebsaat, Norbert and Rousillon, Cristine. *Liliane Karnouk.* La Part des Sables, Mashrabiya Gallery, Cairo, 1989.

LEILA KAWASH

Greenan, Althea. 'Dialogue of the Present,' *Visiting Arts*, No 37, Summer 1998, pp22-23.

Lloyd, Fran (ed). *Contemporary Arab Women's Art: Dialogues of the Present*. London: Women's Art Library and I B Tauris, 1999.

Magna Gallery. *Dawns and Invocations*, Athens, essay by Angela Tamvaki, 1997.

Nashashibi, Salwa Mikdadi. *Forces of Change, Artists of The Arab World*. Lafayette, California: International Council for Women in the Arts, 1994.

SABIHA KHEMIR

Al Hayat, No 13218, Monday 17 May 1999, p23.

Asharq Al-Awsat, Issue 7541, 22 July 1999, p23.

Greenan, Althea. 'Dialogue of the Present,' *Visiting Arts*, No 37, Summer 1998, pp22-23.

Lloyd, Fran (ed). *Contemporary Arab Women's Art: Dialogues of the Present*. London: Women's Art Library and I B Tauris, 1999.

Nashashibi, Salwa Mikdadi. *Forces of Change, Artists of The Arab World*. Lafayette, California: International Council for Women in the Arts, 1994.

Johnson-Davies, Denys. *The Island of Animals*. Illustrations by Khemir, London: Quartet Books, 1994.

NAJAT MAKI

Ahmed, Tina. 'Artistic Evolution and Development in Dubai and the Northern Emirates,' *Eastern Art Report*, Vol IV, No 3, 1996, p28.

Greenan, Althea. 'Dialogue of the Present,' *Visiting Arts*, No 37, Summer 1998, pp22-23.

Howling, Frieda. 'From the Traditional to the Modern and Contemporary - Art in the UAE,' *Eastern Art Report*, Vol IV, No 3, 1996, p24.

Lloyd, Fran (ed). *Contemporary Arab Women's Art: Dialogues of the Present*. London: Women's Art Library and I B Tauris, 1999.

2nd Sharjah International Arts Biennial, 11-22 April 1995, Sharjah, UAE: Department of Culture, 1995.

3rd Sharjah International Arts Biennial, April 1997, Sharjah, UAE: Department of Culture, 1997.

HOURIA NIATI

Al Hayat, No 13218, Monday 17 May 1999, p23.

Ali, Wildan. *Contemporary Art from The Islamic World*, London: Scorpion Books, 1989.

Asharq Al-Awsat, Issue 7541, 22 July 1999, p23.

Chambers, Eddie. *The Art Pack, A History of Black Artists in Britain*, London, 1988.

GEN, London, Issue 2, Spring 1984, *'Interview with Houria Niati,'* pp27-33.

Greenan, Althea. 'Dialogue of the Present,' *Visiting Arts*, No 37, Summer 1998, pp22-23.

Hassan, Salah M. (ed). *Gendered Visions, The Art of Contemporary Africana Women Artists*. Trenton, New Jersey: Africa World Press Inc, 1997.

Hassan, Salah M. 'The Installations of Houria Niati,' *NKA, Journal of Contemporary African Art*, Fall/Winter, 1995, pp50-55.

Lloyd, Fran (ed). *Contemporary Arab Women's Art: Dialogues of the Present*. London: Women's Art Library and I B Tauris, 1999.

Lloyd, Fran. 'Contemporary Algerian Art: Embodiment and Performing the 'Self': Houria Niati and Zineb Sedira,' *Journal of Algerian Studies*, London, March 2000.

Nashashibi, Salwa Mikdadi. *Forces of Change, Artists of The Arab World*. Lafayette, California: International Council for Women in the Arts, 1994.

Mediterranea, Contemporary Art of the Mediterranean Countries. Brussels, Belgium: ARTLIFE for the world, 1999.

Morris, Susan. 'Forms of Intuition,' *Arts Review*, Vol 41, May 1989, p356. *New Visions: Recent Works by Six African Artists*. Eatonville, Florida: The Zora Neale Hurston National Museum of Fine Arts, 1995.

Oguibe, Olu. *Cross/ing, Time.Space.Movement*. Contemporary Art Museum, Florida: University of South Florida, 1997.

Owusu, Kwesi. *The Struggle For Black Arts in Britain*. London: Comedia, 1986.

Parker, Rozsika and Pollock, Griselda (eds). *Framing Feminism, Art and The Women's Movement*. London: Pandora Press, 1987.

3rd Sharjah International Arts Biennial. April 1997, Sharjah, UAE: Department of Culture, 1997.

AZZA AL-QASIMI

Greenan, Althea. 'Dialogue at the Present,' *Visiting Arts*, No 37, Summer 1998, pp22-23.

Lloyd, Fran (ed). *Contemporary Arab Women's Art: Dialogues of the Present*. London: Women's Art Library and I B Tauris, 1999.

3rd Sharjah International Arts Biennial. April 1997, Sharjah, UAE: Department of Culture, 1997.

ZINEB SEDIRA

Greenan, Althea. 'Dialogue of the Present,' *Visiting Arts*, No 37, Summer 1998, pp22-23.

Gallery of Modern Art. *Out of the Blue*, Glasgow, 4 July-21 September 1997, essay by Edith Marie Pasquier, pp20-23.

Lloyd, Fran (ed). *Contemporary Arab Women's Art: Dialogues of the Present*. London: Women's Art Library and I B Tauris, 1999.

Lloyd, Fran. 'Contemporary Algerian Art: Embodiment and Performing the "Self'": Houria Niati and Zineb Sedira,' *Journal of Algerian Studies*, London, March 2000.

London Institute. *Fine Art 1995*, London, June 1995.

Serpentine Gallery. *Is Art Beneath You?* London, August, 1998.

Slade School at Fine Art. *The Slade Journal*, Vol 1, London, June 1997.

Where Are You From? BM Contemporary Art Center, Istanbul, Turkey, 1999.

LAILA AL-SHAWA

Ali, Wijdan. *Contemporary Art from the Islamic World*. London: Scorpion Books, 1989.

Ali, Wijdan. *Modern Islamic Art, Development and Continuity*. Florida: University Press of Florida, 1997.

Bertazzoni, Giovanni, 'The Walls of Gaza': a conversation with Laila Shawa' in *mediterranea, Contemporary Art of the Mediterranean Countries*. Brussels, Belgium: ARTLIFE for the world, 1999.

Bahnasi, Atif, Dr. *Pioneers of Modern Art in the Arab Countries*, (Arabic), Beirut, 1985.

Greenan, Althea, 'Dialogue at the Present,' *Visiting Arts*, No 37, Summer 1998, pp22-23.

Impressions, Norway: H. Aschehoug & Co. 1996.

Khal, Helen. *The Woman Artist in Lebanon*. Beirut: Institute for Women's Studies in the Arab World: Beirut University College Press, 1987.

Laila Shawa Works 1964-1996. Cyprus: MCS Publications, 1997.

Lloyd, Fran (ed). *Contemporary Arab Women's Art: Dialogues of the Present*. London: Women's Art Library and I B Tauris, 1999.

Nashashibi, Salwa Mikdadi. *Forces of Change, Artists of The Arab World*. Lafayette,

California: International Council for Women in the Arts, 1994.
October Gallery. *Shawa and Wijdan.* London, 1994.
October Gallery. *The Transvangarde.* London, 1999-2000.
On The Wings of Peace. New York: Clarion Books, 1995.
Shammout, Ismail. *Art in Palestine* (Arabic). Al-Qabas Press, 1989.
The Right to Hope. UK: Earthscan Publications Limited, 1995.
The Right to Write. Atlanta, USA, Agnes Scott College, 1996.

Contemporary Arab Art
General Bibliography

Aareen, Rasheed. 'New Internationalism' in *Global Visions, Towards a New Internationalism in the Visual Arts,* edited by Jean Fisher. London: Kala/inIVA, 1994, pp3-11.

Abdo, N. 'Women of the Intifada: Gender, Class and National Liberation' *Race and Class*, No 32, 1991.

Abu-Lughod, Lila. *Remaking Women: Feminism and Modernity in the Middle East.* Berkeley: University of California Press, 1998.

Abu-Lughod, Lila. *Writing Women's Worlds: Bedouin Stories.* Berkeley: University of California Press, 1993.

Accad, Evelyne. *Veil of Shame, The Role of Women in the Contemporary Fiction of North Africa and the Arab World.* Quebec: Sherbrooke, Editions Naaman, 1978.

Aharoni, R and Mishal, S. *Speaking Stones; Communiques from the Intifada Underground.* New York: Syracuse University Press, 1994.

Ahmad, Aijaz. *In Theory, Classes, Nations, Literatures.* London and New York: Verso, 1992.

Ahmed, Leila. 'Western Ethnocentrism and Perceptions of the Harem,' *Feminist Studies*, Vol 8, No 3, 1982.

Ahmed, Leila. *Women and Gender in Islam: Historical Roots of a Modern Debate.* New Haven: Yale University Press, 1992.

Ali, Wijdan. 'Artist and Missionary of the Mixed Media,' *Eastern Art Report* Vol 1, Part 4 (16-30 April 1989), pp12-14.

Ali, Wijdan. *Contemporary Art from the Islamic World.* London: Scorpion Publication Ltd, Amman: The Royal Society of Fine Arts, 1989.

Ali, Wijdan. *Modern Islamic Art, Development and Continuity.* Florida: University Press of Florida, 1997.

Alloula, Malek. *The Colonial Harem,* trans. by Myrna Godzich and Wlad Godzich, Minneapolis and London: University of Minnesota Press, 1986.

Archer, Michael *et al. Mona Hatoum.* London: Phaidon Press, 1997.

Art Contemporain Arabe: Collection du Musée du L'Institut du Monde Arabe. Paris: Institut du Monde Arabe.

Atassi, Mouna (ed). *Contemporary Art in Syria, 1898-1998.* Damascus, Syria: Gallery Atassi, 1998.

Atil, Esin. *Patronage by Women in Islamic Art.* Arthur M. Sackler Gallery, Smithsonian

Institution, Vol VI, No 2, New York: Oxford University Press, 1993.

Augustin, Ebba (ed). *Palestinian Women: Identity and Experience*. London and New Jersey: Zed Books, 1993.

Azar, Aimé. *Femmes Peintres d'Egypte*. Cairo: Imprimene Frané+aise, 1953.

Azar, Aimé. *La Peinture Moderne en Egypte*. Cairo: Les Editions Nouvelles, 1961.

Badran, Margot. 'Feminism as a Force in the Arab World' in *Contemporary Thought and the Women*. Cairo: Arab Women's Solidarity Press, 1989.

Badran, Margot. *Feminists, Islam and Nation: Gender and the Making of Modern Egypt*. Princeton, NJ: Princeton University Press, 1995.

Badran, Margot, Cooke, Miriam (eds). *Opening the Gates: A Century of Arab Feminist Writing*. Indiana: Indiana University Press, 1990.

Baker, Alison. *Voices of Resistance: Oral Histories of Moroccan Women*. New York: State University of New York (SUNY), 1998.

Barbican Centre. *Lebanon - The Artist's View, 200 Years of Lebanese Art*. London: Barbican Centre, 1989.

Barbican Centre, Concourse Gallery. *Signs, Traces, Calligraphy, Five Contemporary Artists from North Africa*. Rosa Issa (curator), London, 1995.

Bardenstein, C. 'Raped Brides and Steadfast Mothers; Appropriations of Palestinian Motherhood' in *The Politics of Motherhood; Activist Voices from Left to Right*, edited by Alexis Jetter *et al*, Hanover and London: University Press of New England, 1997.

Batchen, Geoffrey. *Oriental Subjects*, catalogue for the Alternative Museum New York: New York, September 1993.

Beinin, J, Hajjar, L and Rabbani, M. 'Palestine and The Arab Israeli Conflict for Beginners' in *Intifada; The Palestinian Uprising against Israeli Occupation*, edited by Zachary Lockman and Joel Beinin. London: I B Tauris, 1990.

Bernstein, Matthew and Studlar, Gaylan (eds). *Visions of the East: Orientalism in Film*. New Brunswick, New Jersey: Rutgers University Press, 1997.

Betterton, Rosemary. *An Intimate Distance: Women, Artists, and the Body*. London and New York: Routledge, 1996.

Bhabha, Homi K. *The Location of Culture*. London and New York: Routledge, 1994.

Bohm-Duchen, M and Grodzinski, V. (eds). *Rubies & Rebels, Jewish Female Identity in Contemporary British Art*. Barbican Concourse Gallery, London: Lund Humphries, 1998.

Bosca, Joan 'Frida Khalo: Marginalisation and the Critical Female Subject' *Third Text*, No 12, 1990.

Bourdieu, Pierre. *The Algerians*. Boston: Beacon Press, 1961.

Bowman, G. 'A Country of Words: Conceiving the Palestinian Nation from the Position of Exile' in *The Making of Political Identities*, edited by Ernesto Laclau. London: Verso, 1994.

Burgin, Victor. *In/Different Spaces: Place and Memory in Visual Culture*. Los Angeles and London: University of California Press, 1996.

Cairo: 6th Biennale Catalogue. Cairo: 1996.

Candid Arts Trust. *Story Time, An Exhibition by Artists Living in Israel/Palestine*. London, 1998.

Chahine, Richard. *A 100 years of Plastic Art in Lebanon: 1880-1980*, Vol 1 & 2, Beirut, Lebanon: Galerie Chahine, 1982.

Chapman, Helen C. *Memory in Perspective: Women Photographers' Encounters with History*. London: Scarlet Press, 1997.

Chow, Rey. *Writing Diaspora: Tactics of Intervention in Contemporary Cultural Studies*. Bloomington: Indiana University Press, 1993.

Clifford, James. *The Predicament of Culture: Twentieth Century Ethnography, Literature and Art*. Cambridge Mass: Harvard University Press, 1988.

'Contemporary African Art. Camden Arts Centre.' London and New York: *Studio International*, 1969.

Coombes, Annie E. 'Inventing the 'Postcolonial: Hybridity and Constituency in

Contemporary Curating' in *The Art of Art History: A Critical Anthology*, edited by Donald Preziosi. Oxford and New York: Oxford University Press, 1998, pp486-497.

Courtney-Clarke, Margaret and Brooks, G. *Imazighen: Vanishing Traditions of Berber Women*. London: Thames and Hudson, 1996.

Davezac, Shehira Doss. 'Women of the Arab World: Turning the Tide' in *Forces of Change: Artists of the Arab World*, edited by Salwa Mikdadi Nashashibi. Lafayette, California: International Council for Women in the Arts, 1994, pp38-57.

Deepwell, Katy (ed). *Art Criticism and Africa*. London: Saffron Books, 1998.

Deliss, Clémentine (ed). *Seven Stories About Modern Art in Africa*. London: Whitechapel Art Gallery, 1995.

Djebar, Assia. *Women of Algiers in their Apartment*, trans by Marjolijn de Jager. Charlottesville and London: Caraf books, University of Virginia, 1992.

Donald, James and Rattansi, Ali (eds). *'Race', Culture & Difference*. London, California, New Delhi: Sage Publications in association with The Open University, 1992.

El Khalidi, Leila. *The Art of Palestinian Embroidery*, London: Saqi Books, 1999.

El Saadawi, Nawal. *The Nawal El Saadawi Reader*. London and New York: Zed Books, 1997.

El Saadawi, Nawal. *Women at Zero Point*, translated by Miriam Cooke and Margot Badran, 1986.

Fanon, Frantz. *Black Skins, White Masks*. London: Pluto Press, 1986.

Fanon, Frantz. *The Wretched of the Earth,* translated by Constance Farrington. London: Harmondsworth, Penguin, 1967.

Farris-Duprene, Phoebe. *Voices of Colour: Art and Society in America*. New Jersey: Humanities Press, 1997.

Ferguson, Russell *et al. Out There, Marginlization and Contemporary Cultures*. New York: The New Museum of Contemporary Art; Cambridge, MA: The MIT Press, 1990.

Fisher, Jean (ed). *Global Visions, Towards a New Internationalism in the Visual Arts*. London: Kala Press in association with The Institute of International Visual Arts, 1994.

Fullerton, Arlene, Fehervari, Geza. *Kuwait Arts and Architecture*. Kuwait, UAE: Oriental Press, 1995.

Ghoussoub, Mai. ' 'La Culture': The Problem of the Definite Article' in *Prince Claus Fund Journal* Vol 2, June 1999.

Giacaman R and Johnson, P. 'Palestinian Women; Building Barricades and Breaking Barriers' in *Intifada; The Palestinian Uprising Against Israeli Occupation*, edited by Zachary Lockman and Joel Beinin. London: I B Tauris, 1989.

Gilroy, Paul. *The Black Atlantic: Modernity and Double Consciousness*. London and New York: Verso, 1993.

Graham-Brown, Sarah. *Images of Women: The Portrayal of Women in Photography of the Middle East, 1860-1950*. London: Quartet Books, 1988.

Grewal, Inderpal and Kaplan, Caren (eds), *Scattered Hegemonies: Postmodernity and Transnational Feminist Practices*. Minneapolis: University of Minnesota Press, 1994.

Grewal, Inderpal, *Home and Harem: Nation, Gender, Empire and the Cultures of Travel*. Durham, NC: Duke University Press, 1996.

Hall, Stuart. 'Cultural Identity and Diaspora' in *Colonial Discourse and Post-Colonial Theory, A Reader*, edited by P Williams and L Chrisman. Cambridge: Harvester/Wheatsheaf, 1993.

Hall, Stuart. 'New Ethnicities' in *'Race', Culture & Difference,* edited by J Donald and A Rattansi. London, California, New Delhi: Sage Publications in association with The Open University, 1992.

Hassan, Ihab. 'Queries for Postcolonial Studies' *Third Text* Vol 43, Summer 1998, pp59-68.

Hassan, Salah M. (ed). *Gendered Visions: The Art of Contemporary Africana Women*. Trenton, New Jersey: Africa World Press inc, 1997.

Hassan, Salah M. 'The Installations of Houria Niati,' *NKA Journal of Contemporary African Art*. Fall/Winter 1995.

Hejaiej, Monica. *Behind Closed Doors: Women's Oral Narratives in Tunis*. London: Quartet, 1996.

Hélie-Lucas, Marie-Aimée. 'Women, Nationalism and Religion in the Algerian Liberation Struggle' in Badran and Cooke (eds), 1990.

hooks, bell. 'Critical Genealogies Writing Black Art' in *Art on My Mind: Visual Politics*. New York: The New Press, 1995.

Ikon Gallery. *In an Unsafe Light, Charnley, Geogopoulos, Hatoum*. Birmingham, UK, 1988.

Institute of Contemporary Arts/Institute of International Visual Arts.*Mirage, Enigmas of Race, Difference and Desire* ICA/inIVA season, 12 May-16 July 1995, London, 1995.

Irwin, Robert. *Islamic Art: Art, Architecture and the Literary World*. London: Laurence King Publishing, 1997.

Ismail Afifi, Fatma. *Twenty-Nine Artists in the Museum of Egyptian Modern Art*. Egypt: AICA, 1994.

Jad, Islah. 'From Salons to the Popular Committees: Palestinian Women, 1919-89,' in *Intifada: Palestine at the Crossroads*, edited by Jamal R Nasser and Roger Heacock. New York/Westpoint/London/Praegar, 1990, pp125-42.

Jones, Amelia. *Body Art/Performing the Subject*. Minneapolis and London: University of Minnesota Press, 1998.

Jones, Amelia and Stephenson, Andrew. *Performing the Body: Performing the Text*. London and New York: Routledge, 1999.

Kandiyoti, Deniz. 'Identity and its Discontents: Women and the Nation' *Millennium: Journal of International Studies*, Vol 20, No 3, 1991, pp429-43.

Kandiyoti, Deniz (ed). *Women,Islam and the State*. Philadelphia: Temple University Press, 1991.

Kaper, Greta. 'Globalisation and Culture' *Third Text Vol* 37, Summer 1997, pp21-38.

Kaplin, Caren. 'Deterritorializations: The Rewriting of Home and Exile in Western Feminist Discourse,' *Cultural Critique*, No 6, Spring 1987.

Kaplin, Caren. *Questions of Travel: Postmodern Discourses of Displacement*. Durham, NC: Duke University Press, 1996.

Karnouk, Liliane. *Contemporary Egyptian Art*. Cairo, Egypt: American University, Cairo, 1995.

Karnouk, Liliane. *Modern Egyptian Art, The Emergence of a National Style*. Cairo, Egypt: American University in Cairo, 1988.

Katz, S. 'Shahada and Haganah; Politicizing Masculinities in Early Palestinian and Jewish Nationalisms' *Arab Studies Journal*, Fall 1996.

Kennedy, J. *New Currents Ancient Rivers, Contemporary African Artists in a Generation of Change*. Washington: Smithsonian Institution Press, 1992.

Khal, Helen. *The Woman Artist in Lebanon*. Beirut: Institute for Women's Studies in the Arab World: Beirut University College Press, 1987.

Kristeva, Julia. *Strangers to Ourselves*, translated by Leon S.Roudiez, New York: Columbia University Press, 1991.

Kwint, Marius, Breward, C and Aynsley, Jeremy (eds). *Material Memories*. Oxford and New York: Berg, 1999.

LaDuke, Betty. *Africa Through the Eyes of Women Artists*. Trenton: Africa World Press, 1992.

Lewis, Reina. *Gendering Orientalism, Race, Femininity and Representation*. London and New York: Routledge, 1996.

Leyton, Harrie, Damen, Bibi (eds). *Art, Anthropology, and the Modes of Representation, Museums and Contemporary Non-Western Art*. Amsterdam: Royal

Tropical Institute, 1993.

Lippard, Lucy. *Mixed Blessings: New Art in Multicultural America*. New York: Pantheon, 1990.

Lloyd, Fran (ed). *Contemporary Arab Women's Art: Dialogues of the Present*. London: Women's Art Library and I B Tauris, 1999.

Lloyd, Fran. 'Contemporary Algerian Art: Embodiment and Performing the "Self": Houria Niati and Zineb Sedira,' *Journal of Algerian Studies*, London, March 2000.

Lockman, Zachary, Beinin, Joel (eds). *Intifada: The Palestinian Uprising Against Israeli Occupation*. London: I B Tauris, 1990.

MacKenzie, John M. *Orientalism: History, Theory and the Arts*. Manchester and New York: Manchester University Press, 1995.

Madkour, Nazli. *Women and Art in Egypt*. Cairo: State Information Office, 1993.

Mansour and Tamari, Vera. 'Art Under Occupation.' 1990.

Mernissi, Fatima. *Beyond the Veil*. Cambridge, Massachusetts, New York, London: Schenkman, 1975.

Mernissi, Fatima. *The Veil and the Male Élite: A Feminist Interpretation of Women's Rights in Islam*, trans by Mary Jo Lakeland, New York: Addison-Wesley, 1991.

Mernissi, Fatima. *Women's Rebellion and Islamic Memory*. London and New Jersey: Zed Books, 1996.

Mills, Sara. *Discourses of Difference: An Analysis of Women's Travel Writing and Colonialism*. New York and London: Routledge, 1991.

Minh-ha, Trinh T, *Woman Native Other*. Bloomington: Indiana University Press, 1989.

Mirzoeff, Nicholas (ed). *Diaspora and Visual Culture: Representing Africans and Jews*. New York and London: Routledge, 1999.

Mitchell, Timothy. *Colonising Egypt*. Berkeley: University of California Press, 1991.

Mitchell, Timothy. 'Orientalism and the Exhibitionary Order' in *The Art of Art History: A Critical Anthology*, edited by Donald Preziosi. Oxford and New York: Oxford University Press, 1998, pp455-472.

Mohanty, Chandra Talpadé. 'Under Western Eyes: Feminist Scholarship and Colonial Discourses' in *Colonial Discourse and Post-Colonial Theory, A Reader* edited by P Williams and L Chrisman. Cambridge: Harvester/Wheatsheaf, 1993.

Museum Fridericianum. *Echolot: Oder 9 Fragen an die Periperie* (9 Questions from the Margins). Ghada Amer essay by Candice Breitz, Germany, 1998.

Nahid, Toubia (ed). *Women of the Arab World*. London. 1988.

Nashashibi, Salwa Mikdadi. *Forces of Change, Artists of the Arab World*. Lafayette, California: International Council for Women in the Arts, 1994.

Nashashibi, Salwa Mikdadi. *Rhythm and Form, Visual Reflections on Arabic Poetry*. Lafayette, California: International Council for Women in the Arts, 1998.

Nashat, Guity and Tucker, Judith E. *Restoring Women to History: Women in the Middle East and North Africa*. Bloomington and Indianapolis: Indiana University Press, 1999.

Nochlin, Linda. 'The Imaginary Orient' in *The Politics of Vision: Essays on Nineteenth-Century Art and Society*, New York: Harper and Row, 1989.

Oguibe, Olu. *Crossing, Time.Space.Movement*. Florida: Contemporary Art Museum, 1998.

Ostle, Robin, de Moor, Edo and Wild, Stefan (eds). *Writing the self: Autobiographical Writing in Modern Arabic Literature*. London: Al Saqi Books, 1998.

Owusu, Kwesi. *The Struggle For Black Arts in Britain*. London: Comedia, 1986.

Parker, Rozsika and Pollock, Griselda (eds). *Framing Feminism Art and the Women's Movement, 1979-1985*. London and New York: Pandora 1987.

Passia Diary (The Palestinian Academic Society for the Study of International Affairs), Jerusalem: Passia.

Pompidou Centre. *Magiciens de la Terre*. Paris: Editions du Pompidou, 1989.

Pollock, Griselda (ed). *Generations and Geographies in the Visual Arts*. London: Routledge, 1996.

Peetet, Julie. 'Authenticity and Gender' in *The Presentation of Culture, Arab Women, Old Boundaries, New Frontiers*, edited by Judith E Tucker. Bloomington and Indianapolis: Indiana University Press, 1993.

Peretz, Don. *The Intifada Uprising*. Boulder and London: Westview Press, 1990.

Putnam, James and Vivien, V *Time Machine: Ancient Egyptian Art and Contemporary Art*. London: British Museum and Institute of Contemporary Art, 1994.

Ruedy, J. 'Dynamic of Land Alienation, The Transformation of Palestine' in *Essays on the Origin and Development of the Arab Israeli Conflict*, edited by Ibrahim Abu-Lughod. Evanston: Northwestern University Press, 1971.

Rushdie, Salman. *Imaginary Homelands: Essays and Criticism 1981-1991*. London: Granta Books, 1991.

Said, Edward W. *After the Last Sky: Palestinian Lives*. London: Faber and Faber, 1986.

Said, Edward W. *Orientalism, Western Concepts of the Orient*. London: Routledge and Kegan Paul Ltd, 1978.

Said, Edward W. 'Reflections on Exile' (1984) in *Out There, Marginlization and Contemporary Cultures*, edited by Russell Ferguson *et al.* New York: The New Museum of Contemporary Art; Cambridge: The MIT Press, 1990, pp357-366.

Said, Edward W. 'The Voice of a Palestinian Exile,' *Third Text*, Vol 3, No 4, 1988: pp39-50.

Said, Edward W. *Culture and Imperialism*. London: Vintage Books, 1993.

Salman, A. *Modern Art in the Countries of the Gulf Cooperation Council* (Arabic), Kuwait: Gulf Cooperation Council, 1984.

Seoudi, Mona (ed). *In time of War: Children Testify (Drawings by Palestinian Children)*, Beirut, 1970.

Shammout, Ismail. *Art in Palestine*. (Arabic): Al-Qabbas Press, 1989.

Sha'rawi, Huda. *Harem Years: The Memoirs of an Egyptian Feminist*. London: Virago, 1986.

Shehadeh, R. *Occupier's Law; Israel and the West Bank*. Washington DC: Institute of Palestine Studies, 1985.

Shohat, Ella (ed). *Talking Visions: Multicultural Feminism in a Transnational Age*. New York: The New Museum of Contemporary Art; Cambridge, MA: The MIT Press, 1999.

Sijelmassi, M. *L'Art Contemporain au Maroc*. Paris: ACR Edition, 1989.

Silverman, Kaja. 'Fragments of a Fashionable Discourse' in *Studies in Entertainment: Critical Approaches to Mass Culture*, edited by Tania Modleski. Bloomington: Indiana University Press, 1986.

Silverman, Kaja. *The Threshold of the Visible World*. London and New York: Routledge, 1996.

Slaoui, Abderrahman. *The Orientalist Poster: A Century of Advertising Through The Slaouli Foundation Collection*. Casablanca: Malika Editions, 1997.

Spivak, Gayatri C. *In Other Worlds: Essays in Cultural Politics*. London: Metheun, 1987.

Sulaiman, K. *Palestine and Modern Arab Poetry*. London: Zed Books, 1984.

Swedenberg, T. 'The Palestinian Peasant As National Signifier,' *Anthropological Quarterly*, Vol 63, January 1990.

Tamar, Mayer. *Women and the Israeli Occupation; The Politics of Change*. London: Routledge, 1994.

Tamari, Vera. 'Palestinian Women's Art in the Occupied Territories' in *Palestinian Women: Identity and Experience*, edited by Ebba Augustin. London and New Jersey: Zed Books, 1993, pp63-67.

Tawadros, Çeylan (Gilane). 'Foreign Bodies: Art History and the Discourse of 19th Century Orientalist Art,' *Third Text*, No 3/4, Spring/Summer, 1988.

Tawadros, Gilane. 'The Case of the Missing Body' in *Global Visions Towards a New Internationalism in the Visual Arts*, edited by Jean Fisher. London, Kala

Press/inIVA, 1994.

Thornton, Lynne. *Women as Portrayed in Orientalist Painting*. Paris: ACR Edition, PocheCouleur, 1994.

Tucker, Judith E (ed). *The Presentation of Culture, Arab Women, Old Boundaries, New Frontiers*. Bloomington: Indiana University Press, 1993.

Vasseleu, Cathryn.*Textures of Light: Vision and Touch in Irigaray, Levinas and Merleau-Ponty*. Routledge: London and New York, 1998.

Wolff, Janet. *Resident Alien, Feminist Cultural Criticism*. Cambridge, UK: Polity Press, 1995.

Williams, Patrick and Chrisman, Laura (eds). *Colonial Discourse and Post-Colonial Theory, A Reader*. Cambridge: Harvester/Wheatsheaf, 1993.

Yeǧenoǧlu, Meyda. *Colonial Fantasies: Towards a Feminist Reading of Orientalism*. Cambridge: Cambridge University Press, 1998.

Young, G E. 'A Feminist Politics of Health Care: The Case of Palestinian Women under Israeli Occupation 1979-1982' in *Women and the Israeli Occupation; The Politics of Change*, edited by Mayer Tamar. London: Routledge, 1994.

Young, James E. *The Texture of Memory: Holocaust Memorials and Meaning*. New Haven and London: Yale University Press. 1993

Young, Robert. *Colonial Desire: Hybridity in Theory, Culture and Race*. London and New York: Routledge, 1995.

Young, Robert. *White Mythologies: Writing History and the West*. London and New York: Routledge, 1990.

Yuval-Davies, Nira and Anthias, Floya (eds). *Woman-Nation-State*. London: Macmillan, 1989.

Zegher, M Catherine de (ed). *Inside The Visible, An Elliptical Traverse of 20th Century Art*. Cambridge, MA: The MIT Press, 1996.

Zuhur, Sherifa. *Performance, Art, Image and Gender in the Modern Middle East*. Cairo and Florida: American University of Cairo Press and University of Florida Press, I995.

Zuhur, Sherifa (ed). *Images of Enchantment: Visual and Performing Arts of the Middle East*. Cairo: American University of Cairo Press, 1998.

Contemporary cultural magazines

ABWAB, quarterly Arabic magazine, published by Dar al Saqi, London and Beirut: 1994—

African Arts, quarterly, Los Angeles: 1967—

Arts & The Islamic World, London: 1983—

Atlantica, USA.

Banipal: Magazine of Modern Arab Literature, London: 199?—

Eastern Art Report, London: 1989—

El Yassar, Cairo: Arabic/French magazine, 1994—

NKA: Journal of Contemporary African Art, biannual, USA and Nigeria, Lagos: 1994—

Presence Africaine: Revue Culturelle du Monde Noir, Paris: 1947—

Prince Claus Fund Journal: The Hague: 1998—

Qantara: Magazine des Cultures Arabes et Mediterraneene, Institut de Monde Arabe, Paris: 1991—

Revue Noire, Paris: 1991—

Third Text: Third World Perspectives on Contemporary Art and Culture, London: 1987—

List of Illustrations

Illustrations

Batool al-Fekaiki, *Children of the Future*, 1999, installation of painted stone and gravel, from *Dialogue of the Present: Site and Performance*, Pitshanger Manor and Gallery, London, July - August 1999, pp6-7

Sabiha Khemir, *The Happy Island*, 1994 (detail), illustration from *The Island of Animals*, pp8-9

Mary Tuma, *Body Count* (detail), 1995, wire, stockings, tulle, pins, thread, 20 x 32.5 x 12cm, p10

Figures

1.1 Leila Kawash, *Diaspora* (detail), 1992, mixed media collage on canvas, 90 x 75cm, p12

1.2 Malika Agueznay, *Regard,* 1990, zinc etching, 49 x 34cm, p12

1.3 Maysaloun Faraj, *Sisters of Black and Gold,* 1988, glazed stoneware with onglaze and gold metal, height 57cm, width 28cm, p13

1.4 Azza al-Qasimi, *Geometrics 1,* 1997, etching and collage, 75 x 54cm, p14

1.5 Mai Ghoussoub and Souheil Sleiman, *Displaces,* 1998, plaster installation in three rooms, p15

1.6 Saadeh George, *Today I Shed My Skin: Dismembered and Remembered,* 1998, detail of installation, life size, p15

1.7 Zineb Sedira, *'Hide' and 'Seek',* 1999, computer generated photographic image, 21 x 30cm, p16

1.8 Jananne Al-Ani, *Untitled (Veils Project),* 1997, black and white photograph, first of a pair, each 180 x 120cm, p17

1.9 Laila al-Shawa, *Children of War,* 1992-1995, 100 x 230cm, part of *The Walls of Gaza* installation of 10 silkscreens, p17

1.10 Wafaa El Houdaybi, *Meknés,* 1998, work in progress, paint and henna on stretched leather, p17

1.11 Sabiha Khemir, *Shipwreck 1,* Illustration for book cover, *The Island of Animals,* 1994, 12.5 x 32cm, Quartet Books, London 1994, p18

1.12 Mai Ghoussoub, *Diva,* 1999, installation, 200 x 50 x 30cm, p19

1.13 Mai Ghoussoub, *Diva,* 1999, installation, 200 x 50 x 30cm, p19

1.14 Firyal al-Adhamy, *Looking Forward,* 1997, acrylic and watercolour on paper, 55 x 40cm, p19

Facing page
Batool al-Fekaiki, *Ishtar*, 1998
(detail, see colour plate 11)

Illustration

Figures

Illustration

Figures

Illustration

Illustration

Figures

Illustration

Figures

Illustration

Colour Plates

Illustration

Kamala Ibrahim Ishaq, installation detail, *Dialogue of the Present: Site and Performance,* Pitshanger Manor and Gallery, 1999, p139

Illustrations

Notes on Contributors

Mai Ghoussoub is an artist and writer. Born in Beirut, she moved to London in 1979 where she co-founded Al Saqi Books and subsequently studied sculpture. Regularly exhibiting her work since 1985, Ghoussoub is co-editor of *Abwab*, a quarterly cultural magazine published in Arabic (Beirut and London). Author of *Leaving Beirut: Women and the Wars Within* (1998), Ghoussoub is currently working on a forthcoming major installation and performance exhibition (to be shown in Beirut and London) and is co-editing a book on *Imagined Masculinities: Male Identities in the Modern Middle East.*

Sabiha Khemir is an artist, an illustrator, a writer and an Islamic art scholar. Consultant for *Al-Andalus: Islamic Arts of Spain* for the Metropolitan Museum of Art, New York (1992), she has written and presented two documentaries on Islamic Art for Channel Four Television (1993). Her writing on Islamic art includes the forthcoming publication: *Figures and Figurines, Sculpture from the Islamic Lands, 7th-19th Century* (Khalili Collection series, Oxford University Press and Azimuth Edition). She is currently working on a series of short stories with accompanying illustrations.

Fran Lloyd is Head of the School of Art and Design History at Kingston University, London and has published widely on contemporary visual culture. Her publications include: *Deconstructing Madonna* (ed), (Batsford, 1993); *From the Interior: Female Perspectives on Figuration* (ed), (KUP, 1997); *Contemporary Arab Women's Art: Dialogues of the Present* (ed), (Women's Art Library and I B Tauris, 1999); *Secret Spaces, Forbidden Places: Re-thinking Culture* (co-editor), (Oxford and New York: Berghahn Books 2000) and contributor to *Feminist Visual Culture: An Introduction*, edited by Fiona Carson and Claire Pajaczkowska (Edinburgh University Press 2000).

Salwa Mikdadi Nashashibi is the president and founder of the International Council for Women in the Arts, Lafayette, California, established in 1988 to recognise the contributions of Arab women in the visual arts. Organiser of the major American touring exhibition, *Forces of Change: Women Artists of the Arab World* (Washington, 1994-95), she has travelled and worked throughout the Arab world, including a recent two-year residency in Jordan. A leading authority on contemporary Arab art, Nashashibi is a writer, lecturer and curator. She is currently planning an exhibition on *Art and Political Consciousness.*

Houria Niati is an Algerian-born installation and performance artist. Trained in Community Arts in Algeria, she settled in London in 1979 where she subsequently studied fine art. Niati has exhibited widely in Britain, Europe, the United States and North Africa since 1983. Her installations include painting, collage, objects, poetry and her live performances of classical Arab-Andalusian songs. Recent major touring exhibitions include: *Cross/ing: Time.Space.Movement* (United States, 1997-99) and *Dialogue of the Present, the Work of 18 Arab Women Artists* (Britain, 1999-2000).

Tina Sherwell is the former founding director of the Archive of Palestinian Art at the Al-Wasiti Centre, Jerusalem which documents the work of Palestinian artists in Jerusalem, the West Bank, the Gaza Strip and Israel/Palestine. She is completing a PhD on the 'Representations of Palestine' and has published widely on Palestinian art and culture. Trained as an artist at Goldsmith's College, London, she has curated several exhibitions of Palestinian art. Sherwell currently lives in Jerusalem where she works as a freelance curator and writer.

Els van der Plas is director of the Prince Claus Fund, The Hague, Netherlands, established in 1996 to stimulate and support cultural activities which promote international co-operation and debate. She is an art historian, a curator and an art critic. From 1987 to 1997, van der Plas was the founding director of the Gate Foundation in Amsterdam, an organisation devoted to the intercultural exchange of contemporary art. She lectures on contemporary art and has contributed to various catalogues and art journals, including *Art and Asia Pacific* and *Third Text.*

Index

other recent titles from saffron

Beyond Frontiers marks the first ever
attempt to survey the work of contemporary
British artists whose ancestral roots lie in
the countries and cultures of South Asia. For
some, their links with the Subcontinent
remain present and immediate; for others,
they are a barely perceptible trace, filtered
through generations of exile and migration

Always lively, often provocative and lavishly
illustrated, the book contains a heady mix of
scholarly essays, interviews, artists' texts
and specially commissioned works. It aims,
once and for all, to unsettle pat assumptions
about the meaning and significance of ethnic
origin to artists' contribution to
contemporary culture and experience. There
are as many different voices here, as many
different approaches to art and culture as
there are contributions to the book

Artists of three generations join eminent
critics, cultural theorists and art historians
to explore visual art now, against a backdrop
of the centuries-old intertwining of East and
West that informs many of the most vibrant
manifestations of British and European
contemporary culture

ISBN 1 872843 21 2

288pp, 277mm [h] x 210mm [w] Softback

UK price £24.95 **Overseas** £29.95/US$45.00
(including surface mail packing and postage)

Orders to

Saffron Books
Eastern Art Publishing
P O Box 13666
London SW14 8WF, UK

T   +44-[0]-20-8392 1122
F   +44-[0]-20-8392 1422
E   saffron@eapgroup.com
W   www.eapgroup.com

beyond frontiers

contemporary british art by artists of south asian descent

edited by
Amal Ghosh and Juginder Lamba
Asian Art & Society Series | Series Editor Sajid Rizvi

Contents

Art Criticism and Africa

KATY DEEPWELL, ED

ART CRITICISM AND AFRICA

ISBN 1 872843 13 1 [paperback]

Part of Saffron Books African Art and
  Society Series

Series Editor Sajid Rizvi

Focused on contemporary art and
art criticism in Zimbabwe, South
Africa, Nigeria and Egypt, the
book throws light on many
institutional and administrative
issues in contemporary culture:
highlighting the role of public and
private galleries, art magazines,
the press, art schools, groups of
artists and critics and the work of
government

128pp, 38 illustrations, 16 in colour
250mm x 210 mm [portrait]

£14.95 UK
£19.95/US$29 [Overseas]

Orders to

Saffron Books
Eastern Art Publishing
P O Box 13666
London SW14 8WF, UK

T +44-[0]-20-8392 1122
F +44-[0]-20-8392 1422
E saffron@eapgroup.com
W www.eapgroup.com

Table of Contents

El Anatsui: A Sculpted History of Africa

JOHN PICTON, ED

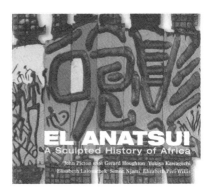

ISBN 1 872843 14 X [paperback]

Part of Saffron Books African Art and Society Series, published in conjunction with the October Gallery, London

Series Editor Sajid Rizvi

Richly illustrated and with texts in English, French, German and Japanese, the book examines the artistic career of the internationally renowned Ghanaian-born sculptor in the context of contemporary African art

Readership level: General to Professional to Postgraduate

96pp, 35 illustrations, 23 in colour
230mm x 248 mm [landscape]

£14.95 UK
£19.95/US$29 [Overseas]

Table of Contents

Orders to

Saffron Books
Eastern Art Publishing
P O Box 13666
London SW14 8WF, UK

T +44-[0]-20-8392 1122
F +44-[0]-20-8392 1422
E saffron@eapgroup.com
W www.eapgroup.com

Hai Shuet Yeung: Innovation in Abstraction

SAJID RIZVI, ED

HAI SHUET YEUNG: INNOVATION IN ABSTRACTION

ISBN 1 872843 11 5 [paper]
ISBN 1 872843 17 4 [cloth]

Exploring the life and work of the internationally renowned and largely self-made British Chinese artist, Guangdong-born Hai Shuet Yeung, the book offers a comprehensive look at issues in contemporary Chinese art and contemporary art in general

The author's main essay, incorporating conversations with the artist on his life and work as well as issues in world art, is supplemented by an introduction by Anne Farrer, formerly at the British Museum, and a critical appraisal of his work from a Chinese perspective by Professor Li Gongming (Guangdong Academy of Fine Arts)

113pp, 105 illustrations, 83 in colour
297mm x 210mm [portrait]

Paperback
£14.95   UK
£19.95/US$29   Overseas

Cloth
£20.95   UK
£26.95/US$39   Overseas

Orders to

Saffron Books
Eastern Art Publishing
P O Box 13666
London SW14 8WF, UK

T   +44-[0]-20-8392 1122
F   +44-[0]-20-8392 1422
E   saffron@eapgroup.com
W   www.eapgroup.com

Table of Contents